Introduction

The Elwha River Fish Restoration Plan (EFRP) is the scientific framework guiding efforts to return successful, reproducing fish to the Elwha River basin following removal of the Elwha and Glines Canyon dams on the Elwha River (Figure 1). The fish restoration effort will provide for the preservation of extant stocks during the dam removal process and the reintroduction of these fish populations into the Elwha River following dam removal. The EFRP has been jointly developed by the Lower Elwha Klallam Tribe (LEKT), Olympic National Park (ONP), Washington Department of Fish and Wildlife (WDFW), U.S. Fish and Wildlife Service (USFWS), and the Northwest Fisheries Science Center (NWFSC) of the National Marine Fisheries Service (NOAA Fisheries Service or NMFS).

Development of the EFRP, including the selection of stocks to be restored and the strategies that will be used to restore them, has considered the physical constraints of dam removal, critical biologic issues, and specific regional management priorities. These fish restoration efforts, which focus primarily on anadromous salmonids, will use both natural recolonization and a variety of hatchery-based enhancement techniques.

The first versions of the EFRP appeared in the Elwha Report (DOI et al. 1994) and in the Draft Environmental Impact Statement for Elwha River Ecosystem Restoration Implementation (DOI et al. 1996). Wunderlich and Pantaleo (1995) also prepared a detailed review of methods that could be used to reestablish naturally spawning populations of salmonids to the upper reaches of the Elwha River. These versions of the EFRP described timelines and cost estimates to restore native anadromous fish populations in the Elwha River following dam removal and identified options for restoring the 10 native anadromous salmonid stocks of the Elwha River.

Cost estimates for the effort were based on hatchery improvements necessary to support fish production and outplanting efforts, and on generic personnel and equipment needs for monitoring adult returns. These versions of the plan did not address Endangered Species Act (ESA) considerations for Chinook salmon (*Oncorhynchus tshawytscha*) or bull trout (*Salvelinus confluentus*), nonsalmonid species, or refinements to the dam removal plan such as implementation of "fish windows" (planned delays in dam removal to reduce sediment transport and impacts to fish), all of which are addressed in this technical memorandum.

Elwha River fish restoration planning efforts have given native or locally adapted stocks priority consideration during the development of restoration strategies (Wunderlich and Pantaleo 1995). Reviews conducted for each species—Chinook, coho (*O. kisutch*), chum (*O. keta*), pink (*O. gorbuscha*), and sockeye (*O. nerka*) salmon; steelhead (*O. mykiss*); coastal cutthroat (*O. clarkii clarkii*), bull trout and Dolly Varden (*S. malma*); and western brook lamprey (*Lampetra richardsoni*) and Pacific lamprey (*L. tridentata*)—are included in the plan, with an evaluation of historical population size and distribution within the drainage, current population size and stock

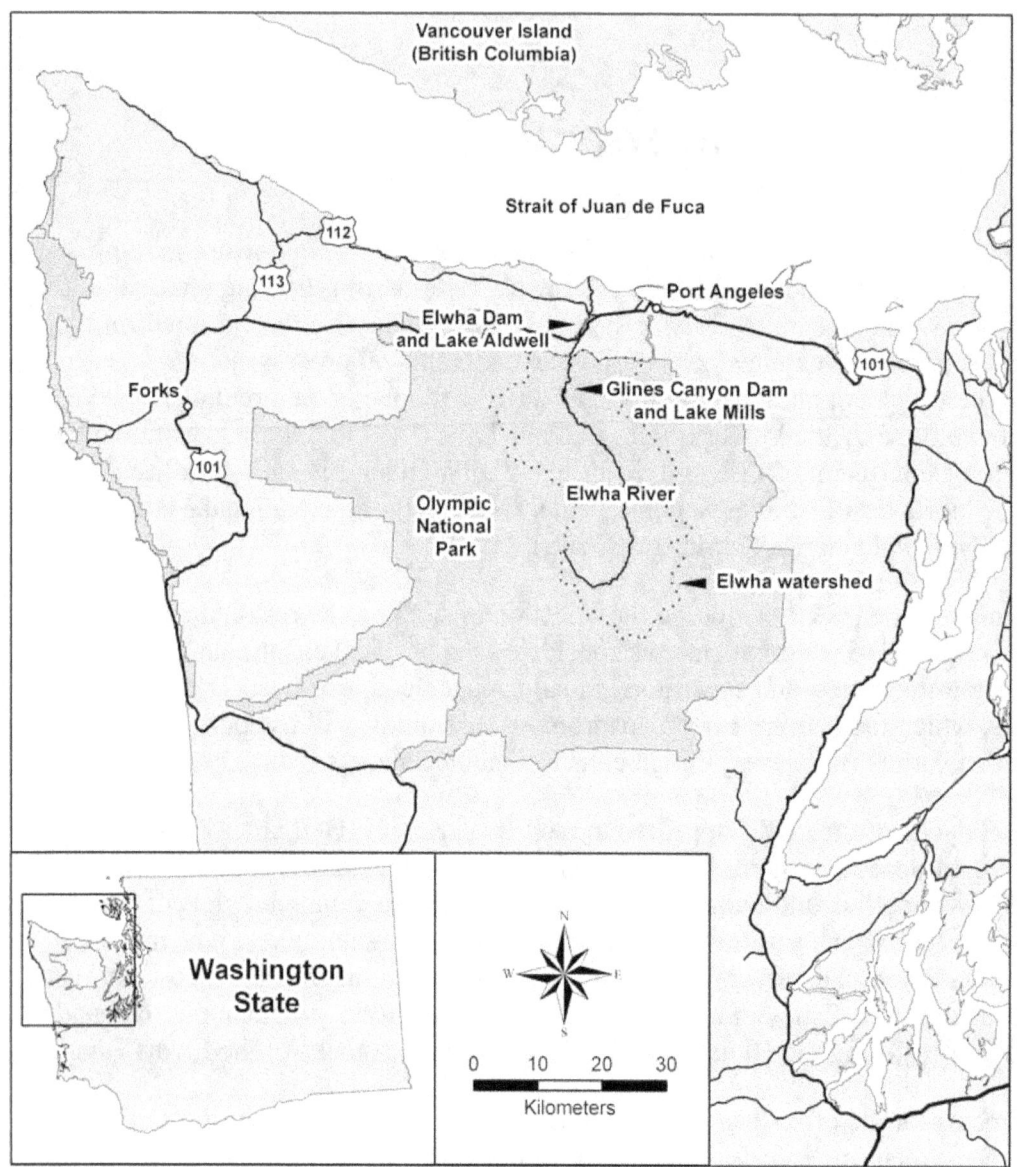

Figure 1. Location of Elwha River watershed.

status, and identified alternate donor stocks. Fisheries experts from local, regional, and international arenas contributed to this evaluation. Throughout the planning process, consideration was given to the genetic composition of stocks, fish health protocols, origin and stock history, hatchery domestication impacts, and the availability of suitable numbers of fish needed to achieve effective breeding populations.

Preferred options were developed for each species and stock, along with the strategy to employ to promote and facilitate restoration (Table 1). The EFRP also identifies alternative stocks and restoration strategies, in the event that the preferred alternative fails to achieve the project goals.

Table 1. Preferred options for Elwha River anadromous fish restoration.

Species	Preferred stock	Stock origin	Description of option*
Winter steelhead	Elwha late-timed component	Natural and hatchery and upriver rainbow trout (*O. mykiss*)	Hatchery enhancement of wild winter steelhead stock Natural recolonization by upriver rainbow trout population Natural recolonization by wild winter steelhead stock
Summer steelhead	Elwha summer	Natural and hatchery and upriver rainbow trout	Natural recolonization by upriver rainbow trout population Natural recolonization by wild summer steelhead stock
Coastal cutthroat trout	Elwha native	Upriver stock	Natural recolonization by existing in-river stock
Bull trout and Dolly Varden	Elwha native	Upriver stock	Natural recolonization by existing in-river stock
Spring Chinook salmon	Elwha summer and fall	Hatchery and natural	Hatchery enhancement of existing stock, rely on natural process to reestablish run timing Natural recolonization by existing in-river stock
Summer and fall Chinook salmon	Elwha summer and fall	Hatchery and natural	Hatchery enhancement and rely on natural process to reestablish native run Natural recolonization by existing in-river stock
Coho salmon	Elwha	Hatchery	Hatchery enhancement Natural recolonization by existing in-river stock
Pink salmon	Elwha	Natural	Hatchery enhancement of existing in-river stock Natural recolonization by existing in-river stock
Chum salmon	Elwha	Natural	Hatchery enhancement of existing in-river stock Natural recolonization by existing in-river stock
Sockeye salmon	Elwha	Natural	Natural recolonization by existing in-river kokanee (*Oncorhynchus nerka*), lacustrine sockeye stock Natural recolonization by existing in-river sockeye stock
Forage fish	Elwha	Natural	Natural recolonization of existing in-river and nearshore stocks
Lamprey	Elwha	Natural	Natural recolonization of existing in-river stocks

* The term "hatchery enhancement" includes a broad array of strategies that may be used to facilitate recolonization of the watershed. Please refer to the Stock Selection and Restoration Strategies section for a detailed description of enhancement options.

In addition to stock selection and restoration alternatives, this plan also provides information on general habitat restoration activities needed to achieve the goals of the Elwha River Ecosystem and Fisheries Restoration Act, Public Law 102-495 (Elwha Act), and the monitoring and assessment actions needed to adaptively manage for changing conditions. The reader is also directed to the proceedings of the technical workshop on nearshore restoration in the Central Strait of Juan de Fuca (Clallam County MRC 2004) and Shaffer et al. (2005) for an overview of nearshore restoration and salmon recovery.

This restoration plan is a working document and is intended to serve as a framework on which to base the preservation and restoration of anadromous fish populations within the Elwha River basin during and after dam removal. Monitoring conducted throughout the duration of the restoration effort will assist resource managers in evaluating success or failure of management actions taken, provide critical information on the capacity of the system to sustain itself, and help managers to maintain a flexible adaptive management approach that can respond to changes in the Elwha River ecosystem as recolonization by anadromous fish populations occurs.

Project Background

Overview

Since 1911 the Elwha Dam, located at RM 4.9 on the Elwha River, has blocked anadromous fish passage to more than 70 miles of mainstem and tributary habitat in the watershed (DOI et al. 1994). In 1927 the Glines Canyon Dam was constructed 8.5 miles upstream of the Elwha Dam. Like the Elwha Dam, the Glines Canyon Dam was built without fish passage capability.

The two Elwha River dams not only block passage of anadromous fish but also have interrupted the natural function of the river ecosystem. Nearly 18 million cubic yards of sediment have been captured in the two reservoirs (DOI et al 1995), affecting not only the lower river system but also the estuarine and nearshore environment to the east and west of the river mouth—an area that extends from Ediz Hook to Crescent Bay (Clallam County MRC 2004). The recruitment of large woody debris (LWD) from the upper watershed has been virtually eliminated and the two reservoirs serve as "heat sinks" during the summer, dramatically increasing water temperature. Consequently, the cumulative effects of the two dams leave the freshwater and marine habitat available to salmon below the Elwha Dam severely degraded. The presence of the two dams has been identified as the single largest factor limiting Elwha River salmon production (WSCC 2000), including Chinook salmon and bull trout, which are listed as threatened under the Endangered Species Act.

The Elwha Watershed Area

The Elwha River watershed encompasses 321 square miles, of which 267 square miles (83%) are protected in perpetuity within ONP. The river itself has a general north-south orientation, flowing north to debouch into the Strait of Juan de Fuca. Mean winter flows average approximately 2,000 cubic feet per second (cfs), while mean summer flows average approximately 600 cfs. Peak flood events have exceeded 40,000 cfs, while base summer low flows may be as low as 200 cfs. Annual precipitation in the basin ranges from 220 inches near the headwaters of the watershed to 56 inches at the river mouth. Substantial snow accumulates in the upper elevations during the winter creating a bimodal flow pattern, with peak flows seen in November (associated with rain or snow events) and June (associated with snowmelt) (Elwha-Dungeness Planning Unit 2005). Over the period of record, the average size of the peak annual flow events has nearly doubled (Figure 2), while the frequency of high flow events is also increasing.

Dam Removal and Salmon Recovery Planning

Applications for licensing the Elwha and Glines Canyon dams were filed with the Federal Energy Regulatory Commission (FERC) in 1968 and 1973, respectively, sparking nearly two decades of debate regarding the impact of the two dams on the fisheries within the watershed

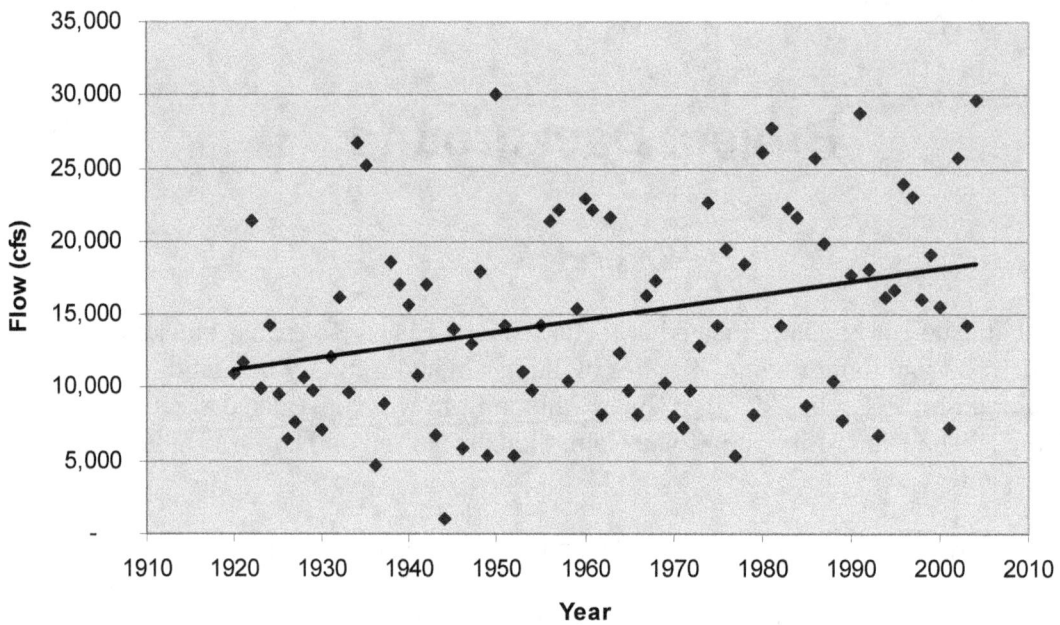

Figure 2. Elwha River peak flow events (USGS unpubl. data). The slope of the regression line
(y = 85.717x − 153368) is statistically different from 0 (F = 8.868; α (2) : 0.01 > α > 0.005).

and the government jurisdiction responsible for oversight of the two facilities. The then
Washington Department of Fisheries (WDF) reached a settlement with the dam owners in 1975
(WDF and Crown Zellerbach 1975), that required the two dams be operated as "run of the river"
and also provided a portion of the construction and annual operation costs for an artificial rearing
facility on the river to produce a maximum of 360,000 pounds of juvenile Chinook salmon each
year.

Although WDF reached a settlement with the dam owners, other governmental agencies
(including the LEKT, ONP, NOAA Fisheries Service, and USFWS) along with various
environmental groups continued to oppose the licensing of the dams. Ultimately, in order to
settle legal disputes regarding jurisdiction and trust responsibilities, Congress passed the Elwha
Act in 1992.

The Elwha Act provided for federal acquisition of the two dams and required a specific
plan to achieve "full restoration" of the Elwha River fisheries and ecosystem. The Department
of the Interior (DOI et al. 1994) subsequently published the Elwha Report, which found that full
restoration could only be achieved through the removal of both dams. In 1995 DOI completed
the first of two environmental impact statements (EISs) regarding dam removal (DOI et al.
1995). The 1995 document evaluated the decision to remove the dams. A second EIS,
completed in 1996, evaluated the physical effects of dam removal (DOI et al. 1996).

Since completion of these three documents, a number of significant actions have
occurred. First, the federal government acquired the two dams from private ownership in 2000.
Second, Puget Chinook salmon, bull trout, and Puget Sound steelhead ESU populations have
been listed as threatened under the ESA. Recovery planning for these species is underway by
NWFSC and USFWS. Recovery planning for Chinook salmon and bullhead species has been

further facilitated by Shared Salmon Strategy for Puget Sound, which submitted draft recovery plans to the two federal agencies in June 2005 (Shared Salmon Strategy for Puget Sound 2005). Third, the State of Washington initiated watershed planning efforts under ESHB (Engrossed Substitute House Bill) 2514 in order to establish the minimum instream flows in state streams needed to protect and restore salmon populations. Fourth, Clallam County completed and adopted its watershed plan for the Elwha River in 2005 (Elwha-Dungeness Planning Unit 2005). Finally, DOI drafted a supplemental EIS to evaluate design changes that are required for the project to address changed conditions since the original EISs were written.

Dam removal is scheduled to begin in approximately 3 to 5 years. Compliance requirements and permits were secured for construction activities, and in 2007 contracts were awarded to construct water treatment facilities on the river for both municipal and industrial water supplies in order to meet requirements of the Elwha Act to protect water supplies during dam removal. The exact start date for dam removal is not known at this time as it depends on completion of two water treatment facilities, cost estimates of final design, dedication of funding by Congress, and administrative requirements for soliciting and awarding the construction contract.

Expected Conditions

Nearly 18 million cubic yards of sediment are stored in the two Elwha River reservoirs (Table 2). As dam removal begins, fine sediments will become suspended in the reservoirs and transported downstream. During the initial phases of removal, it is anticipated turbidity levels will exceed 1,000 parts per million (ppm) for extended periods of time and will spike to levels exceeding 10,000 ppm (Figure 3). Following dam removal, suspended sediment levels may exceed 30,000 ppm for short durations (BOR 1996). Fish exposed to sediment loads between 50 and 100 ppm for an extended period of time may stop feeding, suffer gill abrasion, and experience loss of fitness due to the associated stress (Cook-Tabor 1995). At turbidity levels above 1,000 ppm, direct mortality may result simply from the elevated sediment loads (Cook-Tabor 1995). With sediment loads expected to exceed 10,000 ppm, it was assumed for planning purposes that most or all fish rearing naturally in the Elwha River below Glines Canyon Dam will die during dam removal.

In addition to fine sediment loading, coarser sediments will be released into the lower watershed following dam removal, elevating the bedload (sediment as it slides, rolls, or bounces along a stream or channel bed of flowing water) above natural background levels for up to 10 years (BOR 1996). It is anticipated the stream channel below the dams may destabilize during this time, with a resultant temporary decrease in quality of the natural fish habitat.

Implementation of Fish Windows

So-called fish window periods have been built into the dam demolition schedule to accommodate migration, spawning, and collection of broodstock. During fish window periods, the release or transport of sediment will be curtailed and water quality in the river temporarily improved. These windows correlate to times that fish are entering the river or are emigrating to the Strait of Juan de Fuca. To the extent that the fish window periods coincide with important

Table 2. Reservoir sediments.

Sediment size	Amount (million yards³)	Method of transport	Rate of transport
Silt or clay	9.2	Suspension—all flows	High
Sand	6.2	Suspension—high flows	High
		Bedload—all flows	Medium
Gravels and cobbles	2.3	Bedload—all flows	Slow
Total	17.7		

life history phases of other aquatic species (e.g., forage fish or shellfish), those species will also benefit. However, accommodations in the demolition schedule have only been made to facilitate protection and recovery of the river's salmon species.

Fish window periods will occur three times during each year of the active dam removal process: 1 November to 31 December for coho and chum salmon entry timing, 1 May to 30 June for hatchery-reared juvenile emigration and adult native steelhead entry timing, and 1 August to 14 September for Chinook and pink salmon entry timing (Figure 4).[1] Dam removal activity will also be halted for worker safety during periods of time where stream flows exceed 3,000 cfs.

Role of Hatcheries

The role of the WDFW and Elwha tribal hatcheries throughout the restoration effort is to preserve extant populations during dam removal and to help initiate recolonization of the watershed through the temporary supplementation of key species in the basin following dam removal. These hatchery facilities will be safe havens, serving as gene banks for Elwha River fish populations, protecting fish from predicted high sediment loads in the river during the dam removal process, and ensuring that no year-class of fish is lost because of dam removal activities.

Considerable thought went into determining the preferred role of hatcheries in the recovery process. Evidence from several studies suggests the natural spawning success of hatchery origin fish may be considerably lower than that of the native, natural-origin population (Reisenbichler and McIntyre 1977, Chilcote et al. 1986, Berejikian 1995). Fish reared for extended periods in hatcheries (e.g., to the yearling life history phase) have been shown to survive at lower rates than natural origin fish (Chilcote 2002), potentially through the expression of altered behavioral, genetic, or phenotypic characteristics that may decrease their fitness in the natural environment (Bugert et al. 1992, Campton 1995, Reisenbichler and Rubin 1999).

Fitness and survival effects of hatchery propagation rearing may be less evident, however, depending on broodstock origin, the degree of intervention into the natural life cycle, and the duration of the hatchery program (Kapuscinski and Miller 1993, Arden 2003, Blouin and Araki 2005, USFWS 2005, Ford et al. 2006). Species reared in hatcheries for a minimal time

---

[1] T. Randle, U.S. Bureau of Reclamation, Denver, CO. Pers. commun., 3 December 2005.

Lake Mills surface elevation (meters)

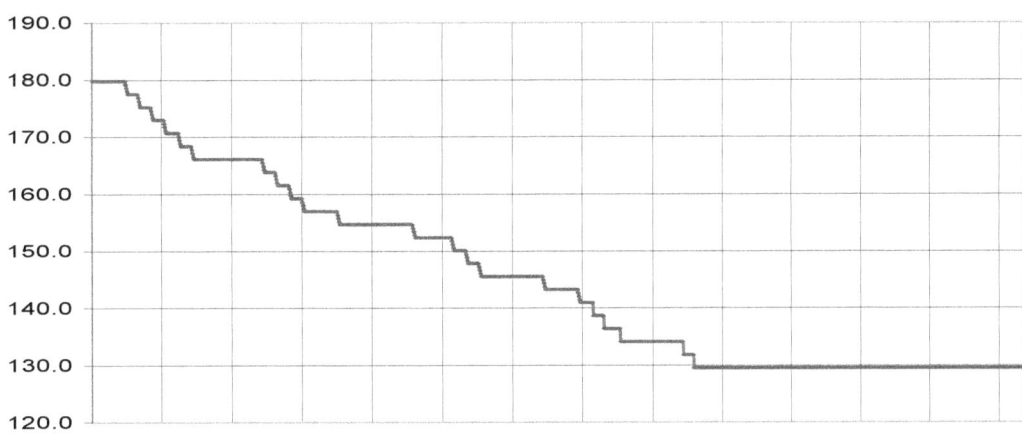

Elwha River discharge (cms)

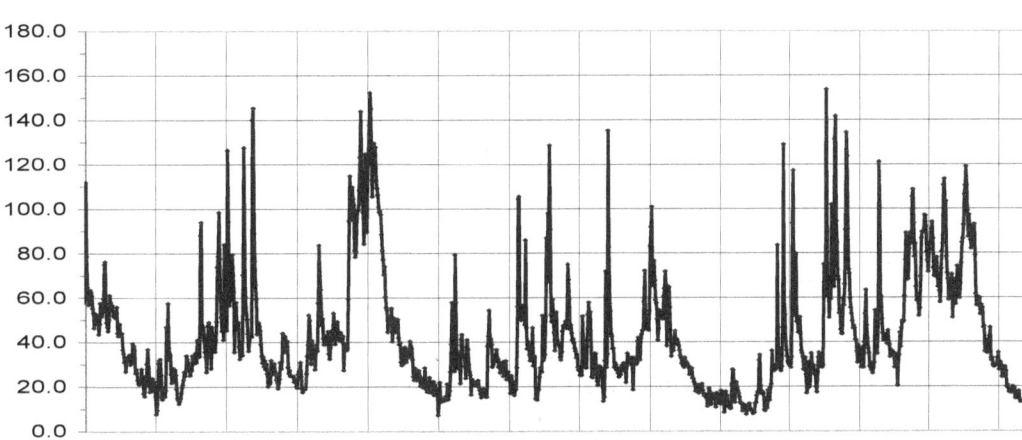

Fine sediment concentration (100s of ppm)

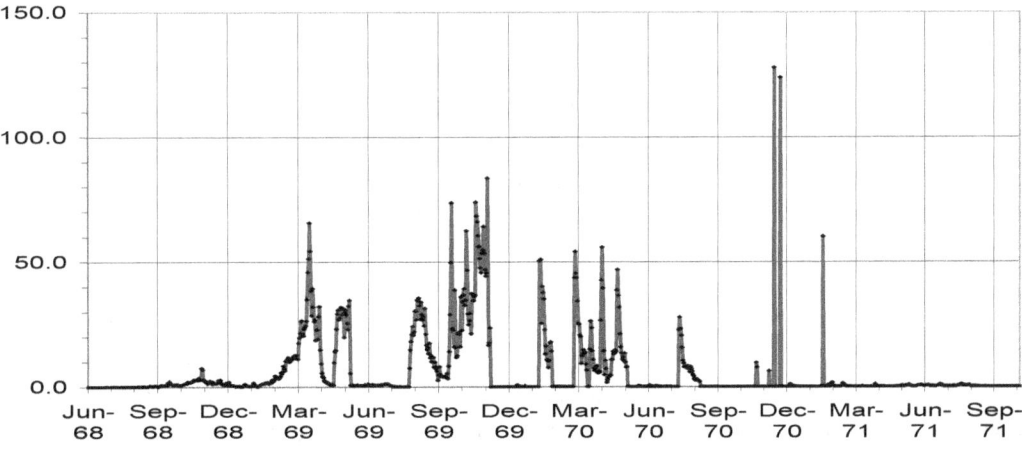

Figure 3. Modeled Lake Mills surface elevations, Elwha River discharge, and suspended sediment concentrations: 1968–1971 flow scenario (BOR 1996).

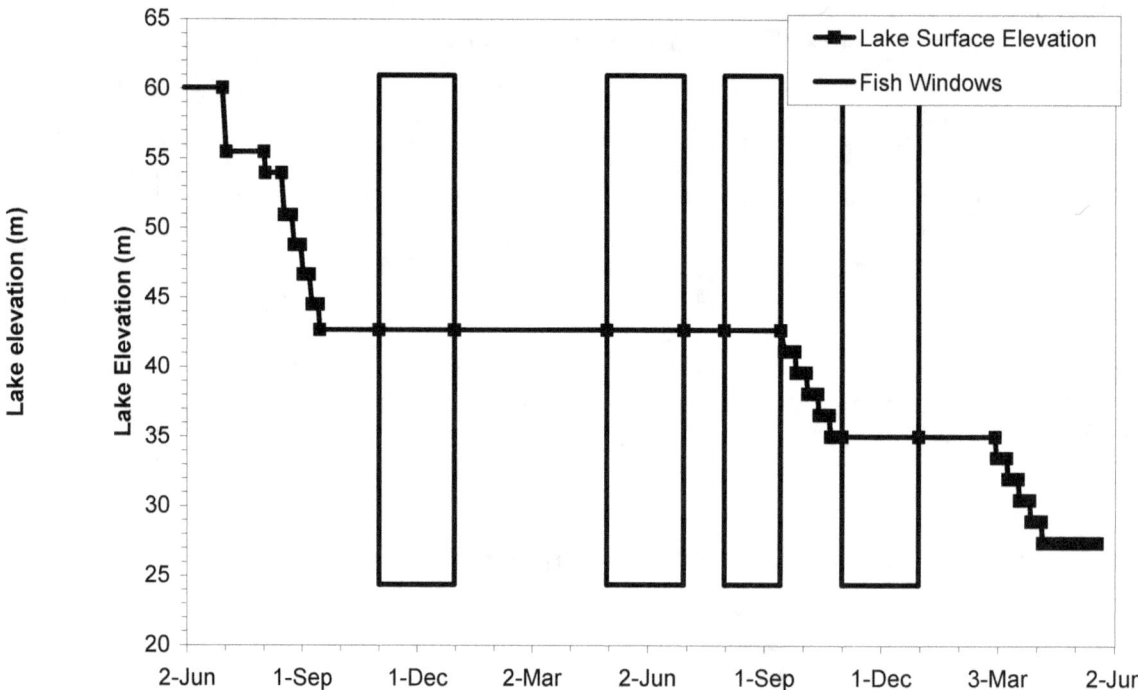

Figure 4. Elwha River drawdown schedule and fish windows.

(e.g., ocean rearing Chinook salmon, chum salmon, and pink salmon) seem to be less likely to change phenotypically and genetically in response to hatchery rearing than are species with longer freshwater rearing times (coho, yearling Chinook, steelhead) (Berejikian and Ford 2004). Results from hatchery-based supplementation and reintroduction programs designed to preserve and restore ESA-listed summer chum salmon indicate that hatcheries can bolster the abundances of naturally spawning and natural-origin fish, and reestablish naturally spawning populations in watersheds where indigenous stocks have been extirpated (WDFW and PNPTT 2003, PNPTC et al. 2005, WDFW and PNPTC 2006).

Restoration of anadromous fish will occur in the Elwha River in the absence of hatchery supplementation, although the time frame for natural recovery is uncertain. The choice to use hatcheries to supplement the restoration effort has been driven by the high risk during dam removal of losing stocks of fish identified as unique, threatened, or endangered. In addition, the Department of the Interior, WDFW, LEKT, and other interested parties want to ensure that significant progress towards fish restoration occurs within a 20 to 30 year time frame.

Identifying and developing the preferred role of hatcheries in the recovery process occurred following extensive consultation with a wide range of scientists and political leaders in the region. Discussions focused on finding a balance between the goals of restoration, preserving stocks of fish unique to the Elwha River, producing fish capable of successfully integrating into the natural environment, and reducing the length of time necessary to achieve restoration.

Hatchery Facilities

The hatchery-based fish preservation and restoration activities described in this plan will rely primarily on two hatchery facilities located within the Elwha River basin: WDFW's Elwha rearing channel and LEKT's Lower Elwha Hatchery. Three out-of-basin hatchery facilities operated by WDFW will be used to support the two in-basin hatcheries as satellite incubation, rearing, and broodstock production locations: Sol Duc Hatchery, Hurd Creek Hatchery, and the Morse Creek rearing and broodstock collection facility.

WDFW Elwha rearing channel

The Elwha rearing channel is located at approximately RM 3.5 on the mainstem Elwha River, immediately downstream of the Port Angeles industrial water supply diversion structure. Water for the facility is largely supplied by the surface water structure, but several small wells also provide water. The channel does not have incubation or early rearing facilities, but can hold up to 3.5 million fingerlings and 200,000 yearlings at the time of release. This facility will be the central focus of the Elwha River Chinook salmon restoration effort.

Lower Elwha Hatchery

LEKT currently operates a fish hatchery near the river mouth. In order to achieve restoration objectives and to ensure successful hatchery operation during and following dam removal, a new tribal facility has been designed and will be constructed prior to dam removal on tribal lands upstream of the present location (RM 1.0). This new facility will be the central focus for restoration efforts of winter steelhead and coho, chum, and pink salmon. It will provide a controlled environment for the receiving, processing, and spawning of adults, incubation of eggs, and rearing of juveniles.

Morse Creek rearing facility

WDFW is planning to construct a small Chinook salmon rearing and recapture facility on Morse Creek. This program is designed to create an Elwha River lineage adult Chinook salmon return to Morse Creek that can serve as a genetic reserve and alternative broodstock source in the event of a catastrophic loss of the donor natural- or hatchery-origin components of the population in the Elwha River during and shortly after the dam-removal period. The Morse Creek rearing and broodstock collection facility will be available for the final rearing of 200,000 yearling Chinook salmon for volitional release into Morse Creek.

Hurd Creek Hatchery

The Hurd Creek Hatchery in the Dungeness watershed will serve as the initial incubation site for fertilized eggs procured from Chinook salmon collected from the Elwha River. Following eyeing, the eggs will be transferred to the WDFW Sol Duc Hatchery.

Sol Duc Hatchery

The Sol Duc Hatchery will conduct final incubation and initial early rearing of Elwha River Chinook salmon. From the Sol Duc Hatchery, fry will be transferred to the Elwha rearing channel for additional rearing, acclimation, and release as subyearlings and yearlings. Fingerlings will also be transferred to the Morse Creek rearing and broodstock collection facility for volitional release as yearlings into the creek.

Fish Release Locations

On-station releases of fish will occur at the Elwha rearing channel and the Lower Elwha Hatchery in the Elwha River basin and the Morse Creek release facility. Off-station releases of fish will occur at Lake Sutherland and at a series of acclimation or release sites throughout the middle and lower portions of the basin. Upper basin sites will be accessed by helicopter and will be used initially for outplanting of Chinook salmon only. Off-station release locations include the following:

- Lake Sutherland sites for release include the public boat ramp and net pens located in the lake.

- The use of formal acclimation ponds located in the middle reaches of the Elwha River is under consideration. The number of acclimation ponds and their exact locations have yet to be determined.

- Middle-reach release sites include primarily side-channel areas on the east side of the river, accessible from the Hot Springs Road.

- The use of upriver helicopter release sites includes 31 outplanting sites previously identified by the USFWS in the 1990s that will be used for upriver release of fish (Wunderlich and Dilley 1990). Outplanting locations extend from RM 19 to RM 42.

Fish Recovery Facilities

Recovery of returning adult fish will occur at the Elwha rearing channel, the Lower Elwha Hatchery, and the Morse Creek rearing and broodstock collection facility. In addition, a weir will be constructed in the Elwha River immediately upstream of the Elwha rearing channel for the purposes of capturing returning Chinook salmon (Figure 5). This facility will only be operated during summer low flow periods and will be supplemented by in-river capture using seines when deemed efficient or necessary.

Hatchery Protocols

Hatchery protocols designed to achieve restoration goals are currently in development. Operational protocols implemented through this plan include hatchery management practices applied for decades, more recently derived practices designed to promote optimal overall fish survival in the hatchery and postrelease, and new conservation-based practices implemented in response to federal ESA listings of several local fish populations. Preliminary details regarding each hatchery program proposed for implementation are provided in draft hatchery genetic management plans (HGMPs) assembled by WDFW and LEKT and submitted for NOAA Fisheries Service evaluation for compliance with ESA 4(d) Rule Limit 6 criteria (LEKT 2003a, 2003b, 2003c, WDFW 2005). The four HGMPs are included in two Puget Sound–wide hatchery resource management plans proposed by WDFW and the Puget Sound Treaty Tribes as

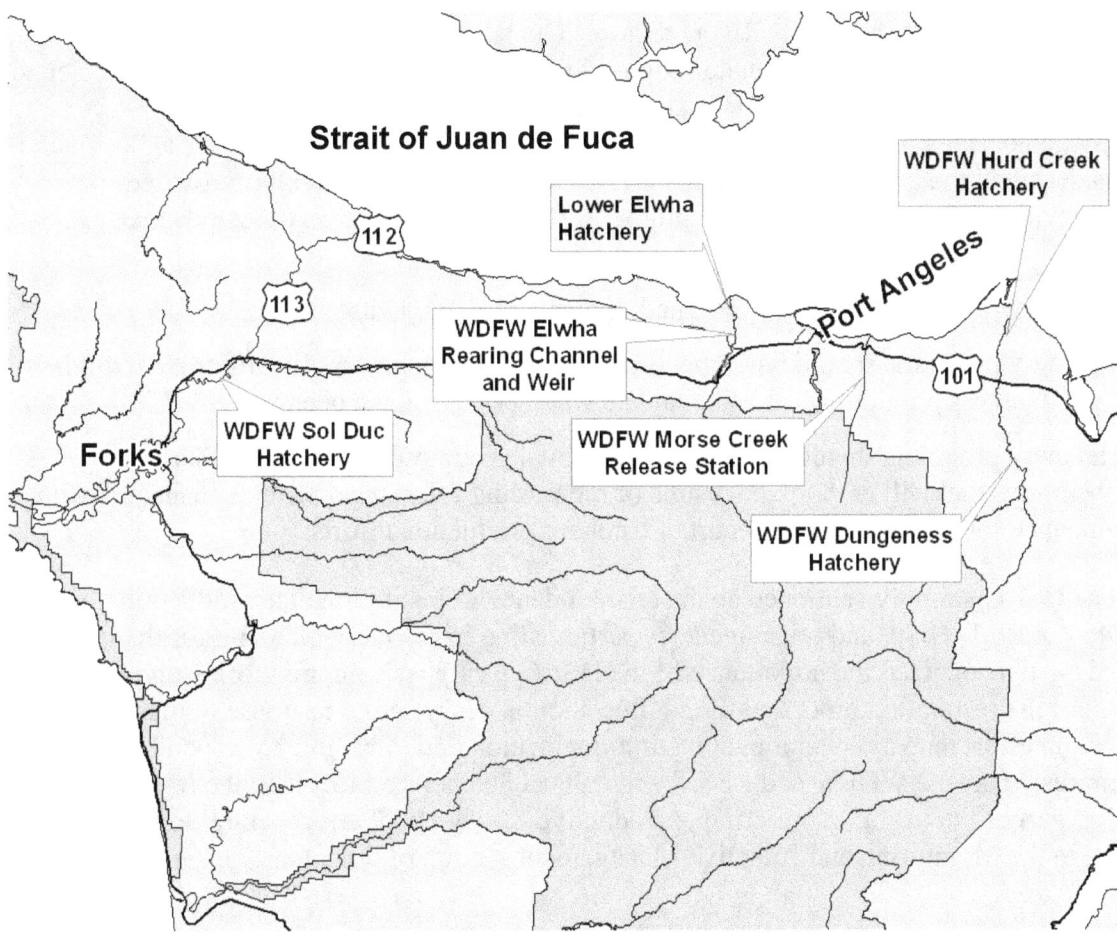

Figure 5. Regional fish culture facilities.

overarching approaches for managing hatchery programs in the region to contribute to the conservation and recovery of ESA-listed Puget Sound Chinook salmon and Hood Canal summer chum salmon ESUs (PSTT and WDFW 2004, WDFW and PSTT 2004).

Hatchery operations and methods under development are designed to incorporate fish culture innovations that increase postrelease survival of fish and increase natural spawning by returning adults in the wild. Operational parameters will emphasize reduced rearing densities, increased flows, and providing structure and cover in rearing units. The potential for biased selection of adults will be limited through broodstock selection methods that are representative of time of arrival, age, size, and sex ratio, and will be used in conjunction with mating protocols that are random with respect to phenotypic traits to preserve genetic variability.

Attempts will be made to match rearing temperature conditions in the hatchery with those in the Elwha River where appropriate, so that hatchery-reared fish do not have a competitive size advantage.

Hatchery protocols under development will make use of innovative rearing technologies and will emphasize the production of fish that maximize effective population size, as recommended by the Hatchery Scientific Review Group (HSRG) during its review of the Eastern

Straits (Discovery Bay to the Elwha River) region. The HSRG is an independent panel of scientists funded by Congress to evaluate proposed reforms to hatchery protocols in Puget Sound and Pacific coastal areas of Washington State. This review of hatchery operations and programmatic goals applied a scientific approach to hatchery management and pointed to a suite of actions designed to help achieve these goals (HSRG 2002). The HSRG has provided additional review of proposed operational protocols (HSRG 2004) and recommends the following:

- Hatchery programs should be designed to meet recovery goals.

- Hatchery programs should have specific measurable benchmarks identified that will be used to assess program goals and evaluate whether goals have been met.

- Hatchery programs should have a formal, annual programmatic review of hatchery operations that will employ the results of monitoring efforts and provide managers with guidance for how to modify or curtail hatchery production efforts.

The HSRG strongly cautioned against the tendency to institutionalize production goals. The WDFW, LEKT, ONP, and other agencies participating in recovery planning for the Elwha watershed have recognized the importance of the HSRG's emphasis on monitoring and evaluation of the restoration process through time and the ecosystem's response to management actions. In an effort to avoid operational institutionalization and to be able to respond to ecosystem response, the WDFW and LEKT will subject hatchery protocols to the review process included as part of the overall monitoring and adaptive management effort central to the discussion in the Monitoring and Adaptive Management section of this plan.

Harvest Management

Management of the harvest of salmon originating in Washington State waters can be generally described as "weak stock management." That is, all fisheries are designed to meet specific escapement and exploitation rate objectives for the weakest "primary" populations, even when managing for these populations may require closures or significant restriction of many fisheries. Prior to the 1990s, application of the weak stock management concept also led to the management of some natural salmon populations as "secondary" to harvest and escapement needs identified for primary populations. These secondary management stocks included certain aggregate hatchery and wild populations, natural populations occurring in low (de minimis) proportions of the total abundance of a particular species in mixed stock fishing areas, and natural populations originating from watersheds where hatchery fish of the same stock predominated. Fisheries occurring in mixed stock and some terminal areas were therefore not managed to meet identified spawning objectives for secondary populations and the populations consequently experienced poor escapements in some years.

The development of initiatives by WDFW and the Puget Sound tribes in the mid-1990s directed at wild salmonid population restoration, and the proposed ESA listing of several salmon populations later that decade, led to changes in harvest management strategies that were based on the secondary management concept. A detailed description of the current approaches applied for harvest management for Chinook salmon in Puget Sound can be found in Appendix B: Chinook Salmon Harvest Management and in the Comprehensive Management Plan for Puget Sound

Chinook (PSIT and WDFW 2004). Coho salmon management is very similar to that described for Chinook salmon in Appendix B, except with different harvest rate targets. Management of sockeye, chum, and pink salmon differs slightly from Chinook and coho salmon, with fisheries more directly governed by the provisions of the Pacific Salmon Treaty (PST). A summary of the current harvest management approach follows.

For management purposes, current fisheries are generally divided into four groups: Alaskan and Canadian interception fisheries, U.S. preterminal interception fisheries, terminal area fisheries, and extreme terminal fisheries. Provisions of the PST direct the Alaskan and Canadian interception fisheries. The PST's annexes, which set objectives for each salmon species, are renewed periodically and updated with new information or new policy standards. The current annexes recognize the depressed status of both Canadian and U.S. Chinook and coho salmon populations, and restrict fisheries accordingly. Fisheries in U.S. waters south of the Canadian border are coordinated through the Pacific Fishery Management Council (PFMC).[2] Salmon fisheries in the U.S. exclusive economic zone (3 to 200 miles offshore) are managed under regulations recommended by the PFMC and implemented by NMFS, while each state and affected tribe is responsible for implementation of regulations for their respective fisheries in waters inshore of 3 miles.

For years the naturally spawning stocks of salmon in the Elwha River were managed as secondary populations, with the hatchery stocks on the river accorded primary status. However, to be consistent with risk averse harvest management approaches applied for other natural-origin populations in the Strait of Juan de Fuca region, LEKT and WDFW agreed, beginning in the 1990s, to manage all naturally spawning salmon populations in the Elwha River as primary populations.

This change helped ensure that all fisheries in U.S. waters south of the Canadian border would be managed to meet natural spawner escapement goals and objectives established for Elwha River salmon populations. In addition when active dam removal begins, the tribe and WDFW have agreed to curtail all in-river fisheries for a period of 5 years. Following this time, the opportunity to recommence limited fisheries in-river will be evaluated, based on stock status. However, all agencies recognize the objective is recovery of healthy, self-sustaining natural spawning populations to the watershed, and in-river harvest activities will be scheduled to avoid interfering with recovery.

Fisheries Restoration Periods

During dam removal the restoration effort will involve three discrete periods. These periods will dictate and define the restoration strategy efforts and direction and will influence the rate of ecosystem recovery. The three restoration periods are before dam removal, defined as all years prior to beginning actual demolition of the dams; active dam removal, a three-year time frame between commencement of demolition and the time when fish may freely swim upstream

---

[2] The PFMC refers to the area south of the U.S-Canadian border as "southern U.S. fisheries." Because it is a fisheries management term, the meaning of "geographic boundaries" varies, depending on context. For the purposes of this plan, this area includes commercial, tribal, and recreational fisheries in marine and freshwater from Washington to California.

through the construction site; and after dam removal, defined as the 10 years following provision of fish passage. Characteristics of each period follow.

Pre-dam-removal Period

Until demolition begins, the dams will remain in place and will be operated by the U.S. Bureau of Reclamation (BOR) to generate power. Upriver and downriver passage by fish is not possible. Hatcheries and the Elwha Surface Water Intake and Elwha Water Treatment Plant will undergo modification, renovation, or replacement during this period. Total hatchery production capacity may be limited either by the status of facility infrastructure renovation or due to water availability. Hatchery-based fish production efforts will emphasize maintaining ongoing enhancement programs or will be increased to boost total future adult returns. Adult capture weirs will be erected seasonally in the river main stem in association with the two Elwha basin hatchery facilities and at the new Morse Creek rearing and broodstock collection facility to facilitate broodstock collection. Both pre-dam-removal monitoring and long-term study design will have been completed.

Dam-removal Period

Dam removal will be initiated and completed during this approximate 3-year period. During the first year, minimal changes will occur to the environmental quality of the lower portion of the Elwha River. As dam removal progresses, elevated levels of turbidity will be common as sediments trapped in the reservoirs become mobilized and are transported downstream (BOR 1996). Habitat quality within the lower 12 miles of the Elwha River basin will be severely reduced by pulses of suspended and bedload sediment interspersed by periods of clearing due to the implementation of fish windows. As removal proceeds and the reservoir surface area is reduced, river temperatures below the dams will approach natural background levels.

Hatchery facilities modifications will have been completed by the start of this period. The Elwha Surface Water Intake and Elwha Water Treatment Plant will be operational and provide hatchery facilities with treated water. Production goals during this period are limited by the production capability of the water treatment facility. Downstream passage by outplanted or natural-origin smolts as well as upstream passage by returning adults will be reestablished. Elwha River sport and commercial fishery harvest will be curtailed throughout this period for all salmon stocks.

Post-dam-removal Period

Dam removal will be completed at the start of this 10-year period. Turbidity in the basin will have stabilized and water quality will approach natural background levels. The shared water treatment facility will have been taken off-line and hatchery facilities will receive untreated surface water. Hatchery production of salmon will no longer be limited by water availability, and fish culture programs will be increased to full restoration production levels. The adult capture weir spanning the mainstem Elwha River will be phased out and greater emphasis will be placed on natural recolonization. Active monitoring programs will assess rates of stock rebuilding. This data will be used to judge the success or failure of restoration efforts and to gauge decisions concerning hatchery outplanting efforts.

Stock Selection and Restoration Strategies

Careful consideration and analysis has been given to the range of strategies that may be appropriate for achieving the goals of preserving and restoring anadromous fish populations in the Elwha River watershed commensurate with dam removal. Wunderlich and Pantaleo (1995) completed the first detailed analysis of methods that might be used to reintroduce salmon into the upper Elwha River. Since that analysis, strategies have been revisited and revised based on new information. These strategies include selection of stocks, methods for preserving populations during dam removal, methods for reintroducing populations into the watershed following dam removal, and alternative actions if preferred methods fail.

During development of the EFRP, guidance was sought from independent scientists, organizations such as the HSRG, state and federal agencies, and resource managers on how to achieve restoration of fisheries and ecosystem function in the shortest time possible. In general opinions regarding how to approach recovery are wide ranging. Roles that hatcheries play in the basin, selection of species and stocks, life history phases that should be released, duration of residency for fish in the hatchery environment, and locations selected for outplanting have all been the subject of debate.

The process of first preserving and then restoring anadromous fish populations to the Elwha River watershed above the Elwha Dam is not a simple task. The dams cannot be removed with the expectation that fish will naturally recolonize the watershed within a "reasonable" time frame, as the potential donor populations that use the river below Elwha Dam are in chronically low abundance and, further, will be dramatically affected by dam removal itself. Without proactive intervention, the conditions that will be present in the river below the dams during and immediately following dam removal may result in mortality rates approaching 100% for any naturally rearing fish, virtually eliminating the local brood source for recolonization (see the Project Background section).

Even if some fish survive the removal process, the abundance is likely to be so low as to create a genetic bottleneck. Fish from other river systems might repopulate the Elwha watershed over time, but for ESA-listed and candidate species (Chinook and coho salmon, bull trout, and steelhead) extirpation resulting from dam removal is not an acceptable option. For other species, such as chum and pink salmon, there is little local evidence that recolonization through straying will occur in the short term, as other potential donor populations are in low abundance. For example, Dungeness River and Morse Creek—two adjacent river systems—have seen steady declines in pink and chum salmon production, with little evidence of straying from outside systems (Small 2004).

Restoration Design

The restoration design for the Elwha River restoration plan comes from two key factors: the spatial arrangement of the watershed and current supplementation practices. The Elwha watershed has been physically partitioned into four general areas since dam construction was completed in 1927: 1) the upper watershed above both dams, 2) the middle reach between the Glines Canyon and Elwha dams, 3) the reservoir sections behind each dam, and 4) the lower Elwha below the Elwha dam. In addition, with the exception of limited stocking activities related to the assessment of downstream passage at the two dams and stocking of resident trout between and above the dams, since the early 1900s anadromous salmonid supplementation has only occurred in the lower Elwha River.

Though supplementation will be used for some salmonids in the lower Elwha following removal, natural recolonization is an integral part of the overall restoration strategy. The spatial partitioning of the watershed in combination with natural recolonization for some of the salmonid species provides the opportunity to develop a restoration design that has three parts: no supplementation, limited supplementation (e.g., one or two generations), and general supplementation (e.g., more than one generation).

Areas beyond the dams—such as the upper Elwha—are considered pristine habitats because they have not been altered by anthropogenic activities and have no ongoing hatchery supplementation activities. The area between the two dams, not including the two reservoirs, is typically considered altered habitat due to the loss of sediment supply from Glines Canyon, historic logging and floodplain encroachment by roads, historic stocking of trout into Lake Aldwell, and ongoing stocking of trout into Lake Sutherland. The reservoirs represent the most physically altered habitats, with evidence that the historic planting of nonnative trout has altered the fish community though there is currently no supplementation. Finally, the lower Elwha has been altered through various land use activities and large-scale salmonid supplementation activities. In addition each of these areas, with the exception of the reservoir sections, has the same basic general habitat types, including mainstem, tributary, and floodplain habitats.

The overall restoration design will be to utilize this natural stratification by designating habitat areas in the following manner:

- No supplementation areas as an indicator of natural recolonization
- Limited supplementation for one to two generation cycles (4 to 8 years) with the focus on the subsequent recovery of native-origin returns (NORs)
- General supplementation for more than two generations

An additional layer of stratification for comparing how different supplementation and habitat restoration techniques succeed will be the general habitat types associated with each of these categories including the main stem, floodplain, and tributary (Table 3). Because different outplanting strategies (e.g., by life stage, location) have different habitat requirements, incorporating the natural habitat hierarchy into the restoration design will enable a better understanding of which restoration strategies have the greatest success in developing the most fit salmonid colonizers. Finally, stratification can occur among species, as different approaches to initiating recolonization may be used for each of the different species.

Table 3. Habitat strata.

Reach	Habitat area (m^2)				Habitat area (%)		
	Pool	Riffle	Glide	Total	Pool	Riffle	Glide
Main stem							
Lower Elwha	121,078	64,788	84,161	270,027	45	24	31
Middle Elwha	61,288	310,499	319,273	691,059	9	45	46
Whiskey Bend	2,150	–	5,121	7,272	30	0	70
Rica Canyon	26,549	26,549	26,549	79,646	33	33	33
Geyser Valley	10,523	48,986	37,031	96,540	11	51	38
Grand Canyon	55,752	55,752	55,752	167,256	33	33	33
Valley	1,754	8,164	6,172	16,090	11	51	38
Canyon	10,619	10,619	10,619	31,858	33	33	33
Press Valley	2,056	29,512	16,701	48,270	4	61	35
Carlson Canyon	15,929	15,929	15,929	47,787	33	33	33
Chicago Camp	6,314	41,044	10,566	57,924	11	71	18
Total	314,014	611,842	587,873	1,513,729	21	40	39
Side channels							
Lower Elwha	49,592	15,966	25,362	90,920	55	18	28
Middle Elwha	22,165	22,627	5,070	49,861	44	45	10
Whiskey Bend	147	104	79	330	45	31	24
Kraus Bottom	6,050	5,155	4,581	15,786	38	33	29
Elkhorn	215	717	1,495	2,427	9	30	62
Camp Wilder	832	1,126	920	2,877	29	39	32
Total	79,001	45,694	37,507	162,202	49	28	23

	Habitat area (m^2)		
	Alluvial main stem	Confined main stem	Floodplain channels
Below dams	270,027	–	90,920
Between dams	698,331	330	49,861
Above dams	218,824	326,547	21,090

Stock Selection

Salmon are known to rapidly colonize new habitat when provided the opportunity (Bryant et al. 1996 and 1999, Burger et al. 2000, Seiler 2000). However, when colonization is aided through artificial means, the selection of the appropriate donor stocks is critical to the ultimate success of the project, as it depends on fundamental biological capabilities of the donor populations (Burger et al. 2000, Chilcote 2003). Elwha River stocks would be the preferred populations to use in the recovery efforts. However, the current condition of the river below the dams certainly differs from historic conditions as well as from conditions currently seen above the dams. Additionally, hatchery programs have been used to aggressively supplement fish production below the dams and have included the introduction of nonnative stocks. Finally, several populations appear to be extirpated from the watershed or are present at such low numbers that recovery based on the use of these stocks may not be feasible. Therefore, it was necessary to carefully evaluate the status of existing populations to determine their fitness for utilization in the recovery plan.

Selection Criteria

When evaluating and selecting potential source populations for the restoration effort, five criteria were qualitatively employed (a detailed summary of background information by species is found in the subsections for each species, see pages 31-74). It is important to note that little or no information exists to directly compare current populations to those present before construction of the Elwha Dam. Therefore, it was necessary to infer historic traits from current information or comparison to other local populations. Table 4 summarizes decisions made regarding the preferred and alternative stocks identified. For some species, importing fish from other watersheds was considered in previous versions of the restoration plan. Those alternatives have been dropped from this plan but may be reevaluated in the future as part of the adaptive management process. The five current selection criteria follow:

1. Current population size: Is the population "large enough" to retain genetic variability needed for successful recovery? In general evidence shows that founder populations of less than 100 mature fish may be too small to ensure adequate genetic variability in the stock (Salmon Recovery Science Review Panel 2001).

2. Genetic analysis: Does the current genetic composition of the population represent an independent population, or has it been homogenized with imported hatchery populations? DNA and GSI data were available for Chinook salmon (Myers et al. 1998), chum salmon

Table 4. Fish stocks utilized for restoration.

Species	Primary restoration stock		Secondary restoration stock	
	Stock	Origin	Stock	Origin
Chinook salmon	Elwha River summer/fall	Natural/ hatchery	–	–
Winter steelhead	Elwha River late-timed	Natural/ hatchery	Upriver rainbow trout	Natural
Summer steelhead	Elwha River	Natural	–	–
Coho salmon	Elwha River	Hatchery*	–	–
Chum salmon	Elwha River	Natural	–	–
Pink salmon	Elwha River	Natural	Dungeness River upriver	Natural
Coastal cutthroat	Elwha River	Natural	–	–
Bull trout and Dolly Varden	Elwha River	Natural	–	–
Sockeye salmon	Unknown origin	Natural	To be identified if necessary	Unknown
Western brook lamprey	Elwha River	Natural	–	–
Pacific lamprey	Elwha River	Natural	–	–
Forage fish	Elwha River	Natural	–	–

*The Elwha hatchery coho population was founded using native Elwha coho salmon as the donor population.

(WDFW 1996), pink salmon (Small 2004), and steelhead and rainbow trout (Reisenbichler and Phelps 1989, Phelps et al. 2001). Bull trout, coho salmon, and cutthroat trout genetic samples are being collected, but no data was available to assist in stock selection.

3. Phenotypic and life history traits: Does the population retain phenotypic and life history traits known or suspected to occur in the original Elwha population (e.g., body size)?

4. Run timing: Is run timing consistent with known historic run timing or with the run timing of similar proximal populations (e.g., Hoh or Dungeness rivers)?

5. Accessibility of broodstock: Is it feasible to obtain adequate brood to incorporate into the restoration strategy?

Restoration Strategies

Two basic strategies were considered in developing the restoration plan: natural recolonization and artificial supplementation. In general natural recolonization was preferred to artificial supplementation where feasible and is used exclusively for some species. However, for populations currently present only below the Elwha Dam, relying solely on natural recolonization was combined with hatchery conservation strategies to preserve populations during the dam removal period.

Artificial supplementation strategies considered included outplanting and release of adults in the middle (between the two dams) and upper basins (above Lake Mills), production and release from hatcheries of multiple age-classes (juveniles), outplanting and release of hatchery-reared juveniles in the middle and upper basins at multiple age-classes (eggs, fry, presmolt, smolt), and using alternate out-of-basin production, release, and recovery sites. Captive brood is also considered for steelhead, pink salmon, and Chinook salmon but is not recommended for Chinook salmon in this plan as it was deemed unduly intrusive, expensive, and ultimately unnecessary. Captive brood will be used for steelhead and pink salmon and has been retained as an alternative strategy for Chinook salmon if other methods fail.

During the development of this recovery plan, there was considerable debate regarding the appropriate release age of juveniles to ensure recovery objectives were met. Available evidence suggested that exposing fish to the minimum possible residence in the hatchery environment would ultimately produce the most successful spawning adults (Waples 1991, 1999). Conversely, given that salmon are known to rapidly colonize a system when provided the opportunity, release strategies that provide the highest adult returns in the first generation would help seed the watershed and speed recovery, although this concept is not synonymous with maximizing the greatest number of fish released.

Maximum returns will be realized through the identification of the most effective life history stage released and the overall habitat capacity of the system (HSRG 2004). Ultimately it was decided to rely on a broad cross section of alternatives in conjunction with careful monitoring. Through annual review and adaptive management, the hatchery program will be adjusted to favor those strategies that return successfully spawning adults to the Elwha River (see the Monitoring and Adaptive Management section).

A brief description of alternative enhancement options considered in the development of this document follows. Table 5 summarizes the strategies selected for each species.

Natural Recolonization

Some level of natural recolonization will occur for all species, either as a result of the natural movement of native Elwha fish within the system, straying of fish from the enhancement program, or straying from outside systems. In addition it will not be feasible to outplant fish throughout the watershed; therefore, many areas must rely on natural recolonization. Specifically, initially only Chinook salmon smolts will be outplanted into the upper watershed above Lake Mills. Other species may also be outplanted in the upper watershed at a much younger age (egg or fry), but the early phases of recovery above Lake Mills will be largely driven by natural recolonization.

Yearling Smolts: On Station

Rates of return of adult Chinook salmon, coho salmon, and steelhead to the Elwha River are consistently greater when large yearling smolts are released (WDFW and tribal coded wire tag data, PSMFC 2006) as opposed to fry or presmolts. The production and release of yearling smolts from hatchery facilities promotes the long-term restoration goal of returning the greatest number of adults to the river. On-station releases will also ensure adequate brood sources for ongoing enhancement needs.

Yearling Smolts: Off Station

As noted above, the highest rate of return of adult salmon to the Elwha River is found with the release of yearling smolts. Release of yearling Chinook smolts at off-station locations has been found to produce lower stray rates than release of presmolts (Hayes and Carmichael 2002) and may speed recolonization of the watershed while minimizing affects of straying.

Yearling Smolts: Morse Creek/Out of Basin

The production and release of yearling smolts in an out-of-basin facility will provide short-term protection against catastrophic losses that may result from avoidance of the Elwha River during peak turbidity levels immediately following the dam-removal phase. Fish and eggs produced at or returning to out-of-basin facilities will be incorporated into Elwha River–origin fish production.

Age-0 Smolts: On Station

Production and release of age-0 Chinook salmon smolts from hatchery facilities ensures that the hatchery program is representative of the known natural life history strategies for this species (age-0 vs. yearling emigration). On-station releases also ensure adequate brood for ongoing enhancement needs.

Table 5. Elwha River fish restoration strategies.

	Chinook salmon	Coho salmon	Chum salmon	Pink salmon	Winter steelhead	Summer steelhead	Sockeye salmon	Cutthroat salmon	Bull trout	Western brook lamprey	Pacific lamprey	Forage fish
Natural recolonization	X	X	X	X	X	X	X	X	X	X	X	X
Yearling smolts: on-station	X	X										
Yearling smolts: off-station	X				X							
Yearling smolts: Morse Creek	X											
Age-0 smolts: on-station	X		X	X	X							
Age-0 smolts: off-station	X	X	X	X	X							
Egg outplants	X	X	X	X	X							
Fry upstream		X			X							
2-year-old smolts: upstream					X							
Captive brood	X			X	X							

24

Age-0 Smolts: Off Station

Production and release of age-0 smolts from appropriate locations is consistent with the restoration goal of releasing multiple age-classes in the basin, but may have unanticipated consequences due to straying that will need to be closely monitored. Hayes and Carmichael (2002) noted that release location, release date, juvenile physiological development, and flows at release time are thought to affect homing of presmolt releases. Using acclimation ponds may increase homing of some species (Tipping 2003).

Egg Outplants

Egg production in excess of hatchery production goals will be designated for outplanting in appropriate locations throughout the river basin. Methods for outplanting eggs may include hatch boxes (also known as salmon condos or Jordan/Scotty salmon incubators, Scott Plastics, Sidney, British Columbia), remote-site incubators, or injection of eggs into the native substrate. Stocking of eggs maximizes the exposure of planted fish to natural selection pressures and may minimize domestication concerns.

Fry Upstream

Production and release of fry from appropriate upriver locations is consistent with the restoration goal of releasing multiple age-classes in the basin.

Two-year-old Smolts Upstream (Steelhead)

Production and release of 2-year-old steelhead smolts at appropriate locations throughout the basin is consistent with the restoration goal of releasing multiple age-classes in the basin and will be used as a production option when growth rates in the hatchery preclude the timely production of yearling smolts.

Captive Brood (Chinook and Pink Salmon, Winter Steelhead)

Captive brood refers to the practice of rearing fish in captivity to full maturity. Captive brood is being retained in this plan for winter steelhead and pink salmon, and as an alternative enhancement strategy to be employed for Chinook salmon in the event that hatchery enhancement efforts fail to achieve production goals, suffer catastrophic loss of fish within the basin, or adults fail to enter the river due to elevated levels of sediment.

Outplanting Strategies

Methods

Outplanting of fish in the Elwha River basin will be conducted using trucks, boats, helicopters, and by foot in conjunction with one of the other methods. Transport trucks will be used as a means to access outplanting and acclimation sites throughout the middle and lower portions of the Elwha River basin. Boats may be used as an outplanting strategy prior to dam removal and during the initial year of dam removal as a method to transport adult fish to the headwaters of Lake Mills and into the upper Elwha River basin. Helicopter use will be restricted to outplant locations in the upper Elwha River basin (RM 16 to 41).

Helicopter outplanting affords an effective means to distribute juvenile fish to the remote upper reaches of the Elwha River basin where foot or horse transport of fish would be impractical. With this method fish may be distributed to appropriate habitats safely and effectively, provided proper fish handling and transport techniques are followed. Past helicopter outplant efforts have resulted in consistently high rates of survival (survival to smolt) of juvenile Chinook salmon, steelhead, and coho salmon outplanted to a variety of sites in the upper Elwha River basin (Dilley and Wunderlich 1990, Wunderlich et al. 1989). Due to the high cost of helicopter transport as well as limitations required to protect listed bird species in the watershed, the use of helicopters will be restricted exclusively to Chinook salmon outplants during the project's initial years and will be limited to 36 flights per year.

Outplanting strategies will include multiple life history patterns including adults, juveniles, and eyed eggs. Selection of life history patterns outplanted is based on stock availability and appropriateness of specific life history patterns to meet outplanting goals. The selection of outplanting strategies employed is dynamic, subject to review by managers, and may shift throughout the duration of the restoration project according to fish response.

Timing

Outplanting strategies will vary depending on the period: before dam removal, during dam removal, or after dam removal.

Pre-dam-removal period

Outplants of juveniles during this period will be limited to eyed egg outplants of chum and pink salmon below Elwha Dam and outplants of steelhead presmolts to selected acclimation sites in middle basin mainstem and tributary locations.

Dam-removal period

Juvenile outplants during dam removal will be expanded to extend into the Elwha River's upper basin and continued in selected acclimation sites in middle basin mainstem and tributary locations.

Post-dam-removal period

Outplanting strategies following dam removal will depend on fish response during previous restoration periods. Initial prioritization of helicopter efforts for outplanting of Chinook salmon may be revised, offering the potential for the outplanting of alternate species if warranted. Outplanting efforts will be phased out gradually in response to adult fish returns and spawning successes in the upper Elwha Basin. Outplanting methods and locations, outplanting densities, species targeted for outplanting, and the size and fish life history pattern outplanted will be adjusted throughout the duration of the restoration project when warranted by the response of fish populations.

Outplanting Locations

Release locations have been selected based on historical distributions of fish, logistical considerations (which sites can be feasibly reached), and genetic concerns (reducing the potential for genetic dilution of intact gene banks). Outplanting densities will strive to match but not exceed habitat-specific seeding rates based on assumed productivity. Outplant sites will be sufficiently distant from one another to allow for maximum fish dispersal. The outplanting locations are divided into three major areas: lower, middle, and upper basin sites.

Lower basin outplanting sites

All outplanting sites in the lower basin will be mainstem sites or side-channel locations accessible by truck and foot outplanting efforts. Sites include the one-way bridge (RM 3.2) and the former Elwha Dam site (RM 4.9).

Middle basin outplanting sites

All outplanting sites in the middle basin will be accessible by truck outplanting or a combination of truck and hand outplanting. Mainstem and side-channel sites in the middle reach section have been selected based on their accessibility, potential for providing successful rearing habitat, and distance from one another. Sites include Highway 101 bridge (RM 7.7), mouth of Little River at Elwha River (RM 7.8), Altaire Campground bridge (RM 12.5), and the former Glines Canyon Dam site (RM 13.4).

Tributary sites for the middle basin include Indian Creek, Lake Sutherland, Little River, and middle-reach side channels. A description of each follows:

- Indian Creek drainage provides extensive outplanting opportunities throughout its length for winter steelhead and coho and chum salmon. Networks of off-channel beaver ponds from Lake Sutherland downstream to the Elwha River are suitable for outplants of all target species.

- Lake Sutherland, located at the head of Indian Creek, will be used for direct releases of steelhead and coho salmon and for formalized acclimation of coho salmon in net pens prior to release.

- Outplanting opportunities exist throughout the lower portions of Little River for winter steelhead and coho salmon. Upriver reaches of Little River contain unique populations of rainbow trout and, in an effort to maintain genetic stock integrity, no enhancement activities will occur within these reaches. It should also be noted that Little River is being considered as a control area (no hatchery planting) in the Monitoring and Adaptive Management section of this plan, meaning no outplanting should occur. This issue will be subject for further discussion by the project participants leading up to full implementation of this plan.

- Middle-reach side channels on the east side of river accessible from the Hot Springs Road will be used.

Upper basin outplanting sites

Upper basin outplanting sites are inaccessible to trucks, and all outplants that occur in this region will be conducted by boat (prior to the full draining of Lake Mills), helicopter, or by foot in conjunction with boat or helicopter. Flight restrictions have been placed on the project to conserve northern spotted owls (*Strix occidentalis caurina*) and marbled murrelets (*Brachyramphus marmoratus*), limiting efforts to 36 helicopter flights per year. Because of this limitation, only Chinook salmon will be outplanted into the upper basin. Site selection for this reach of the river has several constraints and considerations:

- Each site offers suitable shallow, side-channel rearing habitat for young-of-the-year salmonids.

- Each site is considered representative of the excellent rearing conditions in the upper watershed within Olympic National Park.

- The sites are sufficiently distant from one another to allow maximum fry dispersal.

- The total size of the release group will be at or below maximum seeding rates for the species and life stage. This will reduce the likelihood that fish would be displaced downstream into less suitable habitat after outplanting.

Outplant sites for Chinook salmon in the upper basin main stem will be extended from just above the current Lake Mills (RM 16) to the uppermost limit of Chinook salmon mainstem habitat (RM 41). Use of a helicopter fire bucket for outplanting allows greater access than other outplant techniques in this remote section of the river and relatively even distribution of fish. Helicopter outplants may be used in conjunction with hand outplants to better distribute small, discrete populations of fish.

Upper basin mainstem sites include Krause Bottom, Lost River reach, and the Chicago Camp reach (Figure 6). Krause Bottom (RM 19 to 20) offers abundant shallow, side-channel habitat appropriate for age-0 Chinook salmon and will be outplanted at a rate of 100,000 Chinook salmon presmolts (90 fish/lb) per mile. The river in the Lost River reach (RM 24 to 31) tends to remain in a single channel with large substrate; however, there are areas of canyon and wide floodplain habitat. Pool habitat is limited. The target outplanting rate for the Lost River reach is 25,000 Chinook salmon presmolts (90 fish/lb) per mile. The final upper basin site—the extreme upper reach (RM 36 to 41)—extends to the upper limit of historic Chinook salmon distribution (RM 41) to ensure that all available mainstem habitat is seeded. Planting rates for this reach are targeted to reach 27,000 Chinook salmon presmolts (90 fish/lb) per mile.

Initial upper basin enhancement efforts will focus on Chinook salmon in mainstem habitat. Tributaries throughout the Elwha River upper basin offer outplanting opportunities for future steelhead and coho salmon enhancement efforts, but are not planned at this time.

Brood Collection Strategies

In order to maintain the artificial enhancement program during the recovery period, it will be necessary to obtain adequate and appropriate brood. A number of methods have been considered and are incorporated into the plan:

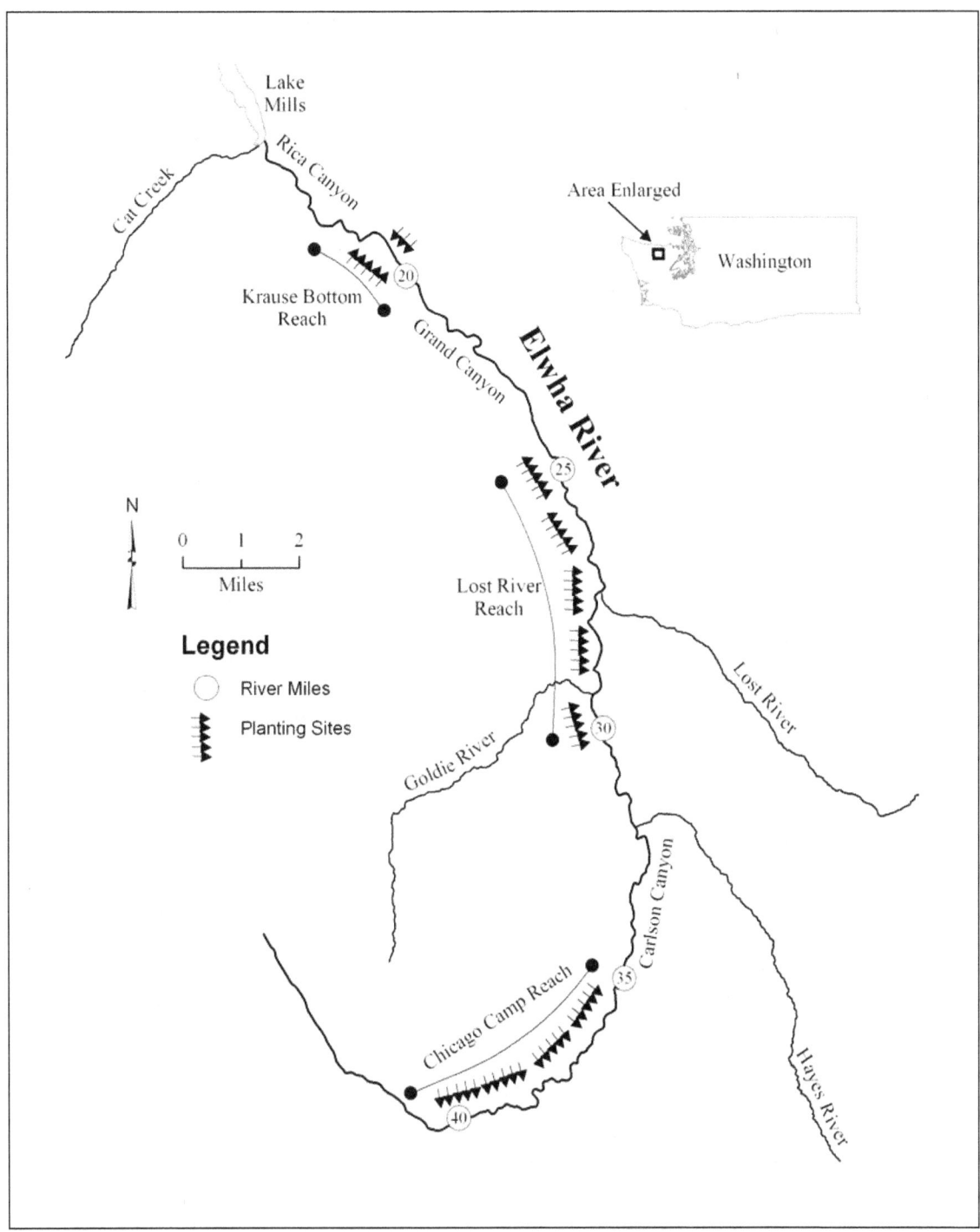

Figure 6. Chinook salmon outplanting locations.

- Hatchery rack: On-station releases of fish are expected to home to their hatchery of origin. A standard collection rack will be used at each facility to capture brood.

- Weir operation: A collection weir will be installed in the Elwha River near the WDFW rearing channel and in Morse Creek near the Highway 101 bridge. These weirs will be operated during summer low flow conditions and are intended to capture returning Chinook and pink salmon.

- Net capture: Gill or seine nets may be used to capture brood during higher flow conditions associated with the return timing of winter steelhead, coho and chum salmon. Gill nets are already being effectively used in side-channel habitats in the lower Elwha River to capture chum salmon brood.

- Redd pumping: The hydraulic pumping of redds is an effective method of collecting fish to incorporate into a captive brood program or to remove fish from the river should conditions associated with dam removal activities warrant. Redd pumping has been initiated to collect winter steelhead and may also be used for pink salmon prior to dam removal.

- Other (hook and line, electrofishing, etc.): A variety of other collection methods may prove useful to support the restoration plan. In particular, hook and line fishing and electrofishing are effective methods for capturing bull, resident rainbow, and resident cutthroat trout in the upper Elwha watershed.

Phase Out of Artificial Supplementation

The objective of using artificial supplementation as a tool in restoring fisheries resources in the Elwha Basin is to maintain existing native fish populations during the period of dam removal, to ensure adequate numbers of fish are available to seed the basin once conditions allow, and to begin to recolonize the basin once the dams are removed. It is envisioned these programs will phase out as natural production recovers.

Phase out of artificial supplementation will be tied to the specific interim (10-year) abundance, productivity, and distribution goals identified in the Monitoring and Adaptive Management section of this plan. In general these goals are defined as abundance levels on a trajectory to long-term recovery goals, natural-origin production in excess of one recruit/spawner, and distribution approximating the historic range. Annual review of the status of each population relative to the interim goals will guide decisions regarding continuation of the supplementation program. For example, if at the end of 10 years it is found that the abundance of naturally spawning Chinook salmon is 4,000 fish, productivity is two recruits per spawner, and Chinook salmon are spawning throughout their historic range, then the hatchery program would be phased down to a low maintenance level or eliminated entirely. Conversely, if abundance and productivity were to remain as above, but Chinook salmon were only spawning in the lower 10 miles of the river, then it would be necessary to carefully evaluate the program and decide on a course of action most likely to ensure recolonization of the historic range is achieved.

A specific end date for the artificial supplementation of populations cannot be set at this time, since the river's response to dam removal is uncertain in the short term. Additionally, each stock is likely to respond differently based on its respective life history strategy, starting population size, dependence on the lower river habitat, and other factors. Therefore, careful adherence to the goals and adaptive management strategies identified in this document will be relied on to guide supplementation activities.

Chinook Salmon Proposed Restoration Approach

Chinook salmon populations in the Elwha River historically displayed a wide range of life history strategies that took advantage of diverse natural habitat conditions present in the river in its pristine state. Remaining components of the historic populations have been retained in what is now believed to be a single population through natural spawning and hatchery enhancement activities. The current population exists in a reduced form: principal entry and spawning dates have been altered over time (shifted to later summer/fall dates) and reduced in the extent of their duration. Elwha Chinook salmon are genetically distinct from other Chinook salmon in the Strait of Juan de Fuca and Puget Sound (Ruckelshaus et al. 2006). Spring Chinook salmon, as expressed by early river entry and large adult body size, have been largely extirpated from the Elwha River (Brannon and Hershberger 1984, Wunderlich et al. 1993). Loss of access to upriver habitat coupled with possible cotemporal spawning with other populations of Chinook salmon in the lower river are thought to be the primary factors responsible for their demise.

Maintenance of a Chinook salmon hatchery program using broodstock collected from natural- and hatchery-origin adult returns provides a composite population on which to base stock restoration (WDFW 2002). Intentional capture and segregation of a discrete spring Chinook salmon component from the greater population was rejected as a restoration strategy due to reduced population size and the potential for selection biases.

A Chinook salmon restoration strategy that treats the population as a single unit, collecting eggs from across the range of the current spawning spectrum followed by outplanting juveniles throughout the basin, will best permit diverse life history types to develop and express themselves in the population. Chinook salmon are known to adapt rapidly to new habitats (Quinn et al. 1996), showing significant shifts in spawn timing in response to new environmental conditions. It is believed this adaptation will be realized by exposing Chinook salmon from across the run-timing spectrum to the upriver regimes of temperature, habitat, and food availability.

Stock Targeted for Enhancement

The existing in-basin composite stock has been identified as the preferred stock for enhancement activities. In an effort to limit risk to the stock, the variety of restoration strategies applied to this species is greater than those applied to other stocks of fish in the Elwha River basin. In the event of a catastrophic failure of recovery efforts using native Elwha River stock, it is noted that a component of the naturally spawning population of Chinook salmon in the Dungeness River may be of Elwha origin and therefore may be an alternative population for consideration.

Stock Status

The Elwha River Chinook salmon population is included as part of the ESA-listed threatened Puget Sound Chinook salmon ESU (NMFS 2005a). As one of only two Chinook salmon populations delineated for the entire Strait of Juan de Fuca biographical region, recovery of the Elwha River Chinook salmon stock to a viable status is considered a requirement for the recovery and delisting of the Puget Sound Chinook salmon ESU (NMFS 2005b).

Harvest Status

No directed harvest occurs on Elwha Chinook salmon. During the 2005 harvest season, the anticipated incidental total exploitation rate was 24%, of which 4.3% was attributable to southern U.S. fisheries directed at other salmon species and populations. Further, in the restoration strategy for Puget Sound Chinook salmon, it has been agreed that no directed harvest shall be permitted for Elwha Chinook salmon, and that the total incidental exploitation rate shall not exceed 10% (PSIT and WDFW 2004). It is anticipated this harvest management strategy shall remain in effect until either the Elwha Chinook salmon population recovers or the harvest rate proves to be in excess of the level that will lead to restoration. A detailed description of Chinook salmon harvest management is provided in Appendix B.

Hatchery Enhancement Efforts

The current hatchery program for Elwha Chinook salmon is designed for stock maintenance. The annual egg-take goal for the program is 3.5 million, with a release goal of 2.5 million age-0 fish (all otolith marked). Following on recommendations from the Hatchery Scientific Review Group (HSRG 2002), the annual hatchery program has recently been modified to also include yearling releases. An initial group of 200,000 yearlings were released into the Elwha River in spring 2005 and in 2006, with the intent to continue to release an additional yearling component of 200,000 fish thereafter. To address the risk of catastrophic loss of the Elwha River population during dam decommissioning, an out-of-watershed reserve Chinook salmon broodstock source is being established in Morse Creek. An initial release of 200,000 yearlings was made in spring 2005, with the program continuing as needed at the 200,000 yearling release level until the risk of stock loss in the Elwha River has passed. All yearlings will be coded wire tagged.

Escapement Level

The current escapement goal for Elwha Chinook salmon below Elwha Dam is 2,900 fish, with an objective of maintaining a natural spawning level of at least 500 fish. Total escapement of adults in 2004 was 3,443 fish. Returns to the hatchery (both volunteer and gaffed or seined) accounted for 1,368 fish, while an additional 2,075 adults spawned naturally. The most recent 5-year average return of adults to the river has been approximately 2,200 adults—just over 75% of the goal. Forecasted adult terminal run size for 2008 is 2,178 fish.

Projected Hatchery Facility Use

Enhancement efforts will take place at the WDFW Elwha rearing channel and at the WDFW Morse Creek facility. Early rearing will occur at the WDFW Sol Duc facility, with fry and fingerling transfers back to the Elwha rearing channel and Morse Creek facility for rearing and release as subyearlings or yearlings.

Elwha River–origin adult fish produced at and returning to the Morse Creek facility will be fully incorporated with Elwha River adult returns as broodstock used to implement Elwha River hatchery-based restoration efforts.

Shared Salmon Strategy Recovery Plan

The EFRP is the primary component of the effort to recover the Elwha Chinook salmon population included in the ESA listing of the Puget Sound Chinook salmon ESU. However, the jurisdiction of this plan is directly linked to removal of the two dams on the Elwha River, and therefore cannot address all the factors that led to the decline of Elwha Chinook salmon or, more broadly, Puget Sound Chinook salmon.

An ESU-wide recovery planning effort was undertaken by Shared Salmon Strategy for Puget Sound, a collaborative group dedicated to restoring salmon throughout Puget Sound (online at http://www.sharedsalmonstrategy.org). Strait of Juan de Fuca Chinook salmon populations, and Elwha Chinook salmon specifically, are included in the Shared Strategy Plan (Shared Salmon Strategy for Puget Sound 2005). Beyond dam removal, the Shared Strategy Plan includes actions adopted through the WRIA 18 Watershed Plan (Elwha-Dungeness Planning Unit 2005), the North Olympic Peninsula Lead Entity Group (NOPLE) Strategy (NOPLE 2005a), and the NOPLE Draft Nearshore Strategy (NOPLE 2005b). Recovery actions included in the Shared Strategy Plan that are not in the EFRP include water use planning, additional habitat restoration actions, nearshore restoration actions, and land use planning. The Shared Strategy Plan can be found in its entirety on the group's Web site, including an Elwha-specific appendix.

Summary

Proposed strategies for Chinook salmon are based on the following production assumptions. Sex ratio is 50:50. Primary age at return is age 4. Ages 3 and 5 contribute to the population. Fecundity is 5,000 eggs per female. Survival rates from the fertilized egg stage are 90% to eyed egg stage, 80% to age-0 smolt, and 72% to yearling smolt.

A summary of the Elwha River Chinook salmon restoration strategies includes:

- on-station releases of yearling smolts

- transfer and release of yearling smolts into Morse Creek

- on-station release of age-0 smolts

- natural spawning of adults

- planting of eyed eggs

- outplanting of fry, age-0 smolts, and yearling smolts in upstream locations

The strategies described for Chinook salmon in this plan are intended to be adaptive, changing based on observed responses of the Chinook salmon population. Therefore, if certain strategies prove to be unsuccessful, they may be discontinued at any time in favor of options that are more likely to produce a healthy, naturally spawning population. Further, specific options, including the release of fish into Morse Creek, will be discontinued as soon as the risk of catastrophic loss of the Elwha River production is passed. Hatchery production proposed for this period will be phased out over time as the natural-origin Chinook salmon population increases to a healthy, self-sustaining level and as seasonal components of the natural-origin population (spring, summer, and fall) reestablish.

Phasing of Chinook Salmon Restoration Strategies

Pre-dam-removal period

The emphasis of the proposed hatchery approach for Chinook salmon is maintenance of the existing hatchery and natural-origin population. Hatchery facilities (in and out of basin) will be modified, with water treatment facilities and delivery systems being constructed during this time to meet production goals. Table 6 summarizes the restoration strategies for the pre-dam-removal period.

Annual production of juvenile fish will be maintained at recent year release levels. At low adult return levels, the enhancement program will prioritize release of yearling smolts. As adult numbers increase, restoration strategies will be expanded to include the production and release of fish from the Morse Creek facility and upper-basin outplants of eyed eggs (beginning 2008). Broodstock collection strategies for adult Chinook salmon during this period will include trapping of adult returns to the Elwha Channel and Morse Creek facilities, in-river net capture of adults, and gaffing of adults on the spawning grounds.

No directed commercial or recreational fisheries on Chinook salmon will occur during this time period.

Dam-removal period

Enhancement strategies during this period will emphasize the maintenance of hatchery-based populations. Hatchery facilities (in and out of basin) will have been modified and releases from these facilities will have begun. Water treatment and delivery systems will be online and treating water. Water quantity available for fish culture activities in the hatchery setting will be periodically limited by water treatment facility capacities. In-river environmental conditions in the lower river will be severely degraded and unsuitable for natural spawning. Hatchery production capabilities will be reduced from the previous period (resulting from water production limitations). Table 7 summarizes the restoration strategies for the dam-removal period.

At low adult return levels, the enhancement program will prioritize release of yearling smolts. As adult numbers increase, restoration strategies will be expanded to include production and release of fish (subyearlings and yearlings) from alternate in-basin facilities as well as from the Morse Creek facility. Other expanded restoration strategies will include upper basin outplants of eyed eggs, fry, and subyearling smolts, yearling presmolts, and yearling smolts.

Broodstock collection strategies for adult Chinook salmon during this period will include trapping of adult returns to the Elwha Channel and Morse Creek facilities, the interception and capture of adults at the in-river adult collection weir, and gaffing of adults on the spawning grounds.

No directed commercial or recreational fisheries on Chinook salmon will occur during this time period.

Post-dam-removal period

Dam removal will have been completed at the start of this period. Turbidity levels in the river will have declined, the water treatment facility will have been taken off-line, and hatchery facilities will be receiving raw, untreated surface water. Hatchery production levels will no longer be limited by water availability during this period. Table 8 summarizes the restoration strategies for the post-dam-removal period.

Hatchery-based restoration strategies will maximize on- and off-station fish production during this period. As the returning Chinook salmon adult population increases, restoration activities will expand to include outplanting of eyed eggs and fry, increased upriver outplanting of presmolts and smolts, and greater numbers of natural spawners throughout the basin. Assessments of fish response to changes in habitat quality and colonization by fish of new habitats will be critical to the management of these restoration programs. Out-of-basin release and captive brood programs will be phased out as turbidity in the lower basin stabilizes and as Elwha River fish populations return at consistent levels to the river. In-basin restoration programs will be phased out in response to successes (increases in natural production and as fish populations begin to achieve self-sustainability) and failures of the actions employed. As adult returns to the river increase, the use of alternate in-basin production will be phased out.

Broodstock collection strategies for adult Chinook salmon during this period will include trapping of adult returns to the Elwha Channel and Morse Creek facilities, the interception and capture of adults at the in-river adult collection weir, and gaffing of adults on the spawning grounds.

No directed commercial or recreational fisheries on Chinook salmon will occur during this time period.

Table 6. Chinook salmon restoration strategies before dam removal. Numbers in boldface are adult escapement levels.

Production facility	Life history pattern	Release location	Chinook production goal at adult escapement levels							
			100	**200**	**500**	**750**	**1,000**	**2,000**	**4,000**	**4,000+**
Elwha Channel	Yearling smolts	On-site	175,000	180,000	200,000	200,000	200,000	200,000	200,000	200,000
Morse Creek	Yearling smolts	On-site		180,000	200,000	200,000	200,000	200,000	200,000	200,000
Elwha Channel	Age-0 smolts	On-site			555,000	1,050,000	1,050,000	2,550,000	3,526,000	3,665,000
Elwha Channel	Natural spawners	Elwha Basin				65	315	565	2,077	5,945
Potential egg production:			250,000	500,000	1,250,000	1,875,000	2,500,000	5,000,000	10,000,000	20,000,000

Table 7. Chinook salmon restoration strategies during dam removal. Numbers in boldface are adult escapement levels.

Production facility	Life history pattern	Release location	Chinook production goal at adult escapement levels							
			100	**200**	**500**	**750**	**1,000**	**2,000**	**4,000**	**4,000+**
Elwha Channel	Yearling smolts	On-site	175,000	180,000	200,000	200,000	200,000	200,000	200,000	200,000
Morse Creek	Yearling smolts	On-site		180,000	200,000	200,000	200,000	200,000	200,000	200,000
Elwha Channel	Age-0 smolts	Upper basin				250,000	250,000	500,000	750,000	750,000
Elwha Channel	Age-0 smolts	On-site			555,000	805,000	855,000	1,250,000	1,250,000	1,250,000
Elwha Channel	Natural spawners	Elwha Basin						903	2,778	6,778
Potential egg production:			250,000	500,000	1,250,000	1,875,000	2,500,000	5,000,000	10,000,000	20,000,000

Table 8. Chinook salmon restoration strategies after dam removal. Numbers in boldface are adult escapement levels.

Production facility	Life history pattern	Release location	Chinook production goal at adult escapement levels							
			100	**200**	**500**	**750**	**1,000**	**2,000**	**4,000**	**4,000+**
Elwha Channel	Yearling smolts	On-site	180,000	180,000	200,000	200,000	200,000	200,000	200,000	200,000
Morse Creek	Yearling smolts	On-site		180,000	200,000	–	–	–	–	200,000
Elwha Channel	Age-0 smolts	On-site			500,000	546,000	805,000	2,200,000	2,200,000	2,200,000
Elwha Channel	Age-0 smolts	Upper basin				120,000	250,000	500,000	750,000	750,000
Elwha Channel	Yearling smolts	Upper basin				100,000	200,000	200,000	200,000	200,000
Elwha Channel	Natural spawners	Elwha Basin			250	250	250	490	2,365	6,303
Potential egg production:			250,000	500,000	1,250,000	1,875,000	2,500,000	5,000,000	10,000,000	20,000,000

Winter Steelhead Proposed Restoration Approach

An aggregate winter and summer steelhead population, influenced by past out-of-basin-origin hatchery steelhead introductions, currently occupies the Elwha River below Elwha Dam. The early returning portion (December through March) of the winter steelhead population is currently supported by LEKT hatchery production, with an annual release target of 120,000 smolts. This hatchery run is an admixture of native Elwha River stock and nonnative Chambers Creek stock. The hatchery stock has a significantly earlier run timing than the later, natural-origin portion of the winter run, and has been found to be genetically similar to the Chambers Creek stock (Reisenbichler and Phelps 1989). The proposed steelhead restoration strategy emphasizes development of broodstock based on the late-timed, natural-origin component of winter steelhead and natural recolonization by upriver rainbow trout populations. Production of the existing hatchery-origin population of winter steelhead will be maintained at the LEKT hatchery to provide recreational and commercial harvest opportunities, but will be managed to avoid conflict with recovery of the natural-origin component and may be phased out over time.

Stock Targeted for Enhancement

The primary stock targeted for recovery efforts is the late-timed, natural-origin component of winter steelhead, which exhibit an April to June spawn timing. These fish are believed to retain the genetic signature of the native Elwha steelhead stock.[3] Additionally, upriver rainbow trout are expected to secondarily contribute to natural recolonization of the river. Upriver rainbow have been observed to exhibit smolting behavior (Hiss and Wunderlich 1994a), with pockets of native-origin stock persisting (Phelps et al. 2001). The hatchery-maintained Chambers Creek steelhead will not be incorporated into the recovery plan.

Stock Status

The naturally spawning winter steelhead stock in the Elwha River is thought to be in relatively poor condition. Limited spawner escapement surveys conducted since 2002 have documented an average of 50–100 redds per year (LEKT 2006). In 2005 61 discrete redds were identified in the lower river. In past years, annual run-size forecasts were generated from hatchery returns and commercial harvest scale analyses. The forecasted natural return was approximately 75 fish in 2002. In more recent years, escapements of naturally produced Elwha River adult steelhead ranged between 100 and 200 fish, based on forecasted abundance levels.

Self-sustaining populations of rainbow trout are known to occur above the Elwha Dam. These populations are thought to originate from native steelhead and rainbow trout populations isolated above the dams after their construction, as well as progeny from past fish planting efforts. Rainbow trout from the McCloud River in California were widely propagated throughout Washington, and the Elwha River is known to have received a series of outplants from Goldendale Hatchery in eastern Washington (Phelps et al. 2001). Smolt outmigration trapping operations conducted during the 1990s captured a number of fish that appeared to express the characteristics of outmigrating steelhead smolts (Hiss and Wunderlich 1994a).

---

[3] G. Winans, NWFSC, Seattle, WA. Pers. commun., 28 February 2007.

An analysis of the genetic relationship of seven populations of resident rainbow trout from within the Elwha River above Elwha Dam showed evidence of successful natural reproduction by hatchery-origin rainbow trout (with the exception of the South Branch Little River population) (Phelps et al. 2001). These fish are likely descendants of past hatchery outplanting efforts, including rainbow trout that originated from California (McCloud River). Despite these effects, the genetic attributes of all steelhead collections in the Elwha River differed significantly from hatchery and natural populations of Washington steelhead (Phelps et al. 2001). The population collected from the headwaters of the Little River was most closely related to wild winter run Washington steelhead and may therefore be a landlocked descendant of native Elwha River steelhead (Phelps et al. 2001).

Harvest Status

No directed harvest currently occurs on the native steelhead stock. A small portion of the run is taken each year during fisheries that target hatchery winter steelhead. Fisheries for hatchery steelhead end no later than 28 February each year.

Hatchery Enhancement Efforts

LEKT initiated an artificial propagation program using the native late-returning winter steelhead population as broodstock beginning in 2005. The program is directed at the preservation and restoration of the native stock and will operate parallel to the existing Chambers Creek lineage steelhead program that the tribe operates for harvest augmentation purposes.

Escapement Level

Average estimated run size for this stock is 333 fish (based on a 12-year average). Annual run sizes are estimated to have ranged between 100 and 200 adult fish in more recent years.

Projected Hatchery Facility Use

Enhancement efforts are taking place at the Lower Elwha Hatchery.

Summary

A summary of the Elwha River winter steelhead restoration strategies includes:

- captive brood program development
- on-station releases of yearling smolts
- upstream passage of adults for natural spawning
- planting of eyed eggs
- outplanting of fry, presmolts, yearling smolts, and 2-year-old smolts in upstream locations

The strategies described for steelhead in this plan are intended to be adaptive, changing based on observed responses of the steelhead population. Therefore, if certain strategies prove to be unsuccessful, they may be discontinued at any time in favor of options that are more likely to produce a healthy, naturally self-sustaining spawning population.

The steelhead population in the Elwha River is included as part of the Puget Sound steelhead ESU that was proposed for listing as "threatened" under the federal ESA on 29 March 2006 (NMFS 2006). The hatchery population derived from late-timed, natural-origin steelhead and produced for use in restoration is included in the ESU and is therefore also proposed for protection under the act. The Puget Sound steelhead ESU was listed as a threatened species under the ESA on 11 May 2007 (NMFS 2007).

Phasing of Winter Steelhead Restoration Strategies

Pre-dam-removal period

Restoration activities during this period emphasize capturing and developing a population of late-timed, natural-origin steelhead capable of returning to the hatchery facility. Enhancement efforts will include both the production of yearlings (1- and 2-year-old fish) and development of a captive brood program to accelerate egg and smolt availability. Hatchery facilities during this time will be limited by both space (incubation and rearing) and water quantity. Broodstock required to sustain this program will be acquired either through mainstem river capture and transport of adult fish to hatchery facilities for maturation and spawning, or through hydraulic mining of redds for fry or eggs. Throughout this phase, sport and commercial harvests of winter steelhead will continue to be limited to only the early returning hatchery-based stock. Table 9 summarizes the restoration strategies for the pre-dam-removal period.

At low adult return levels (<100 adults), enhancement will emphasize the release of smolts from the Lower Elwha Hatchery and captive brood. As adult return numbers increase, enhancement strategies will be expanded to include planting of eyed eggs, the release of presmolts and fry, and the release of adults to permit natural spawning.

Broodstock collection strategies for winter steelhead during this period will include mining of redds to acquire eggs and fry, trapping of adult fish using a weir spanning the mainstem river, hook and line capture of adults at the base of the Elwha Dam, gillnet capture in the mainstem river (stationary and driftnet), and trapping of adult returns to the tribal hatchery facility on the lower Elwha River. Hydraulic redd sampling to retrieve developing eggs and alevins from naturally produced redds will be limited to a small proportion of each redd's total production (limit of 250 eggs or alevins per redd).

The production of Chambers Creek stock to support harvest opportunity will continue at existing levels up to the year prior to dam removal. At that time, production will be ramped back to maintenance levels (20,000–40,000 fish per year).

Dam-removal period

Enhancement strategies will mimic those employed during the pre-dam-removal period. Due to projected adverse environmental conditions, expectations for successful natural spawning of adults in the lower basin are not programmed into the list of enhancement strategies for this phase. Table 10 summarizes the restoration strategies for the dam-removal period.

Broodstock collection strategies for winter steelhead during this period will include trapping of adult fish using a weir spanning the mainstem river, hook and line capture of adults at selected locations throughout the Elwha River basin, gillnet capture in the mainstem river (stationary and driftnet), and trapping of adult returns to the tribal hatchery facility on the lower Elwha River. Redd pumping will continue to be used for egg and alevin collection; however, environmental conditions (turbidity) may preclude this method.

The hatchery production of Chambers Creek stock will be maintained at maintenance levels during the entire dam-removal period, as no fisheries are expected.

Post-dam-removal period

During this phase, dam removal will have been completed, the period of greatest turbidity will have passed, the shared water treatment facility will have been taken off-line, hatchery facilities will be receiving raw surface water, and hatchery production levels will no longer be limited by water availability. Table 11 summarizes the restoration strategies for the post-dam-removal period.

Enhancement strategies at low adult return numbers will emphasize the release of smolts and presmolts from the hatchery. As adult return numbers increase, restoration strategies employed will be expanded to include providing upstream passage of adults, outplanting of eyed eggs, and the upstream release of fry, presmolts, and smolts. Hatchery production proposed for this period will be phased out over time as the natural-origin population increases to a healthy, self-sustaining level.

During this time, sport and commercial harvests will target the early timed component of the run. Harvest of the late-timed component will begin based on stock status assessments that demonstrate achievement by the stock of a population size capable of supporting a directed harvest effort.

Redd pumping may still be used to collect eggs and alevins from the naturally spawning population. The need to collect eggs and alevins from redds to sustain the hatchery program may be reduced, as it is expected that late-run fish needed as broodstock will begin to return directly to the hatchery in addition to spawning naturally in the restored river channel. Other collection strategies for adult winter steelhead during this period will include a capture weir, hook and line capture of adults at selected locations throughout the Elwha River basin, and gillnet collection (stationary and driftnet).

The production of Chambers Creek stock will be maintained to support fishing opportunities in the Elwha River such that it does not interfere with recovery efforts for the native steelhead stock. Production goals and fisheries will be carefully evaluated and monitored according to the Monitoring and Adaptive Management section of this report. Changes shall be made to the program if it appears that natural recolonization is being hindered.

Table 9. Winter steelhead restoration strategies before dam removal. Numbers in boldface are adult escapement levels.

Production Facility	Life history pattern	Release location	Winter steelhead production goal at adult escapement levels					
			100	**500**	**1,000**	**1,500**	**2,000**	**5,000**
Lower Elwha	Yearling smolts	On-site	102,000	125,000	125,000	125,000	125,000	125,000
Lower Elwha	Natural spawners	Lower Elwha Basin		100	577	1,077	1,577	4,577
Lower Elwha	Eyed eggs	Upper basin		100,000	100,000	100,000	100,000	100,000
Lower Elwha	Fry	Upper basin		220,000	250,000	250,000	250,000	250,000
Lower Elwha	Presmolts	Upper basin		20,000	20,000	20,000	20,000	20,000
		Potential egg production:	150,000	750,000	1,500,000	2,250,000	3,000,000	7,500,000

Table 10. Winter steelhead restoration strategies during dam removal. Numbers in boldface are adult escapement levels.

Production Facility	Life history pattern	Release location	Winter steelhead production goal at adult escapement levels					
			100	**500**	**1,000**	**1,500**	**2,000**	**5,000**
Lower Elwha	Yearling smolts	On-site	80,000	100,000	100,000	100,000	100,000	100,000
Lower Elwha	Natural spawners	Lower basin		39	537	1,037	1,537	4,537
Lower Elwha	Eyed eggs	Upper basin		100,000	100,000	100,000	100,000	100,000
Lower Elwha	Fry	Upper basin		272,000	275,000	275,000	275,000	275,000
Lower Elwha	Presmolts	Upper basin	22,000	20,000	20,000	20,000	20,000	20,000
Lower Elwha	Yearling smolts	Upper basin		25,000	25,000	25,000	25,000	25,000
Lower Elwha	2-year-old smolts	Upper basin		15,000	15,000	15,000	15,000	15,000
		Potential egg production:	150,000	750,000	1,500,000	2,250,000	3,000,000	7,500,000

Table 11. Winter steelhead restoration strategies after dam removal. Numbers in boldface are adult escapement levels.

Production Facility	Life history pattern	Release Location	Winter steelhead production goal at adult escapement levels					
			100	**500**	**1,000**	**1,500**	**2,000**	**5,000**
Lower Elwha	Yearling smolts	On-site	80,000	100,000	100,000	100,000	100,000	100,000
Lower Elwha	Natural spawners	Elwha Basin		37	537	1,037	1,537	4,537
Lower Elwha	Eyed eggs	Upper basin		100,000	100,000	100,000	100,000	100,000
Lower Elwha	Fry	Upper basin		275,000	275,000	275,000	275,000	275,000
Lower Elwha	Presmolts	Upper basin	22,000	20,000	20,000	20,000	20,000	20,000
Lower Elwha	Yearling smolts	Upper basin		25,000	25,000	25,000	25,000	25,000
Lower Elwha	2-year old smolts	Upper basin		15,000	15,000	15,000	15,000	15,000
		Potential egg production:	150,000	750,000	1,500,000	2,250,000	3,000,000	7,005,000

Program Implementation

Project background

The Elwha Fisheries Technical Group—comprised of state, federal, and tribal agency biologists who collectively developed responses to technical questions during the planning stages for dam removal—identified the late-timed natural-origin steelhead population as being most appropriate for post-dam-removal supplementation efforts in the Elwha River basin. LEKT has maintained a hatchery steelhead program at its facility since the late 1970s. The program was initiated using eggs transferred from federal hatcheries on the Quinault and Columbia rivers. The tribe currently produces 120,000 yearling hatchery smolts at its facility. These early timed fish were likely of Chambers Creek origin and therefore are not targeted for use in steelhead restoration efforts following dam removal.

A combination of strategies will be used to restore Elwha winter steelhead. These strategies include 1) reducing outplants of nonnative steelhead prior to dam removal, 2) developing conservation hatchery rearing and release strategies using remnant wild steelhead stocks, and 3) an assumed, unknown level of contribution of anadromous smolts from upriver rainbow trout populations.

Project development and implementation

In May–June 2005 LEKT staff in cooperation with WDFW hatchery staff initiated a redd-pumping effort designed primarily to capture fish for genetic analysis. Weekly surveys of the river below Elwha Dam were conducted between 1 April and 15 June to identify steelhead redds. Results of these surveys confirm that the late-timed component of Elwha River steelhead population is at very low abundance. In 2005 a total of 61 discrete redds were identified, distributed over fairly limited spawning habitat. Of the 61 redds identified, at least eight were dewatered during extreme low flow conditions that occurred. For each identified redd, the date of creation was estimated as well as the rate of egg development based on river temperature.

A total of 30 redds were pumped between 26 April and 22 June (Figures 7 through 9). Approximately 1,200 eyed eggs and alevin were successfully obtained from 22 redds. Eggs and alevin from each redd were treated as individual families and reared in vertical incubators at the LEKT hatchery. As eggs and alevin developed to fry they were transferred to individual rearing tanks as families. When fry reached a minimum length of 65 mm, they were photographed, weighed, measured, sampled for genetic material, and tagged with a unique passive integrated transponder (PIT) tag. Once tagged, individual families can be reared together in a larger rearing tank and subsequently released as smolts or retained as captive brood.

Interagency consultation

On 20 October 2005, LEKT staff met with staff from NWFSC and ONP to discuss the ongoing wild steelhead (late-timed, natural-origin) program and provide LEKT staff with program recommendations. Active and passive management approaches were considered, and it was recommended that for active management the tribe implement a two-prong strategy that

Figure 7. Redds being pumped. A pump discharge wand is inserted into the gravel egg pocket. An hydraulic discharge gently forces eggs and fry upwards from the egg pocket into the capture net.

Figure 8. Eggs and fry evacuated from the redd collect in the downstream portions of the capture net. The turbid downstream discharge from the pump site leaves the redd site free for capture of eggs and fry.

included reductions in outplanting of nonnative early timed steelhead (Chambers Creek origin) along with development of conservation hatchery rearing and release using the late-timed run. Such a program has been implemented on the Hamma Hamma River, combining a hatchery supplementation program (captive brood) with novel conservation elements (Berejikian et al.

Figure 9. Captured eggs and fry awaiting transport to the hatchery for rearing.

unpubl. manuscr.). This program, though not yet thoroughly evaluated, shows some promise in conserving and rebuilding unique depleted stocks.

For the Elwha River, fisheries scientists are faced with few other options for rebuilding native steelhead populations. The remaining late-timed run is at a very low population level and may not survive dam removal. Remnant upstream populations of rainbow trout (above the dams) are thought to retain some traits of anadromy (Hiss and Wunderlich 1994a) and will be used as a form of passive restoration. Thrower and Joyce (2004) suggest, although marine survival of resident rainbow smolts derived from an anadromous population in Alaska was low, that significant numbers of smolts and adults can still be produced by populations landlocked for up to 70 years.

Based on these discussions it was recommended that LEKT continue redd pumping programs targeting the late-timed steelhead populations at least through 2008 and perhaps beyond, depending on the start date for demolition of the dams. Pumping programs have been designed to maximize genetic history and minimize effects on extant wild steelhead populations until dam removal begins. It is anticipated that dam removal will occur within the next 3–5 years. Were dam removal to be initiated in 2009 as originally planned, impacts associated with accelerated sediment releases would have negatively affected future broodyears beginning in 2005 (Figure 10). Beginning with the 2005 broodyear, the tribe has reduced its outplanting of early timed Chambers Creek–origin steelhead to 45,000. With these changes in hatchery management, the work group identified a suite of options to consider for wild winter steelhead restoration for the Elwha River, including:

- develop a captive brood program with a target of 200 adults per year

- eventual spawning of captive brood (broodyear + 4) followed by kelt reconditioning and release

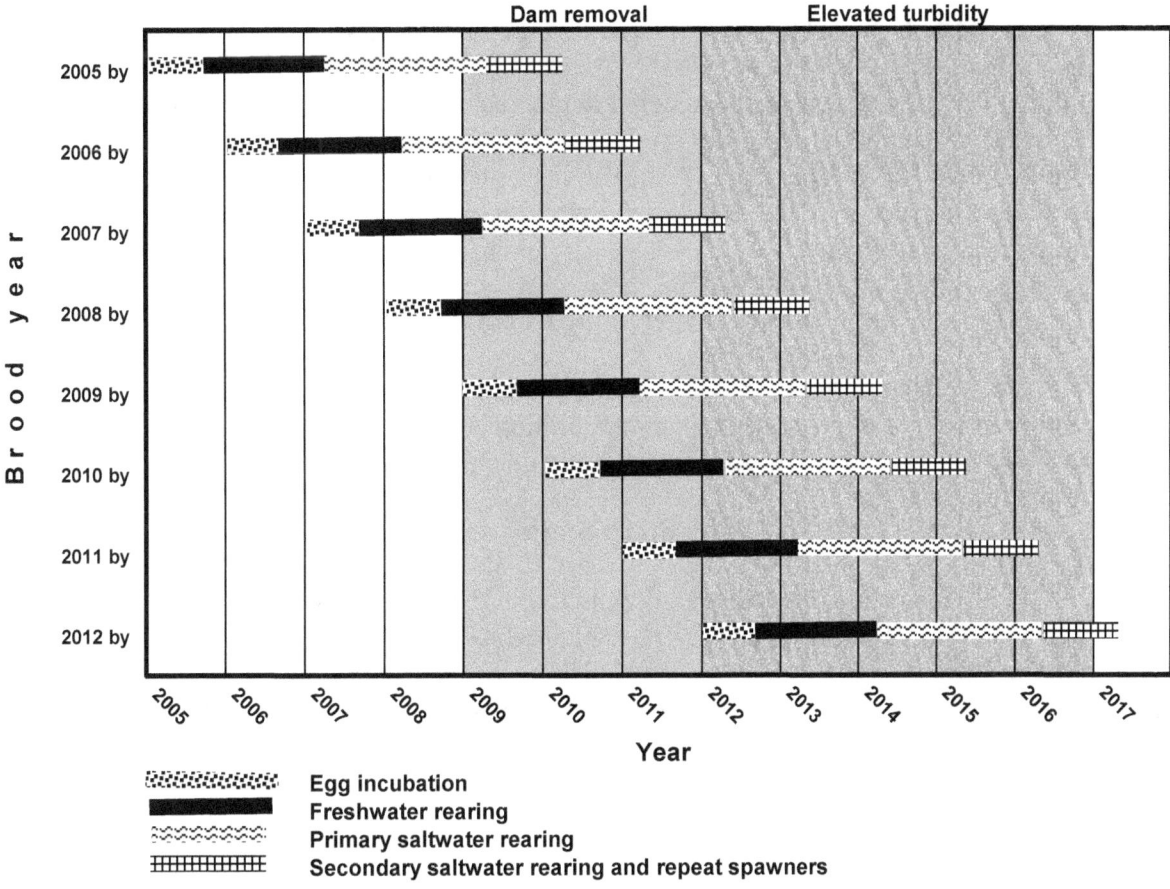

Figure 10. Life history versus dam removal timing for Elwha River wild steelhead based on a previous 2009–2012 timetable for dam removal.

- continued monitoring of natural spawning populations
- smolt release into the Elwha River and into an alternate drainage—either Morse or Ennis creeks

Assuming the original schedule, the work group also identified and proposed these specific strategies by broodyear: 1) the 2005 broodyear will have wild siblings returning to the Elwha River in 2009 and 2) the work group will PIT tag 100% of fish, retain 200 fish to hold as captive brood, conduct genetic analysis on all fish, and release remaining fish as smolts (approximately 750 fish) into the Elwha River. For the 2006, 2007, and 2008 brood years, the strategy was to maximize the number of redds represented in the hatchery, target a maximum capture of 10,000 eggs and fry, limit removal of eggs from individual redds to 250 with minimum target of 40 redds, PIT tag 100% of fish brought into the hatchery, retain 200 fish to hold as captive brood, conduct genetic analysis on all fish, and release remaining fish as smolts into the Elwha River and alternative drainage.

Summer Steelhead Proposed Restoration Approach

Summer steelhead levels are considered depressed, primarily due to the loss of access to upriver habitat. Escapement of naturally produced summer steelhead is unknown, but is estimated at less than 100 fish per year. Annual releases of Skamania stock in the lower basin by WDFW were discontinued in 2001. It is not known if these releases successfully interbred with native Elwha summer steelhead.

Stock Targeted for Enhancement

Summer steelhead restoration will rely completely on natural recolonization. The existing lower river population is the primary restoration stock, while native rainbow trout populations isolated above the dams may represent a genetic reserve.

Stock Status

The status of the summer steelhead population in the Elwha River is unknown but suspected to be at critically low levels. WDFW planted hatchery-origin (Skamania) summer steelhead in the Elwha River for many years. This effort was discontinued in 2001. No efforts have been made to formally document the escapement of summer steelhead within the Elwha River.

Harvest Status

For catch accounting purposes, steelhead returning to the Elwha River from 1 May to 31 October are assumed to be summer fish. With the elimination of the summer steelhead hatchery program, no fisheries remain targeting summer steelhead. Incidental mortality may occur during recreational and commercial coho fisheries in late September and October.

Escapement Level

Average estimated run size for this stock is less than 100 fish.

Coho Salmon Proposed Restoration Approach

Elwha River coho salmon are a mixed-origin stock of composite production associated with hatchery facilities in the lower Elwha River. The river has been heavily planted with out-of-basin hatchery coho salmon, beginning in the early 1950s and continuing to the 1970s (WDFW and WWTIT 1994). Artificial production of the current hatchery stock began with Dungeness and Elwha parents at the WDFW facility in the mid-1970s, but now occurs only at the tribal facility. No genetic analysis has been completed for Elwha River coho to date; however, LEKT, in conjunction with Gary Winans of NWFSC, initiated genetic work in the fall of 2005.

Stock Targeted for Enhancement

The existing in-basin mixed-origin population has been identified as the preferred stock for enhancement activities. In the event of a failure of this stock, Dungeness River coho salmon will be used to supplement Elwha River–origin fish.

Stock Status

The coho stock status is considered healthy (WDFW and WWTIT 1994).

Harvest Status

Preterminal fisheries targeting Elwha River coho salmon are managed primarily to meet the objectives for wild coho salmon production in other Strait of Juan de Fuca streams. Exploitation was limited to a target rate of 40% and a forecasted exploitation rate of 11.6% for natural stocks in 2005 (PNPTC et al. 2005). The objective of the Lower Elwha Hatchery coho salmon program is to augment harvests of returning adult fish in in-river commercial and recreational fisheries, which are managed to meet hatchery broodstock escapement needs. The 2005 total forecasted exploitation rate for Elwha coho salmon was about 50%, with a forecasted in-river exploitation rate of about 30%.

Hatchery Enhancement Efforts

The current hatchery program for Elwha coho salmon is operated for commercial and recreational fisheries harvest augmentation purposes. The egg-take goal for the program is currently 1.2 million, with an annual release goal of 750,000 yearling smolts.

Escapement Level

Terminal run size of Elwha River coho salmon has ranged from 2,000 to 10,000 fish in the last decade. An escapement goal of 1,250 fish to the LEKT hatchery and 250 natural spawners has been established (PNPTC et al. 2003). The 2005 run-size estimate for Elwha coho salmon was 9,865, with an escapement of 4,768 and a harvest of 5,097 fish. The composition of Elwha River coho salmon stock is 90.5% hatchery origin and 9.5% natural-origin (PNPTC et al. 2005).

Projected Hatchery Facility Use

The Lower Elwha Hatchery will be used for coho salmon restoration efforts.

Summary

A summary of the Elwha River coho salmon restoration strategies includes:

- on-station releases of yearling smolts
- natural spawning of adults
- planting of eyed eggs
- outplanting of fry, presmolts, and smolts in off-station locations

The strategies described for coho salmon in this plan are intended to be adaptive, changing based on observed responses of the coho salmon population. Therefore, if certain strategies prove to be unsuccessful, they may be discontinued at any time in favor of options that are more likely to produce a healthy, naturally spawning population. All enhancement activities for restoration purposes are expected to discontinue when natural production is sufficient to achieve recovery goals.

Phasing of Coho Restoration Strategies

Pre-dam-removal period

Enhancement activities for coho salmon will focus on maintaining the existing hatchery program. Hatchery facilities will be undergoing modification and water treatment facilities and delivery systems will be constructed during this time to meet production goals. Fish production will be maintained at historic levels, emphasizing release of smolts from the Lower Elwha Hatchery. Recreational and commercial harvests will be maintained at current levels. Table 12 summarizes the restoration strategies for the pre-dam-removal period. Broodstock collection strategies for adult coho salmon during this period will be restricted to collection of adults returning to the tribal and WDFW hatchery facilities in the Elwha River.

Dam-removal period

In-river environmental conditions in the lower river will likely be severely degraded and may be unsuitable for spawning. Therefore, enhancement strategies during this time will be to maintain the hatchery-based population. Modifications to hatchery facilities and construction of water treatment and delivery systems will be completed during this period. Water availability will be limited periodically by the water treatment facility capacity, which will require coho salmon production levels to be reduced to that supported by the water availability. Table 13 summarizes the restoration strategies for the dam-removal period.

Enhancement will emphasize hatchery release of yearling smolts at low return levels. However, the enhancement program will expand to include passage of adults upstream, outplants of eyed eggs, and the upriver outplants of fry, presmolts, and yearling smolts as numbers of returning adults increase.

Adult coho salmon will be collected at the tribal and WDFW hatchery facilities in the Elwha River and by using gill nets at selected locations throughout the Elwha River basin. Sport and commercial harvest of Elwha coho will be suspended during the restoration period.

Post-dam-removal period

It is assumed that during this period dam removal will have been completed, the period of greatest turbidity will have passed, the water treatment facility will have been taken off-line, hatchery facilities will be receiving raw surface water, and water availability will no longer limit hatchery production levels. Table 14 summarizes the restoration strategies for the post-dam-removal period.

Table 12. Coho salmon restoration strategies before dam removal. Numbers in boldface are adult escapement levels.

Production facility	Life history pattern	Release location	Coho production at adult escapement levels								
			100	**500**	**1,000**	**1,500**	**2,000**	**5,000**	**7,500**	**10,000**	**15,000**
Lower Elwha	Yearling smolts	On-site	225,000	450,000	750,000	750,000	750,000	750,000	750,000	750,000	750,000
	Fishery				166	666	1,166	4,166	6,666	9,166	14,166
Lower Elwha	Eyed eggs	Mid, low basin									
Lower Elwha	Fry	Mid, low basin									
Lower Elwha	Presmolts	Mid, low basin									
Lower Elwha	Yearling smolts	Mid, low basin									
		Potential egg production:	312,500	625,000	1,250,000	1,875,000	2,500,000	6,250,000	9,375,000	12,500,000	18,750,000

Table 13. Coho salmon restoration strategies during dam removal. Numbers in boldface are adult escapement levels.

Production Facility	Life history pattern	Release location	Coho production at adult escapement levels								
			100	**500**	**1,000**	**1,500**	**2,000**	**5,000**	**7,500**	**10,000**	**15,000**
Lower Elwha	Yearling smolts	On-site	225,000	425,000	425,000	425,000	425,000	425,000	425,000	425,000	425,000
	Natural spawners	Upper basin			110	531	1,031	4,031	6,531	9,031	14,031
Lower Elwha	Eyed eggs	Mid, low basin				100,000	100,000	100,000	100,000	100,000	100,000
Lower Elwha	Fry	Mid, low basin			300,000	300,000	300,000	300,000	300,000	300,000	300,000
Lower Elwha	Presmolts	Mid, low basin		15,000	75,000	75,000	75,000	75,000	75,000	75,000	75,000
Lower Elwha	Yearling Smolts	Mid, low basin		10,000	30,000	30,000	30,000	30,000	30,000	30,000	30,000
		Potential egg production:	312,500	625,000	1,250,000	1,875,000	2,500,000	6,250,000	9,375,000	12,500,000	18,750,000

Table 14. Coho restoration strategies after dam removal. Numbers in boldface are adult escapement levels.

Production Facility	Life history pattern	Release location	Coho production at adult escapement levels								
			100	**500**	**1,000**	**1,500**	**2,000**	**5,000**	**7,500**	**10,000**	**15,000**
Lower Elwha	Yearling smolts	On-site	225,000	425,000	425,000	750,000	750,000	750,000	750,000	750,000	750,000
	Natural spawners	Upper basin			286	425	845	2,345	3,845	4,845	9,845
	Fishery							1,500	2,500	4,000	4,000
Lower Elwha	Eyed eggs	Mid, low basin				100,000	100,000	100,000	100,000	100,000	100,000
Lower Elwha	Fry	Mid, low basin			125,000	125,000	125,000	125,000	125,000	125,000	125,000
Lower Elwha	Presmolts	Mid, low basin		15,000	75,000	75,000	75,000	75,000	75,000	75,000	75,000
Lower Elwha	Yearling smolts	Mid, low basin		10,000	30,000	30,000	30,000	30,000	30,000	30,000	30,000
		Potential egg production:	312,500	625,000	1,250,000	1,875,000	2,500,000	6,250,000	9,375,000	12,500,000	18,750,000

The production of juvenile coho salmon from hatcheries will be increased to maximize use of the facilities for coho salmon population restoration purposes. As adult return numbers increase, enhancement activities will be expanded to include fry outplants, increased upriver outplanting of presmolts and smolts, and plants of eyed eggs and greater numbers of natural spawners throughout the basin. The hatchery enhancement program will be phased out in response to increases in natural-origin spawning as the population achieves self-sustainability.

Adult coho salmon will be collected at the tribal and WDFW hatchery facilities in the Elwha River and by using gill nets at selected locations throughout the Elwha River basin.

Sport and commercial harvest of Elwha coho will be implemented as hatchery and natural escapement goals for the basin are met.

Chum Salmon Proposed Restoration Approach

Chum salmon in the Elwha River are considered a native, wild-origin stock (WDFW and WTIT 1994) with a fall run timing. The Lower Elwha Hatchery produced chum salmon beginning in 1975 (Walcott Slough Hood Canal fall stock) but the program was discontinued in 1985. Historic spawner estimates placed population size at many thousands, likely the second most abundant species in the river. Spawner surveys in 1993–1995 indicated the population had declined to 150–300 adults (Hiss 1995). The LEKT Fisheries Department has conducted a broodstock preservation program since 1994. This effort involves collecting 25–40 male and female spawning pairs annually, incubating their fertilized eggs to the eyed stage at the Lower Elwha Hatchery, and transporting eyed eggs to stream-side incubator boxes within side-channel habitats in the lower river for hatching and release of unfed fry.

Stock Targeted for Enhancement

The existing in-basin native stock has been identified as the preferred stock for enhancement activities. Elwha fall chum salmon have two distinct run-timing components—an early population (October-November) thought to be the native stock and a later-entering population (December) that is genetically similar to Hood Canal populations (Wunderlich et al. 1994). It is thought this later component is the remnant of the hatchery-origin population reared at the Lower Elwha Hatchery during the 1980s.

Stock Status

The status of the Elwha chum salmon stock is considered critical.

Harvest Status

No harvest is currently directed at Elwha chum salmon, though some incidental harvest occurs in terminal commercial and sport coho fisheries. During the 2003 coho salmon harvest season, the anticipated incidental in-river exploitation rate for chum was 2.4%.

Hatchery Enhancement Efforts

The current hatchery program for Elwha chum salmon is designed for stock maintenance and restoration. Ripe adults captured in the river are spawned and their eggs are brought into the hatchery and incubated to the eyed stage. Eyed eggs are transported for incubation in stream-side incubator boxes located in side-channel habitats to imprint the chum salmon to river areas suitable for natural chum salmon production. After hatching, incubator-produced fry emigrate seaward into lower river, estuarine, and nearshore marine areas in the Strait of Juan de Fuca to rear.

Projected Hatchery Facility Use

Enhancement efforts will take place at the Lower Elwha Hatchery and at the WDFW Elwha rearing channel.

Summary

Chum salmon proposed strategies are based on the following production assumptions. Sex ratio is 50:50. Fecundity is 3,000 eggs per female. Survival rates are 90% to eyed stage and 80% to age-0 smolt.

A summary of the Elwha River chum salmon restoration strategies includes:

- on-station release of age-0 smolts

- alternate in-basin hatchery releases of age-0 smolts

- planting of eyed eggs in lower and middle Elwha Basin locations

- natural spawning of adults

- outplanting of fry in upstream locations

The strategies described for chum salmon in this plan are intended to be adaptive, with changes based on observed responses of the chum salmon population. Therefore, if certain strategies prove to be unsuccessful, they may be discontinued at any time in favor of options that are more likely to produce a healthy, naturally spawning population. All enhancement activities for restoration purposes are expected to discontinue when natural production is sufficient to achieve recovery goals.

Phasing of Chum Salmon Restoration Strategies

Pre-dam-removal period

Enhancement activities for chum salmon will focus on increasing the population size of the composite chum salmon population produced by and returning to the Lower Elwha Hatchery and the WDFW Elwha rearing channel. Hatchery facilities will be undergoing modification to accommodate new fish production needed for restoration. Water treatment facilities and delivery systems will be constructed during this time to meet production goals. Table 15 summarizes the restoration strategies for the pre-dam-removal period.

Broodstock collection strategies for adult chum salmon during this period include in-river gillnet collection and the collection of adults returning to the tribal hatchery. Fish production strategies will emphasize release of age-0 smolts from the facilities. No harvests will be directed at Elwha River chum salmon during this period.

Dam-removal period

Enhancement activities for chum salmon will focus on increasing the population size of the composite chum salmon population only at the Lower Elwha Hatchery. During this period, modifications to hatchery facilities and water treatment and delivery systems will be complete, although water availability will be periodically limited to the water treatment facility capacity. In-river environmental conditions in the lower river will be severely degraded and will be unsuitable for spawning. Chum salmon production levels will be limited in response to the availability of rearing space and water (due to the treatment capacity of the shared water treatment facility). At low return levels, enhancement will emphasize hatchery release of age-0 smolts. With increased adult return numbers, the enhancement program will expand to include outplants of eyed eggs, passage of adults upstream, and upriver outplants of fry. Table 16 summarizes the restoration strategies for the dam removal period.

Collection strategies for adult chum salmon during this period will include in-river gillnet collection and the collection of adults returning to the tribal hatchery. No harvests will be allowed on Elwha River chum salmon during this period.

Post-dam-removal period

It is assumed that during this period, dam removal has been completed, the period of greatest turbidity will have passed, the water treatment facility will have been taken off-line, hatchery facilities will be receiving raw surface water, and hatchery production levels will be no longer limited by water availability. Based on these assumptions, restoration strategies will emphasize the continued hatchery production of age-0 smolts and outplanting eyed eggs throughout the basin. Returning adults will be encouraged to spawn naturally throughout the basin. Hatchery enhancement of chum salmon will be phased out in response to increases in natural-origin spawning as the population begins to achieve self-sustainability. Table 17 summarizes the restoration strategies for the post-dam-removal period.

Collection strategies for adult chum salmon during this period will include the collection of adults returning to the tribal hatchery and in-river gillnet collection.

Sport and commercial harvest of Elwha chum may be implemented if hatchery and natural escapement goals are met. The benefit of escaping an abundance of chum salmon into upstream spawning areas as a mechanism for enhancing marine-derived nutrients in the Elwha River ecosystem will be factored in any consideration of chum salmon–directed harvests in fisheries.

Table 15. Chum salmon restoration strategies before dam removal. Numbers in boldface are adult escapement levels.

Production Facility	Life history pattern	Release location	Chum Salmon Production Goal at Adult Escapement Levels						
			50	**100**	**200**	**500**	**750**	**1,000**	**2,000**
Lower Elwha	Age-0 smolts	On-site	31,000	75,000	75,000	75,000	75,000	75,000	75,000
WDFW	Age-0 smolts	On-site		40,000	100,000	450,000	450,000	450,000	450,000
Lower Elwha	Eyed eggs	Lower/middle Elwha Basin			75,000	100,000	100,000	100,000	100,000
Lower Elwha	Natural spawners	Lower basin					250	500	1,500
Lower Elwha	Age-0 smolts	Elwha Basin							
		Potential egg production:	37,500	150,000	300,000	750,000	1,125,000	1,500,000	3,000,000

Table 16. Chum salmon restoration strategies during dam removal. Numbers in boldface are adult escapement levels.

Production Facility	Life history pattern	Release location	Chum Salmon Production Goal at Adult Escapement Levels						
			50	**100**	**200**	**500**	**750**	**1,000**	**2,000**
Lower Elwha	Age-0 smolts	On-site	31,000	75,000	165,000	500,000	650,000	650,000	650,000
Lower Elwha	Eyed eggs	Lower basin			100,000	100,000	100,000	100,000	100,000
Lower Elwha	Natural spawners	Lower basin				20	140	460	1,460
Lower Elwha	Age-0 smolts	Elwha Basin							
		Potential egg production:	37,500	150,000	300,000	750,000	1,125,000	1,500,000	3,000,000

Table 17. Chum salmon restoration strategies after dam removal. Numbers in boldface are adult escapement levels.

Production Facility	Life history pattern	Release location	Chum Salmon Production Goal at Adult Escapement Levels						
			50	**100**	**200**	**500**	**750**	**1,000**	**2,000**
Lower Elwha	Age-0 smolts	On-site	31,000	120,000	240,000	300,000	300,000	300,000	300,000
Lower Elwha	Eyed eggs	Lower basin				250,000	250,000	250,000	250,000
Lower Elwha	Natural spawners	Lower basin				83	333	292	1,292
Lower Elwha	Age-0 smolts	Elwha Basin						350,000	350,000
		Potential egg production:	37,500	150,000	300,000	750,000	1,125,000	1,500,000	3,000,000

Pink Salmon Proposed Restoration Approach

Elwha River pink salmon populations declined to critical levels following dam construction and subsequent river channelization and flood control efforts. Pink salmon historically were the most numerous salmonid in the Elwha River and their recovery is critical to the overall success of the restoration effort. The historic Elwha River pink salmon population is estimated to have numbered in the hundreds of thousands of adult fish. Although given a small average weight as adults (1–2.5 kg), the sheer numbers of fish provided large amounts of marine-derived nutrients to the Elwha ecosystem. Pink salmon have the least amount of life history variation of all Pacific salmon, with a two-year life and only brief residency in freshwater (Hard et al. 1996). Pink salmon are also unique among the Pacific salmon in that they are the smallest yet most abundant, have generally limited freshwater migrations, have the fewest number of chromosomes, and are reproductively isolated by their two-year life history (Groot and Margolis 1991).

As throughout almost all of Puget Sound, the odd-year cycle is dominant in the Elwha. However, small numbers of pink salmon are occasionally observed in the Elwha River on the even-year cycle. Two life history patterns are presumed for Elwha pink salmon: an early timed (summer) entry associated with upriver spawning populations and a later timed (fall) population associated with lower river spawning habitats. While pink salmon have not had access to the upper Elwha River in nearly 100 years, this entry timing pattern persists today and is similar to pink salmon populations in the adjacent Dungeness River.

Remarkably, Elwha populations of pink salmon were considered extirpated by the late 1980s. However, the recent discovery of what appears to be a persistent population and new genetic analysis of tissue collected in 2001 and 2003 (Small 2004) indicate Elwha River pink salmon are a unique population and genetically distinct from neighboring Puget Sound pink salmon populations. This information supports a renewed effort to conserve and rebuild native Elwha pink salmon stocks through dam removal. Because of the very low numbers of pink salmon and the potential for impacts from elevated sediment yield during and following dam removal, maintenance of the native gene pool through a captive brood program will be the highest priority for this species.

Genetic Diversity

Genetic analysis indicates pink salmon populations around the Pacific Rim tend to separate by three broad groups: 1) Asia, 2) Alaska and northern British Columbia, and 3) southern British Columbia and Washington (Beacham et al. 1985, 1988, Shaklee et al. 1991). These regional populations appear to be subdivided as well. For southern British Columbia and Washington populations, Hard et al. (1996) concluded there are four distinct groups of odd-year spawners: 1) Olympic Peninsula, 2) southern British Columbia, 3) Puget Sound, and 4) Fraser River. The highest levels of genetic diversity are associated with populations from the Olympic Peninsula. Hard et al. (1996) noted Olympic Peninsula pink salmon populations are at the southern end of the species range and may be critical to maintaining the overall integrity of the Puget Sound population as a whole. It should be noted that at the time of these analyses, Elwha pink populations were considered extirpated and tissue was not included in any of the analyses.

Additional genetic analysis of Olympic Peninsula pink salmon populations has recently been completed. Small (2004) used microsatellite DNA techniques to compare populations of pink salmon from the Elwha (summer and fall), Dungeness (summer and fall), and Morse Creek. Elwha River and Morse Creek pink salmon collections were genetically differentiated from each other and genetically differentiated from Dungeness River summer and fall pink salmon stocks.

Conservation Strategy

The existing Elwha River stock will be utilized in a captive brood program in order to maintain native gene pools and to develop future sources of broodstock to colonize restored habitats. The native, odd-year Elwha River pink salmon population is the preferred stock for use in restoration, given recent information indicating it is genetically distinct from other Puget Sound pink salmon populations. The population is currently at very low abundance levels (<200 adults) and may not survive sedimentation impacts associated with dam removal. If this were to occur, restoration options would be limited to two alternatives: natural recolonization or the reintroduction of pink salmon using a nonnative stock.

Natural recolonization through straying is considered a viable alternative and will be monitored in the Elwha River through spawning ground surveys and tissue (microsatellite DNA) analysis. However, straying of pink salmon populations appears to be somewhat of a paradox. While the species is known to readily invade habitats in large numbers, such as those recently exposed by deglaciation in Glacier Bay, Alaska (Milner and York 2001), and following 35 years of blockage from the upper Fraser River (Vernon 1966), their overall straying rate is thought to be low (Quinn 1993). An experimental movement of returning hatchery adults found that 91% of the adult pink salmon intentionally displaced from Olsen Creek, Alaska, returned to that site (Helle 1996). In contrast to these studies, a genetic analysis of 37 subpopulations in northwestern Alaska (Gharrett et al. 1988) found very little evidence of genetic heterogenerity, even amongst Aleutian Island populations separated by as much as 1,000 miles. The authors hypothesized that frequent straying may prevent the genetic divergence of these spatially separated populations. The Elwha River itself serves as an example, as the Elwha population has remained at extremely low abundance levels for many years without any obvious indication from genetic analysis of straying.

Natural recolonization may take some time, given the relative isolation of the Elwha River, apparent low straying rates, and depressed population sizes of adjacent pink salmon populations. Hatchery reintroductions using an outside stock is considered the least desirable alternative, but has been maintained as an option in the event of failure of the captive brood and natural recolonization to rebuild pink salmon populations. It should be noted that pink salmon have been widely transplanted, and success rates over the long term have been low. The most successful introduction of pink salmon was the result of an accidental spill of pink fry in the Great Lakes. In contrast, attempts to establish pink salmon populations within their native range have mostly failed. Hard et al. (1996) cite the failure despite repeated attempts to establish even-year pink salmon runs in Puget Sound.

Stock Status

Elwha pink salmon stock status is considered critical based on chronically low escapements. This stock level is currently considered depressed with recent escapements ranging from approximately 200 fish in 2001 to less than 50 in 2005. There is no formal escapement goal for pink salmon in the Elwha River. Escapement estimates for the Elwha River have historically been provided as an estimated percentage of the Dungeness pink salmon run. Population declines in both systems have resulted in an Elwha River estimate of 50 fish used as a placeholder, indicating the run was believed to exist at a very low level.

Pink salmon numbers remained relatively high after dam construction. However, between 1950 and 1970 there was a loss of spawning habitat due to large-scale river manipulation such as channelization, removal of snags and logjams, and floodplain logging that led to a loss of channel sinuosity (Johnson 1997, Pohl 1999). These activities and resultant effect are also coincident with the final collapse of pink salmon in the Lower Elwha during the 1960s (McHenry et al. 1996). The last sizeable escapement of 40,000 fish to the Elwha River was recorded in 1961. The estimated spawning population in the river declined to as low as one fish by the early 1970s. This poor status continued through the 1980s, with only four individuals observed during escapement surveys in 1989. Detailed escapement surveys conducted by the LEKT Fisheries Department since 1991 have documented the appearance of a persistent population of between 100 and 1,000 fish in odd years.

In the early 1990s, cursory surveys conducted by LEKT's Fisheries Department were unable to identify any spawning pink salmon. From the late 1990s through the 2001 pink salmon run, the tribe's surveys indicate the population may be growing. However, in 2003 the tribe estimated that Elwha pink salmon escapement was only 150 fish, and flood impacts likely reduced the survival of their progeny to very low levels. Similar trends were observed within the Hunt Road complex, a large side-channel complex entering on the western bank of the Elwha River. Peak live counts of pink salmon increased from only 8 fish in 1997 to as high as 160 adults in 2001. The last two cycles in 2003 and 2005 were 55 live fish and 16 live fish, respectively, observed within the Hunt Road Channel. Based on estimates generated through smolt trapping in 2006, LEKT estimates an outmigration of 19,000 pink salmon smolts.

Harvest Status

No terminal harvest is currently directed at Elwha River pink salmon. The Elwha River is closed to all fishing during the period of river entry and through spawning. Mixed stock sport and commercial fisheries in the Strait of Juan de Fuca and off Vancouver Island likely intercept Elwha pink salmon, but the impacts are not currently known.

Hatchery Enhancement Efforts

There has never been an historic hatchery program for Elwha River pink salmon and introductions of nonnative pink salmon have not occurred.

Alternate Stocks Targeted for Enhancement

Because the availability of the native Elwha River stock is uncertain due to chronically low population numbers, Dungeness River (summer) and Finch Creek (Hood Canal early component) pink salmon stocks will be considered as an alternate broodstock for use in the restoration program. These options will only be pursued in the event that the native Elwha pink salmon are extirpated and if significant natural colonization does not occur within five generations (10 years) following dam removal. If stock transfers are pursued, Dungeness River summer pink salmon are preferred for transfer to the Elwha, primarily because of geographic proximity, but also because of similar life history expressions. The Finch Creek stock would only be pursued as a last resort if insufficient numbers of Dungeness pink salmon were available for transfer.

Dungeness River (summer)

The upriver Dungeness River summer pink salmon (peak spawning late August) has been identified as the preferred alternate stock for enhancement activities based on its proximity (18.5 miles) to the Elwha River, upstream migratory patterns, and adult run timing. It is currently considered depressed with escapements ranging from 1,556 in 1993 to 69,272 in 2001. No terminal harvest is currently directed at Dungeness River pink salmon. Hatchery enhancement efforts for the Dungeness River fall pink salmon population were discontinued following the 2001 cycle. Total escapement of adults in 2003 (summer and fall populations) was 15,148 fish. Total escapement of both populations in the Dungeness River in 2005 was 8,667 fish.

Finch Creek (Hood Canal, early component)

Finch Creek pink salmon were previously identified as the secondary alternate stock for enhancement activities. This stock is a hatchery-origin composite stock originating from pink salmon from the Dungeness and Dosewallips rivers. The Finch Creek stock is not considered genetically distinct from the original donor and other regional pink salmon populations. Since 1991 the combined total annual estimated harvest of Finch Creek (Hoodsport) pink salmon has ranged from 1,100 to 4,800 adults. The current annual juvenile fish release goal for the program is 500,000 fingerlings. Recent escapements back to the Hoodsport Hatchery (1991 to 2003) have ranged from 7,600 to 68,000 adults. The current escapement goal for Finch Creek pink salmon is 920 fish.

Projected Hatchery Facility Use

Conservation and potential future supplementation efforts for pink salmon will take place initially at the existing Lower Elwha Hatchery, transitioning to the new LEKT facility. If capacity is limited during 2007–2008, it may be necessary to use the WDFW facility at Hurd Creek as a backup rearing site.

Phasing of Pink Salmon Restoration Strategies

Pre-dam-removal period

Conservation activities for pink salmon during this period will focus on stock protection and developing the capabilities to manage a captive brood program. With only a few cycles remaining prior to dam removal, emphasis will be placed on developing a captive brood program. Collection techniques will be implemented to maximize genetic diversity and prevent potential inbreeding depression. Genetic sampling will be conducted for every fish collected. Table 18 summarizes the restoration strategies for the pre-dam-removal period.

All collection techniques will be considered. However, due to potential mortality from capturing and handling adults as well as selection factors related to the small population size, emphasis will be placed on collection of eggs and fry through redd pumping or collection of outmigrating smolts at the rotary screw trap. Redd pumping and smolt collection have the advantage of maximizing available genetic diversity of the extant populations. Additionally, these techniques can be managed to minimize impacts on the existing natural populations.

The LEKT hatchery, water treatment facilities, and delivery systems will be constructed during this time but will not be ready during the initial development stages of the captive brood program. It is not certain whether the current LEKT hatchery has sufficient space and water to maintain the captive brood effort. In the event that space is not available, the WDFW Hurd Creek facility would be used to rear fish.

Dam-removal period

During the dam removal period, activities for Elwha pink salmon will continue a focus on genetic conservation using primarily a captive brood program. However, as environmental conditions in the lower river will be severely degraded and will be unsuitable for spawning as sediment yields peak immediately following dam removal, capture of adults will be attempted. Progeny will be either incorporated into the captive brood program or released into the river as fed fry. Table 19 summarizes the restoration strategies for the dam-removal period.

Collection of pink smolts from the broodyear just before the initiation of dam removal will be attempted using the screw trap and redd pumping. Collection goals will be to maximize genetic diversity for the captive brood program. Depending on the success of the captive brood program, some numbers of adult pink salmon from broodstock collected in years prior to dam removal will be available to initiate outplanting programs including the release of adults to upstream refuge habitats. Alternatively, if sufficient numbers of captive brood adults are available, these fish may be spawned and their progeny released as smolts or outplanted as eyed eggs.

Modifications to hatchery facilities and water treatment and delivery systems will be completed during this period, although water availability may be periodically limited to the water treatment facility capacity. No harvests will be directed at Elwha River pink salmon during this period.

Post-dam-removal period

During this period, turbidity levels in the river will be returning to background levels. The water treatment facility will be taken off-line, and hatchery facilities will be receiving raw surface water. The availability of water will no longer limit hatchery production levels. Based on these assumptions, pink salmon restoration strategies may be able to move from genetic conservation to stock rebuilding. Monitoring programs will provide critical information regarding recolonization rates and genetic makeup of Elwha pink salmon populations. Returning adults will be encouraged to spawn naturally throughout the basin and captive brood fish will be used to supplement the population. Hatchery enhancement of pink salmon may be considered if populations are not responding.

Conversely, if natural populations are expanding, hatchery programs will be phased out in response to increases in natural-origin spawning and as the population begins to achieve self-sustainability. In a worst case scenario, where both captive brood programs and natural recolonization fail to occur, a decision to import out-of-basin stocks will be considered. In a best case scenario, where rebuilding occurs rapidly, limited fisheries designed to harvest Elwha River pink salmon may be implemented if escapement goals are met. However, the benefit of escaping an abundance of pink salmon into upstream spawning areas as a mechanism for enhancing marine-derived nutrients in the Elwha River ecosystem will be factored into any consideration of pink salmon-directed harvests in fisheries. Table 20 summarizes the restoration strategies for the post-dam-removal period.

The strategies described for pink salmon in this plan are intended to be adaptive, changing based on observed responses of the pink salmon population. Therefore, if certain strategies prove to be unsuccessful, they may be discontinued at any time in favor of options that are more likely to produce a healthy, naturally spawning population.

Sockeye Salmon Proposed Restoration Approach

Historically, Elwha River sockeye salmon used Lake Sutherland for spawning and rearing (FERC 1993). Construction of the Elwha Dam blocked anadromous access to Lake Sutherland, leading to the extirpation of anadromous Lake Sutherland sockeye population. Although adult sockeye salmon are annually observed in the Elwha River, the origin of these fish is unknown and they are not thought to be a viable population. They may be strays or possibly returning adults derived from kokanee smolts (*Oncorhynchus nerka*), lacustrine sockeye outmigrating from Lake Sutherland.

Lake Sutherland is currently home to a self-sustaining population of kokanee salmon that is thought to be native (DOI et al. 1994). WDFW hatchery records indicate the release of nonnative kokanee in Lake Sutherland from 1934 until 1964 (Hiss and Wunderlich 1994b). The influence of nonnative kokanee releases on the native kokanee and sockeye population is not fully understood, but tissue samples were collected for genetic analysis in 1994, 2005, and 2006. Analysis of the 1994 samples indicated that Lake Sutherland kokanee displayed a unique composite haplotype (Powell 1997). For the 2005–2006 samples, data for 15 microsatellite loci were collected and compared with data from Lake Whatcom and Lake Ozette kokanee. The

Table 18. Pink salmon restoration strategies before dam removal. Numbers in boldface are adult escapement levels.

| | | | **Pink Salmon Production Goal at Adult Escapement Levels** | | | | | | |
			50	**100**	**200**	**500**	**750**	**1,000**	**2,000**
Production facility	**Life history pattern**	**Release location**							
Lower Elwha	Captive brood	On-site	1,000	1,000	1,000	1,000	1,000	1,000	1,000
Lower Elwha	Natural spawners	Lower basin	36,500	74,000	149,000	374,000	561,000	749,000	1,499,000
		Potential egg production:	37,500	75,000	150,000	375,000	562,000	750,000	1,500,000

Table 19. Pink salmon restoration strategies during dam removal. Numbers in boldface are adult escapement levels.

| | | | **Pink Salmon Production Goal at Adult Escapement Levels** | | | | | | |
			50	**100**	**200**	**500**	**750**	**1,000**	**2,000**
Production facility	**Life history pattern**	**Release location**							
Lower Elwha	Captive brood	On-site	1,000	1,000	1,000	1,000	1,000	1,000	1,000
Lower Elwha	Age-0 smolts	On-site	30,000	60,000	120,000	300,000	450,000	600,000	650,000
Lower Elwha	Eyed eggs	Lower basin							100,000
Lower Elwha	Natural spawners	Lower basin							391
		Potential egg production:	37,500	75,000	150,000	375,000	562,000	750,000	1,500,000

Table 20. Pink salmon restoration strategies after dam removal. Numbers in boldface are adult escapement levels.

| | | | **Pink Salmon Production Goal at Adult Escapement Levels** | | | | | | |
			50	**100**	**200**	**500**	**750**	**1,000**	**2,000**
Production facility	**Life history pattern**	**Release location**							
Lower Elwha	Captive brood	On-site	1,000	1,000	1,000	1,000	1,000	1,000	1,000
Lower Elwha	Age-0 smolts	On-site	30,000	60,000	120,000	300,000	450,000	600,000	650,000
Lower Elwha	Eyed eggs	Lower basin							100,000
Lower Elwha	Natural spawners	Lower basin							
Lower Elwha	Age-0 smolts*	Elwha Basin							391
		Potential egg production:	37,500	75,000	150,000	375,000	562,000	750,000	1,500,000

*When escapement reaches adequate levels, the release of age-0 smolts to off-station locations in the Elwha Basin will be considered.

2005 and 2006 Lake Sutherland collections were highly similar, but statistically different from the Whatcom and Ozette collections. The results of both studies suggest the Sutherland stock is unique and that previous out-of-basin plantings may not have affected the Sutherland population genetically. Additional comparisons will be made between these stocks and the adjacent population in Lake Crescent in the coming years (Winans et al. in press).

Stock Status

Sockeye salmon in the Elwha River are extinct.

Harvest Status

Lake Sutherland is currently open for harvest year-round for resident trout and kokanee.

Hatchery Enhancement Efforts

There are currently no hatchery programs for Elwha River sockeye salmon populations.

Escapement Level

There is no formal escapement goal for sockeye salmon populations in the Elwha River.

Summary

The preferred Elwha River sockeye salmon population restoration or reestablishment strategy is natural recolonization by remnant kokanee. The period required for natural recolonization is uncertain, commencing when upstream and downstream access to Lake Sutherland becomes feasible for kokanee currently inhabiting the lake when the dams blocking anadromous fish access are fully removed. In order to encourage recovery, it may be necessary to curtail recreational fisheries in Lake Sutherland for a period of years and eliminate plants of nonnative fish in the lake (either kokanee or trout).

Coastal Cutthroat Trout Proposed Restoration Approach

Coastal cutthroat trout populations in Western Washington are typified by both anadromous and resident life history strategies. The preferred Elwha River coastal cutthroat trout restoration strategy is natural recolonization. Natural recolonization of the upper river is expected to occur over an uncertain period once access to the upper river is reestablished. Resident forms of coastal cutthroat exist in the upper Elwha River basin and may contribute to reestablishment of native anadromous populations after dam removal on the Elwha River.

Stock Status

The status of coastal cutthroat trout is unknown. Coastal cutthroat have likely been negatively impacted by loss of access to the upper river, lack of small tributaries in the lower river where the population is sequestered for spawning and rearing, and habitat degradation in the lower river due to the Elwha Dam. Hatchery introductions of out-of-basin-origin cutthroat trout from the Bureau of Fisheries hatchery at Lake Crescent were widespread in the early portion of the twentieth century. A population of westslope cutthroat (*O. clarkii lewisi*) has been documented in Long Creek (Adams et al. 1999). Populations of landlocked or resident coastal cutthroat have been documented in Indian Creek and Lake Sutherland, Little River, and the middle reaches of the Elwha River (Morrill and McHenry unpubl. manuscr.). Resident cutthroat trout, though present in the upper watershed, appear to be at very low abundance levels. No genetic analysis of the composition of this stock has been conducted to date.

Harvest Status

Coastal cutthroat trout populations are currently subject to recreational harvest.

Hatchery Enhancement Efforts

There are currently no hatchery programs for Elwha River coastal cutthroat trout populations.

Escapement Level

There is no formal escapement goal for coastal cutthroat trout populations in the Elwha River.

Bull Trout/Dolly Varden Proposed Restoration Approach

Anadromous and resident (fluvial and adfluvial) life history strategies typify bull trout and Dolly Varden populations in Western Washington. Bull trout and Dolly Varden are recognized as separate species of char, although they are both often referred to interchangeably as "native char." In Western Washington, both sympatric and allopatric populations may occur. In the Elwha River, limited genetic and morphological analysis of a few specimens indicates the presence of only bull trout (Leary and Allendorf 1997). However, other Olympic Peninsula river systems such as the Sol Duc River are known to have Dolly Varden but no bull trout. Conversely, the Quinault Basin has both bull trout and Dolly Varden (Leary and Allendorf 1997). For the purposes of this document, the Elwha River is assumed to support only bull trout.

Stock Status

Bull trout populations in the Elwha may exhibit fluvial, adfluvial, and anadromous life history strategies. Fish found in the lower Elwha River basin (below Elwha Dam) are thought to be anadromous, while adfluvial and fluvial populations inhabit the basin above Elwha Dam.

According to Mike McHenry, LEKT Fisheries Department, few bull trout are observed in the river below the Elwha Dam and only one redd has been documented. George Pess, NWFSC, identified three char fry and a handful of adults (10″–24″) during snorkel surveys initiated in 2000. This population has likely been negatively impacted by loss of access to the upper river, habitat degradation in the lower river, nearshore, and estuary, and potentially to harvests in the lower river.

Construction of the mainstem dams isolated populations of bull trout in both the middle and upper Elwha River basins. The creation of lakes Aldwell and Mills also modified habitat features, resulting in the establishment of adfluvial populations in these lakes. Population size in the upper basin is unknown, although bull trout appear to be relatively prevalent throughout the upper watershed and have been observed as high as RM 43.9 (ONP Fish Distribution Database). They are also found in at least seven of the mainstem tributaries.

Elwha River bull trout are included in the Coastal Puget Sound distinct population segment (DPS), which is listed as threatened under the ESA. In the draft recovery plan, the USFWS (2004) identified a number of "core areas," thought to be strongholds for the population, which must be protected and restored. The USFSW identified the Elwha River as a core area with one identified local population and one potential local population in Little River (USFWS 2004). Based on professional judgment, knowledge of bull trout distribution in drainages, availability of suitable habitat, and extremely low numbers of char observed in this system in recent years, the USFWS rates the lower Elwha River subpopulation as "depressed." The USFWS also thinks that migratory bull trout may persist in the Elwha core area, but the dams block connectivity between the populations and to the marine environment. Without connectivity between the populations or the marine area, there is an elevated risk to the population.

Biological Opinion and Management Prescriptions

USFWS issued a biological opinion in February 2000 covering bull trout during dam removal. It found the project will not result in jeopardy for the listed populations in the Elwha River, as they would benefit over the long term through dam removal. However, they did find that a small "take" was likely to occur and therefore required ONP comply with the following terms and conditions to minimize the take:

1. Develop and implement a bull trout rescue and removal plan for the affected area (Lake Mills to the mouth of the Elwha River) to reduce the level of take from the release of reservoir sediments (see USFWS Recovery Action 1.2.5 below).

2. Determine the origin of bull trout using the lower Elwha River through a genetic analysis (microsatellite DNA) of these fish, for example, from the tribal test fishery, tribal hatchery, and WDFW rearing channel (see USFWS Recovery Action 4.1.1 below).

3. Determine by genetic analysis whether bull trout from the lower Elwha River are distinct from the upper Elwha River or the lower Dungeness and Gray Wolf river subpopulations (see USFWS Recovery Actions 4.1.1 and 4.2.1 below).

4. Determine the genetic signature of the lower Dungeness and Gray Wolf river subpopulations. This information is presently unavailable and is necessary to properly relocate bull trout rescued and removed from the lower Elwha River. Potentially, bull trout from the lower Dungeness River and Gray Wolf river subpopulations may use the lower Elwha River. Their placement above Lake Mills must be avoided (see USFWS Recovery Actions 4.1.1 and 4.2.1 below). (Note: DNA samples from the Dungeness and Elwha rivers are being analyzed at the USFWS Abernathy Fish Technology Center in Longview, Washington.)

5. Replace or modify Hot Springs Road culverts that limit or block access to tributaries that could be used by bull trout as refuge habitat when the high sediment load and turbidity levels occur in the Elwha River. Any culvert should be sized for the 100-year flood event

and installed to safely and effectively pass both juvenile and adult bull trout (see USFWS Recovery Action 1.2.3 below).

6. Using appropriate, USFWS-approved methodologies, monitor sediment levels before and after project, above and below the project area for a period of 10 years, or less if sediment levels in the affected areas reach levels similar to those comparable to those prior to dam construction sooner.[4] Periodically monitor the condition of the Elwha River and determine whether suspended solids and bedload levels have returned to levels similar to those prior to dam construction. By the end of the 10-year monitoring period, if sediment levels have not returned to levels comparable to those before dam construction, implement additional measures (e.g., grading, seeding, or replanting) to reduce the input and transport of sediment from the project area.

The USFWS also suggested that the following conservation measures be implemented by the Olympic National Park:

1. Minimize the removal of trees and shrubs and other impacts to sensitive areas (see USFWS Recovery Action 1.3.1 below).

2. Use only native plant species when reseeding disturbed or unstable areas (see USFWS Recovery Action 1.3.1 below).

3. Conduct night snorkeling surveys to determine local bull trout distribution and seasonal use within the Elwha River main stem and its tributaries (see USFWS Recovery Action 1.3.2 below).

Harvest Status

Bull trout populations are currently subject to incidental takes during recreational and commercial harvests targeting other fish species. Within the Elwha River, fishing for bull trout is prohibited by state, tribal, and ONP fishing regulations. All bull trout must be immediately released if they are incidentally captured.

Hatchery Enhancement Efforts

There are no hatchery programs for Elwha River bull trout populations.

Escapement Level

There are no formal escapement goals for bull trout populations in the Elwha River and the population abundance is unknown. Further, information is needed to describe the underlying productivity of the population on which an escapement goal might be based. In lieu of this information, the USFWS (2004) advised that an interim goal of maintaining a minimum population size for a core population of between 500 and 1,000 adults be established to minimize the deleterious affects of low abundance and a minimum population size of 50–100 adults for localized spawning populations (Rieman and Allendorf 2001). USFWS further suggested that recovery will require an increasing trend in productivity from existing levels.

---

[4] Part of the research being done by physical scientists is to estimate levels prior to dam construction by making inferences from current conditions above the dams.

The preferred bull trout restoration strategy is natural recolonization. Recovery of bull trout is expected to occur naturally throughout the basin, once access to the upper river is reestablished. It is anticipated removal of the dams will allow currently isolated upriver populations to reestablish anadromous life history strategies. The time required to achieve recovery depends on the actual status of the existing bull trout populations, limiting factors affecting bull trout, implementation and effectiveness of recovery actions, and responses to recovery actions. A tremendous amount of work will be required to restore impaired habitat, reconnect habitat, and eliminate threats from nonnative species. Three to five bull trout generations (15–25 years), or possibly longer, may be necessary before recovery is achieved (USFWS 2004).

USFWS Bull Trout Recovery Plan

The primary purpose of the EFRP is to describe fisheries restoration activities that are specifically related to the implementation of the Elwha Act. However, USFWS has crafted a draft recovery plan for the Coastal Puget Sound bull trout DPS that contains specific actions targeting the recovery of entire distinct population segments. Some of the measures of the USFWS plan address the Elwha River core population and are relevant to the removal of the two dams on the Elwha River. These actions were generally captured in the biological opinion for the dam removal project and have been noted above. However, other measures of the USFWS plan for the Elwha River subpopulations are beyond the scope of dam removal. Therefore, if they are to be implemented, it must be through the appropriate jurisdictions outside of the authority of the Elwha Act (tribal, local and state governments, and federal agencies). Key components of the USFWS plan are included on pages 67-71 for informational purposes and to identify areas where the activities associated with the Elwha Act coincide with the USFWS recovery plan. Excerpts from the draft plan have been provided by USFWS.[5]

The overall goal of the USFWS draft recovery plan is "to ensure the ongoing long-term persistence of self-sustaining, complex, interacting groups of bull trout distributed across the species' native range so that the species can be delisted" (USFWS 2004). The key elements describing a recovered bull trout population, covered in the following discussion, are adult abundance, productivity (trends or population growth rate), spatial structure (distribution of local populations within the core area), and diversity (connectivity allowing for the expression of the migratory life history of bull trout). For further details, see Recovery Strategy, Goals, and Objectives, p. 133–147 of the draft recovery plan (USFWS 2004). USFWS bases bull trout recovery within each management unit on the concept of core areas. A core area accordingly represents the combination of both a core population (i.e., one or more local populations of bull trout inhabiting a core habitat) and core habitat (i.e., habitat that could supply all the necessary elements for the long-term security of bull trout, including spawning and rearing as well as foraging, migrating, and overwintering) and constitutes the basic unit on which to gauge recovery.

---

[5] S. Spalding, USFWS, Lacey, WA. Pers. commun., 6 July 2006.

Abundance

In the USFWS recovery plan, the recovered abundance for bull trout is based on two requirements. The first requirement is the minimum number of adult spawners in the core area needed to avoid the deleterious effects from genetic drift. The EFRP has adopted the USFWS minimum population size of between 500 and 1,000. The second requirement is the minimum size of the localized spawning populations to minimize inbreeding effects. The EFRP has also adopted the USFWS minimum population size of 50–100 adults for localized populations.

Productivity

The USFWS recovery plan states that a stable or increasing population is key for recovery of bull trout. Measures of a population trend (the tendency to increase, decrease, or remain stable) include population growth rate or productivity. For a population to be considered viable, its natural productivity should be sufficient for the population to replace itself from generation to generation. Because estimates of the total population size are rarely available, the productivity or population growth rate is usually estimated from temporal trends in indices of abundance (i.e., redd counts) at a particular life stage.

There is a lack of available information to describe current or historical productivity of bull trout in the Elwha River. For planning purposes in the Elwha River, USFWS suggests recovery will require an increasing trend in productivity from existing levels, but recognizes it may take 15 years or more to begin to determine the trend.

Local populations

The distribution and interconnection of multiple local populations throughout a watershed provide a mechanism for spreading risk from random, naturally occurring events and allows for potential recolonization in the event of local extirpations. Based in part on guidance from Rieman and McIntyre (1993), bull trout core areas (or watersheds) with fewer than 5 local populations are at increased risk of local extirpation, core areas with between 5 and 10 local populations are at intermediate risk, and core areas with more than 10 interconnected local populations are at diminished risk (USFWS 2004). Based on limited information and local expertise, the USFWS identified one local population in the Elwha watershed. In addition, one potential local population in Little River in the Elwha core area has been proposed.

Connectivity

The presence of the migratory life history form on the Olympic Peninsula was used as an indicator of the functional connectivity of the unit. If the migratory life form were absent, or if the migratory form were present but local populations lacked connectivity, the core area was considered to be at increased risk. If the migratory life form persists in at least some local populations, with partial ability to connect with other local populations, the core area was judged to be at intermediate risk. Finally, if the migratory life form was present in all or nearly all local populations and had the ability to connect with other local populations, the core area was considered to be at diminished risk (USFWS 2004).

Migratory bull trout may persist in the Elwha core area, but dams block connectivity. As described earlier, no upstream passage at either dam prevents migration of bull trout. The bull trout above the Elwha Dam are unable to connect and migrate to marine waters. Removal of the dams should reestablish connectivity and restore the anadromous life history form of bull trout in the Elwha core area.

Specific Recovery Actions that Apply to the Elwha River

The following are recommendations from the USFWS draft recovery plan (USFWS 2004) that apply specifically to the Elwha River core area. Those recommendations that are the responsibility of the Elwha Dam removal project, either in part or in full, are identified with an asterisk (*). The material quoted from the draft plan is enclosed in quotation marks, followed by commentary as it relates to the Elwha Plan. Notes in brackets ([ ]) are intended to express specific concerns or issues that may exist with how the recovery action is implemented. The recommendations follow.

1.1.3* "Implement measures to restore natural thermal regime." Removal of the dams will restore the natural thermal regime.

1.1.5* "Encourage reestablishment of marine-derived nutrients." In the Elwha River, dams have blocked the migration of salmonids and other fish, resulting in a decrease of marine-derived nutrients. Removal of the dams would enable connection to the ocean. In the meantime, the USFWS recommends dispersing hatchery salmon carcasses to increase availability of marine-derived nutrients. [Note: Jurisdictional conflicts related to this recommendation must be resolved prior to dispersing carcasses throughout the watershed.]

1.1.6* "Monitor water quality and meet water quality standards for temperature, nutrient loading, dissolved oxygen, instream flow, and contaminants." The Elwha River is on the 303(d)—referring to section 303(d) of the federal Clean Water Act—list of waters in the state. It has been impaired by high temperature and the toxin PCB-1254 (polychlorinated biphenyl [54% CL]). Monitoring water quality should continue in the Elwha core area including the area between the Elwha and Glines Canyon dams and to the mouth of the Elwha River downstream of the Elwha Dam. [Note: Water quality monitoring will be implemented to the extent that the need is either directly related to the presence of the two dams or to the impacts associated with removal activities.]

1.1.9 "Adopt and implement a storm water strategy for the lower Elwha watershed." Areas that may be affected include the estuary, road corridors associated with Highway 101, State Route 112, Olympic Hot Springs Road, and the Little River and Indian Creek basins.

1.2.2* "Identify diversions that block fish passage and provide fish passage where feasible." The two dams on the Elwha block migration of salmonids. [Note: The Elwha Dam removal project will also be responsible for the modification of the City of Port Angeles's existing surface water diversion structure, improving both upstream and downstream fish passage to standards required by NOAA Fisheries Service, USFWS, and WDFW.]

1.2.3* "Eliminate culvert barriers." USFWS suggests removing or modifying the culvert at Hot Springs Road in Griff and Madison creeks in the Elwha core area. [Note: USFWS in its biological opinion for the project included this task, though not directly related to dam removal.]

1.2.5* "Restore bull trout passage over dams and other related fish passage barriers." Assess man-made barriers that impact fish movement in the Elwha core area, including the estuary and nearshore environment (proposed Glines Canyon and Elwha dam removals).

1.2.6 "Improve instream flows." Restore connectivity and opportunities for migration by securing or improving instream flows or acquiring water rights. One of the priority rivers identified to date is the Elwha.

1.3.1* "Restore and protect riparian areas." Identify degraded riparian sites and revegetate to restore shade and canopy, riparian cover, and native vegetation to improve or maintain both occupied and potentially suitable bull trout habitat. The removal of the dams will necessitate the reestablishment of riparian vegetation along all newly formed streambank areas. [Note: The Elwha Dam removal project will implement restoration of riparian areas to the extent that the need is either directly related to the presence of the two dams or to the impacts associated with removal activities.]

1.3.2 "Identify, evaluate, and restore overwintering habitat in the mainstem rivers and tributaries." In all core areas, identify specific overwintering areas used by bull trout in the mainstem rivers, estuaries, and tributaries, and classify general overwintering habitat for use, current condition, and restoration potential.

1.3.4 "Reduce stream channel degradation and aggradation." Identify streambanks susceptible to excessive mass wasting (downslope movement of rock, regolith, sediment, and soil due to gravity) and bank failure. On ONP and Olympic National Forest lands, use road network surveys and watershed analyses to identify and map all stream reaches with actively eroding streambanks that likely result from management activities and are susceptible to excessive failure during high flow events. Identify all head-cuts (the upstream movement of a waterfall or a locally steep channel bottom due to the erosion caused by rapidly flowing water) and incidences of mass wasting that may negatively impact riparian areas and inhibit natural stream functions.

1.3.5* "Practice nonintrusive flood control and flood repair activities." A priority core area is the Elwha River. Provide technical assistance to county conservation districts (as defined by the Natural Resources Conservation Service) and private landowners to develop options for fish friendly flood-repair techniques to improve or restore channel processes benefiting bull trout or their habitat. To restore floodplain connectivity, where feasible, prevent future armored or riprapped banks, dikes, and levies and remove existing armoring. [Note: To the extent practicable, the practice of nonintrusive flood control or flood repair activities will be implemented by the Elwha Dam removal project to the degree that the need is either directly related to the presence of the two dams or to the impacts associated with removal activities.]

1.3.7 "Reduce transportation corridor impacts on streams." Reduce impacts from the legacy of highway and railroad encroachment, channel straightening, channel relocation, and undersized bridges. Where necessary and feasible, remove existing bank armoring (bulkheads and riprap) and channel constrictions (e.g., dikes and levies) associated with transportation corridor construction. Plan and develop future transportation corridors that eliminate the need for armoring and channel constriction. Relocate riparian roads and bridge constrictions out of the floodplain. Where possible, move roads out of floodplains or away from streams having local populations of bull trout or streams that have been identified as essential for reestablishing local populations of bull trout. Where roads cannot be moved, provide drainage, recontour road fill slopes, plant woody vegetation, and seed with native vegetation to prevent slumping. Add adequate surface materials if needed to prevent sediment movement. Bridges that restrict channel movement can severely restrict channel function. The lower Elwha River floodplain is a suggested area for initial focus.

1.3.9 "Restore natural stream channel morphology." Conduct stream channel restoration activities if they are likely to benefit native fish and only where similar results cannot be achieved by other less costly and intrusive means. The Elwha River is a priority core area.

1.3.10* "Restore instream habitat." Increase or enhance instream habitat by restoring habitat diversity. Projects should focus on the enhancement of habitat elements, such as LWD, logjams, and complex channels in the short term, and restoration of processes supporting these habitat elements in the long term. The systematic restructuring of the lower and middle Elwha River with LWD is needed to control sediments from degrading pools and spawning gravels once the dams are removed. [Note: The Elwha dam removal project will include habitat restoration efforts to the extent that the need is either directly related to the presence of the two dams or to the impacts associated with removal activities and funding allows.]

1.4.1* "Reduce reservoir operational impacts." Review reservoir operational concerns (water-level manipulation, minimum pool, etc.) and provide and implement operating recommendations for lakes Mills and Aldwell. [Note: DOI, owner of the two Elwha River dams, has already implemented this measure.]

1.4.2 "Provide instream flow downstream from dams." Maintain or exceed established instream flows downstream from Glines Canyon and lower Elwha dams.

1.6.1 "Implement projects that are key to restoring nearshore habitats." Key restoration projects for the Elwha River's nearshore and estuary habitats include providing or improving beach nourishment (i.e., accumulation of sand and gravel materials for forming habitat); removing, moving, or modifying artificial structures (e.g., bulkheads, riprap, dikes, tide gates); using alternative shoreline erosion and flooding protection measures that avoid or minimize impact to natural nearshore processes; and restoring estuaries and nearshore habitats such as eelgrass and kelp beds.

2.1.1 "Review effectiveness of current fish stocking policies." Eliminate planting nonnative fish species in areas draining into bull trout habitat. Reduce negative effects of fish stocking to bull trout and monitor for increased fishing pressure, alterations to prey base, competition, etc., that could impact bull trout.

2.3.1 "Discourage unauthorized fish introductions." Implement educational effort describing the problems and consequences of unauthorized fish introductions, especially brook trout (*Salvelinus fontinalis*).

2.3.2 "Develop a public information program about bull trout." Place broad emphasis on bull trout ecology and life history requirements and a more specific focus on regionally or locally important recovery issues.

2.5.1 "Determine distribution and abundance of nonnative fish (i.e., brook trout) and identify overlap with bull trout." Brook trout interbreed with bull trout and may outcompete them under certain conditions. Where information is lacking and the risk is high (e.g., bull trout populations are depressed, habitat is degraded, and brook trout are present), conduct surveys in high lakes or tributaries to determine distribution of brook trout and degree of interbreeding or potential for interbreeding between bull trout and brook trout.

2.5.3 "Remove established brook trout populations impacting bull trout." Where necessary and feasible, implement experimental removal of brook trout from selected streams and lakes.

3.1.1* "Integrate research and monitoring results into fish management plans and related salmonid information resources." [Note: Information generated through the Elwha dam removal project will be shared with appropriate agencies.]

3.1.2 "Protect remaining bull trout strongholds and native species complexes." Protect the integrity of areas with well established bull trout populations and intact native species assemblages (e.g., upper Elwha River).

3.1.3* "Provide increased forage opportunities in freshwater." Establish improved forage opportunities by managing for increased salmon spawning escapement complementary to related habitat improvements to increase salmon productivity and abundance.

3.2.1 "Develop reporting requirements for recreational, commercial, and tribal fisheries to evaluate bull trout catch and incidental mortality during fisheries for other species."

3.2.2 "Evaluate and minimize incidental mortality of bull trout from recreational, gill-net, and other fisheries." Continue to develop and implement sport angling regulations and fisheries management plans, guidelines, and policies that minimize incidental mortality of bull trout in all waters, especially gillnet fisheries concentrated at the mouths of Olympic Peninsula rivers. Conduct research and develop more selective gear and seasons for salmon gillnet fisheries that will minimize incidental mortality of bull trout, such as adjusting net mesh sizes or duration of having nets out, placement of nets to minimize incidental capture of bull trout, and develop incentives to increase likelihood of bull trout being released alive from gillnet fisheries. It is important to provide extra monitoring of the Elwha River gillnet fishery following removal of the dams on the Elwha River and, if necessary, reduce capture of bull trout in the lower river.

3.3.1 "Monitor and evaluate the effects of salmon and trout hatchery production, stocking, and associated fisheries on bull trout." Salmon and trout stocking or hatchery production occur in all core areas. Evaluate effects on bull trout from competition, predation, disease, and related increased angling effort resulting from stocking salmon and trout.

4.1.1* "Develop and implement a genetic study plan for future collection and analysis of genetic samples from local populations." Use molecular analysis to delineate and describe the genetic population structure of bull trout populations in the Olympic Peninsula, both among core areas and among local populations within core areas. Incorporate this information into future management strategies. Genetic information is necessary to determine whether bull trout from the lower Elwha River are distinct from the upper Elwha River or the lower Dungeness and Gray Wolf rivers subpopulations of bull trout. This genetic information will help address if and where bull trout from the lower Elwha could be relocated. [Note: This task, though not directly related to dam removal, was included by USFWS in its biological opinion for the project.]

5.1.2* "Implement a program to monitor and assess biological responses and changes in habitat from recovery actions." A standardized monitoring and assessment program needs to be developed and implemented to evaluate recovery criteria, assess and improve management actions, and ensure a coordinated strategy for the future of bull trout across their range within the conterminous United States. The program should include a protocol to reliably estimate bull trout abundance and population structure over time. [Note: See the Monitoring and Adaptive Management Section of this document.]

5.2.1* "Investigate bull trout temporal and spatial movement to describe the distribution of juvenile, subadult, and adult bull trout in freshwater, estuarine, and nearshore habitats." Bull trout use of nearshore marine areas, estuaries, and lower mainstem rivers and their associated tributaries is poorly understood; questions remain regarding bull trout habitat preferences (e.g., depth, salinity, substrate), range of migration, and foraging requirements, among other factors, in these areas. Continue implementation of existing bull trout population abundance and distribution studies and initiate new studies. The highest priority is to identify and map all spawning and rearing areas within core areas such as the Elwha River. For anadromous and fluvial bull trout, continue to determine full extent of foraging, migration, and overwintering habitat. Use this information to update and revise recovery recommendations. [Note: This task, though not directly related to dam removal, was included by USFWS in its biological opinion for the project in the form of a "rescue plan" requirement.]

Lamprey Proposed Restoration Approach

Western Brook Lamprey

Western brook lamprey populations in Western Washington display resident characteristics in their life history strategies. The western brook lamprey is nonparasitic and ranges from southern California to British Columbia (Scott and Crossman 1973).

Western brook lamprey reside in freshwater their entire life (Scott and Crossman 1973, Kostow 2002) and display a high degree of site specificity. Individuals move very little during their lives, the most significant movement occurring as passive downstream movements prior to spawning.

Spawning occurs in the spring in small redds located in small gravels upstream of riffles. Hatching occurs in 15 to 20 days and is temperature dependent (Kostow 2002). Larvae emerge after 2 months of incubation, at which time they move into silty areas to burrow. As western brook lamprey increase in size, they migrate from sites further upstream and in finer silt deposits to substrates that are richer in organic materials and sandier in composition. Throughout this period of time they function as filter feeders. This life history stage lasts from 1 to 3 years (Scott and Crossman 1973). Metamorphosis to the adult phase occurs during fall and adult lampreys reside deep in burrows in the sediment until spawning in the spring. Following spawning, adults die—females after one week, males after one month (Kostow 2002).

Management prescriptions

Although USFWS declined to list western brook lamprey on the endangered species list (DOI and USFWS 2004), the director of the USFWS Pacific Region asked resource managers to continue to assess the distribution and status of western brook lamprey throughout the west in an effort to enhance the understanding of lamprey.

The distribution and status of western brook lamprey throughout the Elwha basin need to be determined in order to evaluate the potential impacts associated with dam removal, and develop management actions that will promote the maintenance and rehabilitation of western brook lamprey.

Stock status

The status of western brook lamprey is unknown. No directed harvest or use of western brook lamprey is reported on the Elwha River. Little survey work has been carried out to assess the distribution and status of western brook lamprey populations in the Elwha River. Most likely, populations of western brook lamprey are isolated from other populations of western brook lamprey on the Strait of Juan de Fuca and display unique population structure.

Hatchery enhancement efforts

There are no current hatchery programs for western brook lamprey in the Elwha River.

Summary

The preferred restoration strategy for western brook lamprey in the Elwha River is natural recolonization. A secondary strategy, implemented if the downriver Elwha River population is decimated during dam removal and associated sediment transport and deposition, would be supplementation using an out-of-basin-origin western brook lamprey population as donor broodstock.

Pacific Lamprey

Pacific lamprey inhabiting the north Olympic Peninsula have received little attention from researchers and little is known about the structure of the area's populations or distributions. Generally, the Pacific lamprey is known to display an anadromous life history strategy and, as adults, are found in marine waters from California to Alaska (Scott and Crossman 1973). They spawn in freshwater and rear in larval form in appropriate freshwater habitat for an extended period of time (2 to 7 years).

Spawning occurs in low gradient reaches of mostly gravel and rock and occasionally sand at the head of riffles and in pool tailouts (Stone et al. 2002). Larvae hatch, burrow, and feed in fine substrates. Larval ammocoetes metamorphose to macrothalmia and begin their downstream migration. In landlocked populations, macrothalmia finish their metamorphosis into a parasitic adult and spend their adult life preying on resident fishes (Scott and Crossman 1973).

Adult marine lampreys are predacious, feeding on fishes and marine mammals. Mortality in fishes preyed on by lamprey is estimated to be from 1.6 to 1.8%. Marine residency time varies, lasting from 1 to 3 years (Scott and Crossman 1973).

In contrast to Pacific salmon, spawning migrations of adult lampreys from marine to freshwater are not directed by an innate tendency to home to natal streams. Rather, Pacific lamprey adult migration into freshwater is driven by a response to pheromones released by larval lamprey present in watersheds tributary to marine waters where the adults are present. Before adult lampreys are sexually mature they are sensitive to pheromones released from conspecific larval lampreys (Bjerselius et al. 2000, Close 2002). Absence or lack of larval lamprey in a system will reduce or eliminate migrations of adult lamprey into specific rivers or basins. Reintroduction programs for Pacific lamprey in which adult Pacific lampreys were outplanted in order to reestablish larval abundance in selected river basins have resulted in successes in spawning, production of, and dispersal of larval lamprey in the basins and low outmigrations of macrothalmia. Numbers of upmigrating adults from these efforts have to date been negligible (Close 2002).

The construction of dams in the Elwha River has negatively impacted Pacific lamprey by curtailing upriver access to lampreys and by reducing the complexity and quantity of habitat necessary for spawning and rearing.

Stock status

The status of Pacific lamprey is unknown.

Harvest status

No harvest efforts currently are directed toward Pacific lamprey.

Hatchery enhancement efforts

There are no current hatchery programs for Pacific lamprey populations in the Elwha River.

Escapement level

There is no formal escapement goal for Pacific lamprey populations in the Elwha River.

Summary

The preferred restoration strategy for Pacific lamprey in the Elwha River is natural recolonization. A secondary strategy, implemented if the downriver Elwha River population is decimated during dam removal and associated sediment transport and deposition, would be supplementation using an out-of-basin-origin adult Pacific lamprey population as donor broodstock.

Habitat Restoration

In the Elwha watershed and nearshore area, habitat restoration that complements dam removal and focuses on restoring the physical processes that create and maintain habitats is critical to achieving the objectives of this plan. Because the Elwha River contains relatively minor amounts of low gradient tributary habitat, maintenance and restoration of floodplain habitats and processes by which they are created are vital to habitat recovery. Restoring and maintaining physical processes that form habitat in the mainstem Elwha River is the highest priority following dam removal. These processes include lateral migration (channel migration across the flood plain, perpendicular to the direction of the stream flow) that will result in the interaction between river channels and floodplain forests. As sediment transport and LWD recruitment increase over time, increasing rates of lateral migration will result in the formation of new channel morphologies such as braiding and anastomosing (multiple intersecting channels). These channel morphologies are characterized by a combination of groundwater, surface flow, and overflow types that are essential for fish production.

Hydrodynamic processes of wind, tidal, current, and riverine flow form the Elwha nearshore, which is dominated by sediment processes. As with the riverine environment, restoring and maintaining physical processes that form nearshore habitat is the highest priority following dam removal. The Elwha nearshore includes a portion of the central Strait of Juan de Fuca that includes approximately 14 miles of shoreline extending from the western shore of Freshwater Bay east to the tip of Ediz Hook (Schwartz 1994). It includes the area of tidal influence to 30 m MLLW (mean lower low water) and tidally influenced portions of the riparian zone (Clallam County MRC 2004, Shaffer et al. 2004, 2005). Habitats of the Elwha nearshore include the lower river and associated estuary, intertidal and shallow subtidal sand, and cobble habitats. Kelp (*Agarum fimbriatum*, among others) and eelgrass (*Zostera marina*) beds are the dominant nearshore vegetation of the central Strait of Juan de Fuca, including the Elwha nearshore (Thom and Hallum 1991, Shaffer 2000, VanBlaricom and Chambers 2003, Clallam County MRC 2004).

History of Impacts

Analysis of channel and floodplain morphology over time indicates that several factors have significantly altered the Elwha River below Elwha and Glines dams. These factors include the near cessation of fluvial gravel recruitment caused by construction of the two dams, the chronic loss of functional large wood, and channel alterations such as dike construction, meander truncation, and LWD removal. These activities were particularly prevalent in the lower river and have been well documented by Johnson (1997). Analysis of the aerial photo record since 1939 (the earliest available photo) shows a dramatic loss of stored sediment in gravel bars, reduction in the number of side channels, loss of sinuosity, and a reduction in age of floodplain forest (Pohl 1999). Truncation of alluvial sediment supplies has lead to a coarsening of both freshwater and nearshore habitats. Loss of suitable spawning gravel is chronic below the dams. Because these actions took several decades to manifest, it provides a plausible explanation for the delay in collapse of some stocks of salmon in the lower river (i.e., pink and chum salmon and eulachon [*Thaleichthys pacificus*]) immediately following dam construction.

The armoring of the feeder bluffs to the east of the river mouth has further degraded the Elwha nearshore. This armoring began in the 1930s with the installation of the industrial waterline (and concomitant armoring) along the shoreline from near the mouth of Dry Creek east to Ediz Hook. At present nearly 9,000 feet of the Elwha nearshore is armored, while the western estuarine habitat at the river mouth was truncated by the 1965 construction of a flood protection levee. In response, nearshore habitats have shifted from sand and gravel to cobble dominated, resulting in wide-ranging shifts in biological communities (Ging and Seavey 1995).

Concurrent with the anthropogenic changes in the Elwha Basin, climatic changes have altered the flow profile for the river, with a doubling of the average peak annual flow event from 1924 to present (USGS unpubl. data). The increased frequency and size of large high water events have altered the channel-forming processes of the river, increasing scour and bank erosion even in areas of the basin considered pristine. These changes have been magnified by human activities, particularly in the lower river.

Current Conditions

The cumulative effects of dam construction, land use, changes in flow patterns, and water withdrawals over time continue to influence habitat conditions in the Elwha River. Operation of two mainstem hydroelectric dams at RM 4.9 and RM 13.7 truncates the fluvial transported sediment and large wood to the middle and lower river areas. This truncation represents the loss of one of the primary physical processes by which large river floodplain habitats are formed. It also creates a synergistic reaction with other channel alterations (meander truncation and diking) and floodplain management (logging) that continues to degrade habitat in these areas. A lack of suitable spawning habitat, limited numbers of side channels (in the lower river), very low levels of woody debris, disconnected floodplain (from channel incision), and altered temperature patterns characterize current habitat conditions. Generally speaking, habitat quality increases moving in an upstream direction (Table 21).

The Elwha nearshore has been significantly degraded due to large-scale chronic sediment starvation and alterations to the habitat-forming features of the lower sections of the river and marine shoreline. Sediment sources for the Elwha nearshore include the Elwha River and the adjacent marine feeder bluffs between the river mouth and Ediz Hook (Schwartz 1994), which have been almost completely armored beginning in the 1940s. Armoring of remaining intact feeder bluffs may occur in the next 5 years. Additionally, nearly 10% of the historic estuary remains isolated by the levee located on the western shore of the river mouth.

Table 21. Current relative habitat conditions in lower, middle, and upper Elwha River.

Reach	Temperature	LWD levels	Side channel/mile	Spawning habitat
Lower	Altered	Low	1.6	Low
Middle	Altered	Moderate	7.7	Abundant
Upper	Pristine	High	Unknown	Abundant

Response to Dam Removal

Removal of the dams will restore the sediment supply to the middle and lower river and partially restore the sediment supply to the nearshore marine environment, though several years will be required to reach an equilibrium between sediment supply and transport capacity. Dam removal will also immediately correct long-standing alterations in water temperature throughout the lower and middle river. Dam removal, however, will not immediately affect the deficit of functional large wood resulting from intentional removal, logging, and channelization. Riparian forest stands in much of the lower and middle Elwha Rivers are composed of younger, primarily deciduous species that are incapable of providing functionally sized LWD to support habitat-forming processes in the Elwha River. Additionally, because the reservoir areas inundated by lakes Aldwell and Mills were logged prior to dam construction, at least 6 miles of the Elwha main stem will have little recruitable wood for several decades. Some large sunken wood may be scattered across the reservoir bottom; however, it is not known whether this wood will be of a quality or quantity to affect habitat-forming processes. The reservoir areas will likely be highly unstable for several years following dam removal.

In the lower river, habitat conditions will initially degrade immediately following dam removal. Dramatic increases in suspended sediment supply will increase turbidity levels, degrading water quality. Increases in bedload sediment will result in bed aggradation that will fill pools and reduce the quality of rearing habitat. Bed aggradation of 1–4 feet has been estimated in the lower river (DOI and BOR 1996). This level of aggradation will affect channel morphology by increasing the width to depth ratio of the channel cross section. It is anticipated that this will induce a greater rate of lateral migration across the floodplain. An anastomosing or braided (Leopold et al. 1964) channel network characterized by a multithread channel may evolve. Interstitial filling of the gravel beds with fine sediment will degrade spawning areas.

Mainstem spawning habitat area has steadily eroded in the Elwha River since dam construction. McHenry et al. (unpubl. manuscr.) estimated that between 1939 and 1990 mainstem spawning area declined from 87,585 m^2 to 12,108 m^2, a reduction of 86%. Side-channel habitats in the lower and middle rivers areas will be somewhat buffered from sediment effects and should offer refugia. Accelerated sedimentation will impact the middle reach for a shorter time period because there is less supply (only sediment from Lake Mills) and the gradient is steeper. This steeper gradient causes an increase in stream power that accelerates the transport of sediment through this reach.

Another important difference is that the relative channel incision is less in the middle reach than in the lower river. Relative incision can be examined by comparing the number of side channels between the lower and upper middle reaches (Table 21). The abundance of side channels in the middle reach strongly suggests the river is still strongly connected with its floodplain. Salmonids (all species) will quickly colonize these refugia. Once sediment supply equilibrates with river transport capacity, habitat quality should increase dramatically. Pool depths will increase as excess sediment is transported, spawning habitat will improve dramatically as new gravel deposits are recruited, the supply of fluvially transported LWD will increase, and water quality will improve.

Sediment is the dominant limiting factor of the Elwha nearshore. Dam removal will fully restore riverine sediment delivery, though that is only a portion of the overall nearshore sediment process. The extent of restoration response in the Elwha nearshore depends on temporal scale and geographic scale, and is defined largely by remaining limiting factors of armoring and lower river alterations.

Temporally there are two anticipated main restoration windows in the nearshore. The first will be associated with sediment delivery associated with dam removal, with approximately 5 million cubic yards of sediment reaching the nearshore within 5 years of dam removal. About 10% of this material is expected to be sand or gravel, while finer sediments will dominate the remainder (Randle et al. 1996, 2003). The second temporal event is the long-term sediment transportation that will occur once the Elwha system is stabilized and sediment processes are restored, which is expected to occur about 10 years after dam removal (Stolnack and Neiman 2005). This period represents a return to the historic background riverine delivery of sediment to the nearshore.

Geographically the extent of restoration depends also on the nearshore area examined. The lower river will be partially restored with the exception of the west estuary, which is currently completely occluded by a dike. Nearshore subtidal and intertidal habitats will experience varying levels of restoration depending on location.

Goals of Habitat Restoration

The goals of the habitat restoration efforts on the Elwha River are to accelerate the recovery of habitat-forming processes in synchrony with dam removal planned under the Elwha Act. Because habitat conditions in the Elwha have been degraded as a result of both dam construction and land-use activities over a 90-year period, and because dam removal alone will not immediately result in preproject conditions, active restoration is recommended.

Past Habitat Restoration Efforts

The LEKT Fisheries Department initiated habitat restoration efforts in the Elwha River from 1994 to 1996, initially focused on lower river side-channel habitats including Bosco and Boston Charley creeks. These projects were relatively small scale, but proved successful. Reestablishment of flows to Bosco Creek in particular resulted in increased fish production for steelhead and coho and chum salmon (LEKT 2006). Recent restoration efforts (1999–2005) have focused on restoration of floodplain features through construction of engineered logjams, floodplain reforestation, and removal of impediments to channel migration in the floodplain. To date, 22 logjams have been constructed in the mainstem Elwha River. These structures proved to be stable, cost effective, and capable of positively affecting habitat. Monitoring data also indicates that constructed logjams support two to five times the densities of juvenile salmonids compared to similar habitat types without wood (Pess et al. in press). The Salmon Recovery Funding Board (SRFB), created by the Washington State Legislature in 1999 to administer grant funding targeting salmon habitat restoration, has supported these active restoration efforts, as well as efforts to document their effects on fish habitat and populations.

Proposed Habitat Restoration Strategies and Treatments

In order to accelerate habitat recovery following dam removal, a series of active restoration projects are proposed for the lower and middle reaches. Some of these projects are within the scope of activities planned under the Elwha Act. For planned activities outside of the scope of the Elwha Act, funding must be sought from other sources such as the SRFB. Planned additional restoration actions include additions of LWD, floodplain reforestation, removal or modification of floodplain dikes, and acquisition of floodplain habitat for long-term conservation. Additionally, establishing instream flows that conserve fish recovery needs will be critical to the long-term success of the overall restoration effort.

Large Woody Debris Placement

Recent research has described the critical role that large wood plays in habitat-forming processes in large Pacific Northwest rivers. Abbe and Montgomery (1996) described 17 logjam morphologies in the Queets River. The most stable logjam types strongly influenced channel morphology and were closely associated with development of habitat features important to anadromous fish. Additionally, some logjams were associated with development of old growth coniferous forest patches within the active floodplain. In order to restore these processes to the Elwha, some of these features will need to be created in appropriate locations. These locations will likely include the two reservoirs and the lower river below RM 4.

Additional restoration efforts using large wood should also be considered in Indian Creek and Little River. Historic land use activities including logging, road construction, and housing development have altered wood loadings in these systems. In small streams large wood can influence pool development, sediment storage, and other features salmonids favor (Montgomery and Buffington 1993). Because impacts not associated with the Elwha dams degraded these two midriver tributaries, funding for these projects may be secured through other mechanisms.

Floodplain Reforestation

As a companion project to the addition of LWD, reforestation of the Elwha River is important to restoring the interaction between floodplain forests and river habitat. Most of these efforts are planned for the reservoir surfaces that will be exposed immediately following dam removal. These efforts include extensive replanting of native trees, control of exotic vegetation, relocation of woody debris, and monitoring, and are documented in the revegetation plans for lakes Aldwell and Mills (DOI and ONP 2006).

Dike Removal and Modification

The effect that various floodplain structures (e.g., dikes, roads) have had on habitat-forming processes in the Elwha watershed has been documented (Pohl 1999). While some of these structures are necessary to protect private property, others provide questionable levels of flood protection. The supplemental EIS (DOI 2005) proposes to maintain their current flood protection status, largely through increasing their heights to match expected changes in bed aggradation. Some consideration should be given to the removal or alteration of the following structures that are believed most detrimental to habitat-forming processes:

- Spur dike at RM 8.5. This 90 meter dike provides no flood control function, but redirects water away from historic side channels and potential off-channel sites.

- Gabions at RM 3.1. A series of gabions were constructed on the west side of the river near the infiltration gallery site. These structures appear to provide no flood protection but limit lateral migration.

- Spur dike at RM 2.9. This structure is located on the east bank of the river below the one-way bridge. It provides limited flood control function, but affects channel meander for at least three meander sequences downstream, largely by diverting water away from its historic meander pattern.

- Push-up dikes between RM 1.5 and 3.0. A series of relict unreinforced dikes from meander truncation activities have been left in the Elwha floodplain. These structures still exist and represent barriers to channel migration.

- Dike at tribal hatchery infiltration site at RM 1.5. This dike provides protection for the current infiltration gallery. Alterations to the LEKT hatchery may make this structure unnecessary.

- Tribal hatchery outfall at RM 0.3. Spoils from the construction of the hatchery outfall were formed into a perpendicular dike along the length of the outfall (upstream side).

- Nonfederal levee at RM 0.1. This structure provides limited flood protection and could be altered to increase access to 30 acres of historic estuary habitat.

Nearshore Restoration

The list below represents potential nearshore habitat restoration activities that would contribute to the long-term restoration goals for the Elwha ecosystem. Table 22 depicts the relationship of dam removal to restoration of nearshore processes and the potential for additional restorative actions beyond dam removal.

- Restore process of eastern feeder bluffs. Options may include development of soft armoring techniques that optimize upcoming sediment pulse associated with dam removal, forestalling the need for additional armoring along intact feeder bluffs.

- Remove landfill material that is threatened by bluff erosion.

- Reroute industrial waterline away from the beachfront.

- Initiate a conservation easement program along the bluff shoreline to limit need to protect existing or new housing.

Floodplain Acquisition and Conservation Easements

In addition to the active restoration projects identified above, consideration should be given to developing a long-term strategy for the purchase or development of conservation easements on floodplain and estuarine property outside of ONP. Unconstrained reaches of the Elwha River where lateral migration can occur should be of the highest priority. These areas support the majority of functional side channels that continue to function despite loss of alluvial

Table 22. Nearshore habitat restoration summary.

Habitat	Nearshore reach	Habitat restoration response	Dam removal process and habitat restoration	Additional habitat restoration need
Feeder bluffs	Elwha bluffs–Ediz Hook	Sediment delivery and retention may be impacted by existing rock and by further additional new armoring.	Only partially restored	Significant need, but little opportunity for additional restoration
Estuary	Elwha River mouth	Dependant on levees. If left intact, sediment is transported to east river and nearshore.	Only partially restored	Significant need and opportunity for additional restoration
Rocky reefs and shoreline	Freshwater Bay	Initial sediment contribution will result in partial shift from rock cobble (kelp) to sandy gravel (mixed eelgrass and kelp).	Largely restored	Little anticipated need and little opportunity for additional habitat restoration

sediments from dam construction. These areas are critical to recovery as they are sites of high productivity and offer refugia during floods and periods of high sedimentation.

Significant parcels of floodplain are privately owned, some of which may not be adequately protected by local land use regulations to meet the goals of river restoration. These lands may be logged or converted to housing or other uses that are not compatible with long-term restoration. It is conceivable that a corridor from the ONP boundary on the south to the LEKT reservation could be targeted for protection in cooperation with an appropriate partnership between land owners and conservation organizations. If successfully implemented, such a corridor would link floodplain and estuary habitats in the lower river with pristine habitats within Olympic National Park. The Elwha River could represent one of the largest, largely intact watersheds in the conterminous United States.

Instream Flow Conservation

Conservation of flows necessary to optimize fish spawning and rearing is necessary on the Elwha River, particularly during late summer and early fall. Although the Elwha River has an average annual flow of 1,500 cfs, base flows as low as 200 cfs are common—particularly during low snow pack years. Consumptive water rights in the basin are in excess of base flows. The State of Washington has issued water rights to various parties totaling 212 cfs, with additional water used by LEKT, which is not subject to state water law. The largest water right is owned by the City of Port Angeles, which has a total of 150 cfs for industrial purposes and another 50 cfs for municipal drinking water. While Port Angeles does not currently use its entire water right and leases a portion for nonconsumptive uses (WDFW rearing channel), the magnitude of the water right poses a risk to the fisheries resources in the Elwha River.

Clallam County recently adopted the WRIA (Water Resource Inventory Area) 18 Watershed Plan (Elwha-Dungeness Planning Unit 2005), which was drafted in response to Washington State legislation (ESHB 2514). SHB 2514 legislation was intended to facilitate local participation in the establishment of minimum instream flows for the state's rivers and streams.

The WRIA 18 plan specifically recommends that no additional water rights be issued for the Elwha watershed until dam removal is completed. Then after the river channel stabilizes, it suggests that IFIM (Instream Flow Incremental Methodology) or a similar tool be used to establish the minimum instream flow for the Elwha River under its restored condition. Finally, the plan recommends that the City of Port Angeles, as the primary water purveyor in the watershed, should complete a water conservation strategy for low flow periods that incorporates the needs of fish as the primary trigger. The WRIA 18 Watershed Plan has been endorsed by Clallam County and all of the initiating governments party to the plan (City of Port Angeles, LEKT, Jamestown Klallam Tribe, Agnew Irrigation District, and the Washington Department of Ecology).

Recovery Estimates

Ten stocks of anadromous salmon and trout once used the Elwha River watershed (winter and summer steelhead, coho, summer/fall and spring Chinook, pink, chum, and sockeye salmon, and cutthroat and bull trout), in addition to a variety of other anadromous species including lamprey and forage fish. The Elwha River was legendary for its production of huge Chinook salmon; fish in excess of 100 pounds were recorded as late as 1930, 18 years after closure by the Elwha Dam (Brannon 1930). The Elwha River was also known for its diversity of species. Unfortunately, beyond oral histories and qualitative estimates, little quantitative data exists regarding historic abundances of fish returning to the Elwha River.

At the time Elwha Dam was constructed, limited documentation existed on salmonid utilization of the Elwha River, with no technical information on salmonid abundance or distribution. Certainly members of the Elwha Tribe were intimately familiar with the river's salmon as were other locals, but they were not consulted until years or decades later (Lane and Lane Associates 1990). Records from the original Elwha Hatchery provided some information on fish abundance and species diversity in the years immediately following dam construction, but they are limited in scope. Specifically, during its operation more than 22 million eggs were collected by the hatchery staff from fish captured at the base of the dam (Hosey and Associates 1988a) (Table 23). Fish collected were likely only those that were ripe on the day of capture and therefore do not represent the total population that likely reached the dam in any given year. It is not clear from the records available if eggs were collected throughout the year or only at certain times of the year. By 1923 though, the numbers of fish ascending to the dam had declined to a point that the operation was deemed no longer feasible (Johnson 1997).

The impetus to estimate historic production of the Elwha watershed was initially only partially driven by a desire to restore the watershed. Of equal importance was a desire by the State of Washington to estimate damages caused by the dams. Without direct information available to describe historic production, it was necessary to make estimates based on available habitat and comparisons to other watersheds (Table 24). The first detailed analysis of potential production was completed by WDF in 1971 (WDF 1971), with subsequent efforts made by WDG (1973), the U.S. Bureau of Indian Affairs (BIA) (Chapman 1981), Hosey and Associates (1988a), the Joint Fish and Wildlife Agencies (JFWA 1988), the Federal Energy Regulatory Commission (FERC 1993), and the Department of the Interior et al. (1994). In some cases, estimates of available habitat were made directly by on-the-ground surveys of lineal accessible distance (WDF 1971, Hosey and Associates 1988a). In other cases, estimates of available habitat were made by mapping exercises, estimates of watershed area, flow-based habitat modeling, or simple comparisons to "similar" basins.

Table 23. Hatchery egg takes (thousands) and approximate adults used during 1914–1923.

Year	Coho eggs	Adult coho[a]	Chinook eggs	Adult Chinook[b]	Steelhead eggs	Adult steelhead[c]	Chum eggs	Adult chum[d]	Pink eggs	Adult pinks[e]	Total eggs	Adult total
1914	601	400	0	0	0	0	0	0	0	0	601	400
1915	1,050	700	160	70	433	290	0	0	0	0	1,643	1,060
1916	5,263	3,500	305	135	139	90	0	0	0	0	5,707	3,725
1917	4,148	2,750	0	0	0	0	0	0	0	0	4,148	2,750
1918	60	40	945	420	441	290	0	0	240	320	1,685	1,070
1919	40	30	376	170	361	240	0	0	0	0	777	440
1920	0	0	0	0	0	0	2,120	1,400	0	0	2,120	1,400
1921	143	100	137	60	178	120	3,997	2,650	0	0	4,455	2,930
1922	60	40	185	80	139	90	0	0	1,278	1,700	1,662	1,910
1923	0	0	0	0	67	45	0	0	0	0	67	45
Total	11,365	7,560	2,108	935	1,758	1,165	6,117	4,050	1,518	2,020	22,865	15,730

[a] Adult coho calculated by assuming 3,000 eggs/female and a 1:1 male:female ratio.
[b] Adult Chinook calculated by assuming 5,000 eggs/female and a 1:1 male:female ratio
[c] Adult steelhead calculated by assuming 3,000 eggs/female and a 1:1 male:female ratio.
[d] Adult chum calculated by assuming 3,000 eggs/female and a 1:1 male:female ratio.
[e] Adult pink calculated by assuming 1,500 eggs/female and a 1:1 male:female ratio.

Table 24. Production estimates (NA = no estimates made).

Method	Chinook	Coho	Steelhead	Pink	Chum	Sockeye	Bull trout	Cutthroat
WDF 1971	8,500	NA	NA	91,000	15,000	NA	NA	NA
WDG 1973	NA	NA	5,100	NA	NA	NA	NA	9,990
Chapman 1981	1,284	3,520	483	3,147	9,042	NA	NA	NA
Hosey and Assoc. 1988a	6,720	6,860	3,616	12,000	0	85	1,000	1,000
JFWA 1988	17,493	19,143	NA	137,600	25,600	NA	NA	NA
FERC 1993	6,900	12,100	5,757	96,000	18,000	NA	3,709	NA
DOI et al. 1994	6,900	12,100	5,757	96,000	18,000	6,000	NA	NA

As might be expected, each method provided a different estimate of production, with substantial variability between methods. For example, Chapman (1981) provided a minimal estimate of 1,284 Chinook spawners above Elwha Dam, while JFWA (1988) calculated a spawning potential of more than 17,000 Chinook salmon. Estimates of chum salmon provided by WDF (1971), JFWA (1988), and FERC (1993), ranged from 15,000 to 25,600 spawning chum. On the other hand, Hosey and Associates (1988a) believed chum salmon recovery simply wasn't possible due to the limited estuarine area. Similar variability was seen for the other species.

Observations by Klallam elders and early settlers provide qualitative information to compare with contemporary estimates of production and distribution of salmon in the Elwha River. Ed Sampson, a Klallam native who grew up on the Elwha, said when interviewed in 1976 (Lane & Lane Associates 1990) that "the fish were so plentiful that there was no need to select 'good' areas." He also said "When I went out fishing with my grandmother, I would catch 50 fish. She would catch 100. We'd carry them back in a wheelbarrow."

Other early homesteaders to the area reported that pink salmon were so abundant in Little River (a tributary near the head of Lake Aldwell) that horses shied and refused to cross the channel (Brown 1982). Martin Humes, whose homestead was located upstream of Rica Canyon near the mouth of Idaho Creek, wrote to his sister on November 9, 1897, "The salmon lay there with their backs out of water. All I had to do was to reach over them, hook the hook in their back and pull them out. They are the hook bill (coho) salmon and have just come from salt water. We look for lots of them to run now as this run has just commenced." Joe Sampson, a Klallam native, reportedly made expeditions to Chicago Camp and found large salmon there (Adamire and Fish 1991). Based on these, other similar historic accounts, and evaluation of the main river and tributaries relative to known fish swimming and leaping abilities, we agree that the JFWA and FERC estimates of production are reasonable, if not definitive.

Despite historic reports, questions continued to exist about the ability of salmon to access the upper reaches of the Elwha. WDF (1971), based on its physical surveys of the river, believed salmon could ascend upstream to RM 41. However, the owners of the dams questioned whether or not salmon could pass beyond Grand Canyon (RM 21.5) (Katz et al. 1975) or even Rica Canyon. In order to assess the ability of fish to colonize the watershed and pass through these potential barriers, USFWS radio-tagged adult summer steelhead (Wampler 1984) obtained from WDG, and released them at various locations in the upper watershed. Releases were timed during the summer months (July to September) with flows ranging from 590 cfs to 1,800 cfs. In all cases, fish released in Lake Mills were observed to readily pass through both Rica Canyon and Grand Canyon, ascending to at least the Goldie River, located above RM 29. A fish released near Camp Wilder ascended upstream to RM 37.

This work, combined with the snorkel surveys conducted by Hosey and Associates (1987) confirmed fish could pass through Rica and Grand canyons, upstream to near the headwaters. The only limitation identified is for pink and chum salmon which may not be able to ascend through Rica Canyon, which has several cascades and falls up to 2 m (WDF 1971). If this assumption is incorrect, the production numbers noted above could be low.

The response of fish populations to dam removal is expected to vary between populations. With more than 70 miles of mainstem and tributary habitat available to anadromous species after dam removal, much of it in pristine condition, the rate of recolonization will depend on existing population sizes, the fitness of the founder populations, the amount of new habitat becoming available to a given stock, interactions with other recovering fish populations, and outside effects (marine harvests, nearshore productivity, climate, ocean conditions, etc.). However, it is important to provide an estimate or "recovery goal" for expectations of recovery rates and long-term abundance in order to evaluate the success of efforts used to facilitate recolonization following dam removal.

For the purposes of this plan, recovery expectations have been defined in terms of total production of anadromous adult salmon (including those fish subject to harvest in Canadian and U.S. waters) and rates of recovery. Assumed harvest rates are applied for each species, with subsequent spawning escapement values. However, neither the harvest rates nor the escapement values should be considered "goals" per se, as the harvest rates are simply assumed values based on information available when models designed to estimate fisheries harvest impacts and outcomes were first developed. The escapement levels are simply the result of applying the assumed harvest rate to the anticipated adult production.

True productivity, escapement, and harvest goals will be developed at a later date, when specific information is available for the Elwha Basin. More importantly, initial goals for total production and rates of recovery will be updated as the recolonization process proceeds and information is gathered regarding the inherent productivity of the Elwha watershed. Monitoring activities will be expected to provide important feedback on initial modeling efforts (see the Monitoring and Adaptive Management section).

Chinook Salmon

Potential Production Estimates

The Elwha River is currently the largest producer of Chinook salmon in the Strait of Juan de Fuca, although the majority of the run is the result of artificial enhancement efforts. Following dam removal, it is estimated Chinook salmon (combined spring and summer/fall stocks) will use mainstem habitat up to RM 42.9 as well as 14.1 miles of tributary habitat (FERC 1993). A number of methods have been used to estimate the potential production of Chinook salmon, once fish are allowed access to the entire watershed (WDF 1971, Chapman 1981, Hosey and Associates 1988a). Hosey and Associates (1988a) reviewed known values of spawners per mile for Oregon, Washington, and British Columbia river systems and found a wide variation in spawner densities coastwide—from 84 to 410 Chinook salmon per mile.

After review of the range of spawner densities seen in other river systems, it was decided it would be inappropriate to use either the entire range of values presented by Hosey and Associates (1988a) or a mean value to estimate potential spawner abundance in the Elwha (FERC 1993). This choice was made primarily because it was recognized that the Elwha River represents a nearly pristine watershed, while the values found throughout the Pacific Northwest were heavily impacted by land use. Therefore, it was decided that if it was possible to identify a single river comparable to the Elwha River, a more realistic estimate might be obtained.

A review of the Hoh River on the north Washington coast indicated many shared characteristics with the Elwha River. Both the Hoh and Elwha rivers originate in the Olympic Mountains with their headwaters located within a few miles of one another. Both rivers are influenced by glaciers with high turbidity levels and heavy spring runoff. These rivers are also comparable in watershed area and miles of mainstem and large tributary habitat. The Elwha watershed comprises 321 square miles while the Hoh River contains 299 square miles. The Elwha watershed contains a total of 57 miles of mainstem and tributary stream habitat considered usable by Chinook salmon spawners. The Hoh River contains 59 miles of habitat used by Chinook salmon (WDF 1981). The two rivers presently support, or historically supported, comparable Chinook salmon runs with spring, summer, and fall components.

Based on values for the Hoh watershed, as well as a 1971 WDFW survey of the upper Elwha Basin, estimates of 368 spawners per mile for mainstem habitat areas and 121 spawners per mile for tributary areas were used to derive an estimate of escapement under "pristine" conditions (i.e., the number of Chinook salmon spawners with no harvest). These values for spawner abundance per mile, in conjunction with the mainstem and tributary habitat estimates, were used by FERC (1993) to estimate spawner capacity in the areas above the two dams:

Mainstem escapement = 42.9 miles × 368 spawners per mile = 15,787 spawners

Tributary escapement = 14.1 miles × 121 spawners per mile = 1,706 spawners

Total spawning escapement = 15,787 + 1,706 = 17,493 Chinook salmon spawners

Rebuilding Curves

LEKT Fisheries Department staff used a spawner-recruit model and constants cited in FERC's draft staff report (1993) with some further refinements to develop rebuilding curves based on the potential production estimate developed. Total production estimates for the population were derived from these curves, with resultant estimates of escapement and harvest levels for the population. A starting value of 200 naturally spawning Chinook salmon was assumed, with outplanting of juveniles not reflected in the recovery model. The model assumes no in-river harvest during the first cycle of recovery (i.e., 4-year, first cycle of recruits from initial 200 spawners reach the spawning grounds immediately after passage is restored) and a gradual ramping up of fisheries following that time. In addition, it was assumed that returning Chinook salmon spawners would disperse in the watershed for effective use of the newly available habitat.

It is important to note that when the FERC model was first developed in the late 1980s, harvest rates on Chinook salmon were much higher than at present, and it was assumed that populations could sustain these high rates. In essence the FERC model assumes a very high underlying productivity. Subsequently, the model results reflect a harvest rate of 65% in the first cycles following dam removal, increasing to 78%. Although it is unlikely that a naturally spawning population of fish can sustain these high levels of harvest, it is also true that actual harvest rates on Chinook salmon have declined dramatically in recent years (Appendix B). Therefore, the 25-year recovery time frame predicted by the FERC model is believed to be reasonable (Figure 11). Successful outplanting activities are expected to shorten recovery time further and help ensure that Chinook salmon colonize the entire watershed.

As a further example of how quickly Chinook salmon could be reintroduced into the upper and middle reaches of the Elwha River, the introduction of Chinook salmon into the upper South Fork Skykomish River in the late 1950s was reviewed. An impassable barrier, Sunset Falls, exists at RM 49.6. WDFW developed a trap and haul facility in order to extend anadromy upstream of this barrier falls. Chinook salmon were found to rapidly colonize the habitat (10–15 years), based on returning adults to the trap (Seiler 1991). Chinook salmon production in the South Fork Skykomish has varied since initial increases in the mid-1970s, but ups and downs of returns above Sunset Falls appear to reflect the overall production of Chinook salmon within the greater Snohomish River watershed as a whole.

Though the Skykomish River differs greatly from the Elwha River, that is, steeper with more confined valleys dominated by bedrock, it serves as one of the few examples where new production of anadromous salmonids was developed merely by establishing passage into the habitat. Numbers of fish returning to the trap and haul facility have been recorded since the inception of the facility in the early 1950s. These data points were used to create a sigmoid curve relationship that was subsequently applied to the Elwha Chinook salmon scenario, applying a 2.9 multiplier to the Sunset Falls data to represent Elwha escapement, and a 13.3 multiplier to represent total production. These ratios are based on the theoretical endpoints of Chinook salmon escapement and total production predicted by FERC's recovery model (escapement = 6,900, total production = 31,364) (FERC 1993) (Figure 12).

Given these two model scenarios, escapements of Chinook salmon to the Elwha River could range from a spawning population of 6,900 (78% exploitation rate) to a high of just over 17,000 spawners (unexploited population). Harvest management of impacting fisheries will be

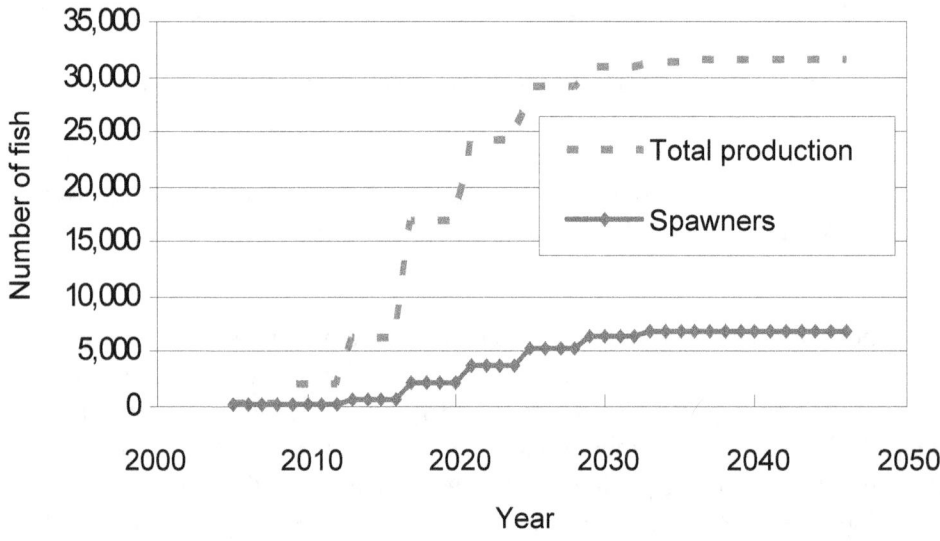

Figure 11. Predicted recovery of Elwha River Chinook salmon stocks using a spawner-recruit model.

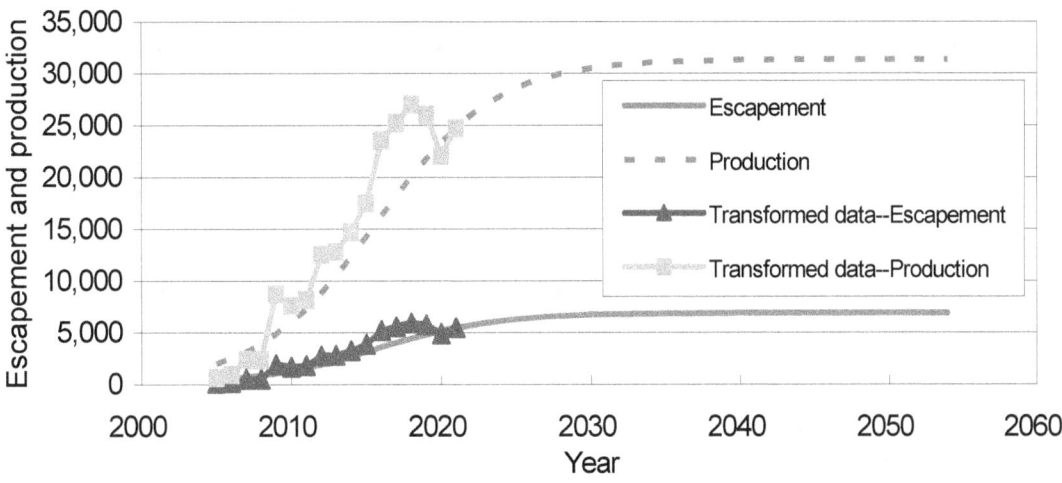

Figure 12. Transformed Sunset Falls data and curve fitting relationships to predict recovery periods for Elwha River Chinook salmon.

an integral part of fisheries restoration. Chinook harvest restrictions in the Elwha River would probably be in place for at least the first two complete cycles (8–10 years). Additional harvest restrictions in localized marine fisheries (e.g., area closures in the Freshwater Bay vicinity) might be necessary during the same period.

Harvest restrictions in other Washington sport and commercial fisheries or Canadian fisheries to specifically accommodate Elwha restoration are not likely, as the depressed status of many other native Western Washington, Columbia River, and Canadian Chinook salmon stocks would probably have a larger influence in shaping fisheries for the foreseeable future. Current harvest management planning ensures that harvest rates within the southern U.S. waters would not exceed 10% for Chinook salmon stocks of the Strait of Juan de Fuca (PSIT and WDFW 2004). Additional harvest is controlled by the provisions of the U.S./Canada Salmon Treaty. Given these constraints on international harvest, a reasonable restoration goal should be based somewhere between these two points (6,900 to 17,000 spawners with a midpoint at approximately 12,000 spawners).

Steelhead

Potential Production Estimates

The Elwha River is currently the largest producer of steelhead in the Strait of Juan de Fuca although, like the river's Chinook salmon production, the majority of the run is the result of artificial enhancement efforts. Following dam removal, it is estimated steelhead (winter or summer) will use mainstem habitat up to RM 42.9, as well as all accessible tributary habitat available, or more than 75 linear miles of stream (FERC 1993).

As cited in FERC (1993), the parr production potential (PPP) method (Gibbons et al. 1985) was used to estimate the potential steelhead production level for the Elwha River watershed. The PPP is a habitat-based method of estimating the carrying capacity of a river system. For the Elwha River, total habitat area (m^2) was apportioned into tributary and mainstem strata, with the mainstem habitat further subdivided into gradient zones (Hosey and Associates 1988a). Potential parr production was then estimated by assigning values of parr per meters squared (parr/m^2) as presented by Gibbons et al. (1985) for each of the strata and summing across the watershed.

Rebuilding Curves

Using the PPP values, Gibbons et al. (1985) proposed a method to modify both Ricker spawner-recruit and Beaverton-Holt stock-recruitment models to estimate total adult recruits and ultimately the maximum sustained yield (MSY) escapement goals. For the Elwha River, total production was calculated to be 10,100 adult recruits, with a MSY harvest rate of 43% and resulting escapement of 5,757 (FERC 1993). Based on these estimates, recovery of steelhead in the Elwha River is expected to occur 15 to 20 years following initialization of dam removal (Figure 13).

The South Fork of the Skykomish River was used to evaluate the modeled recovery of steelhead in the Elwha River with actual returns above Sunset Falls following introduction in 1958. Returns increased through 1980, from 88 adults to well over 1,000 fish in a matter of 22 years (Figure 14).

Coho Salmon

Potential Production Estimates

FERC (1993) used the average of two separate methods to estimate the potential production of coho salmon for the Elwha River. The first method was a habitat-based analysis of potential smolt production developed by Zillges (1977) for estimating smolt density. Using this

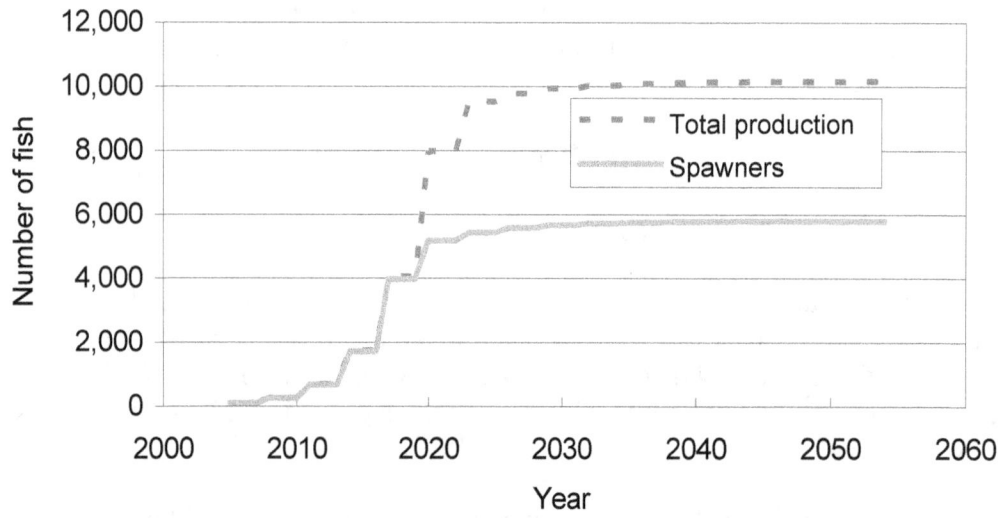

Figure 13. Predicted recovery of Elwha River steelhead stocks using spawner-recruit model.

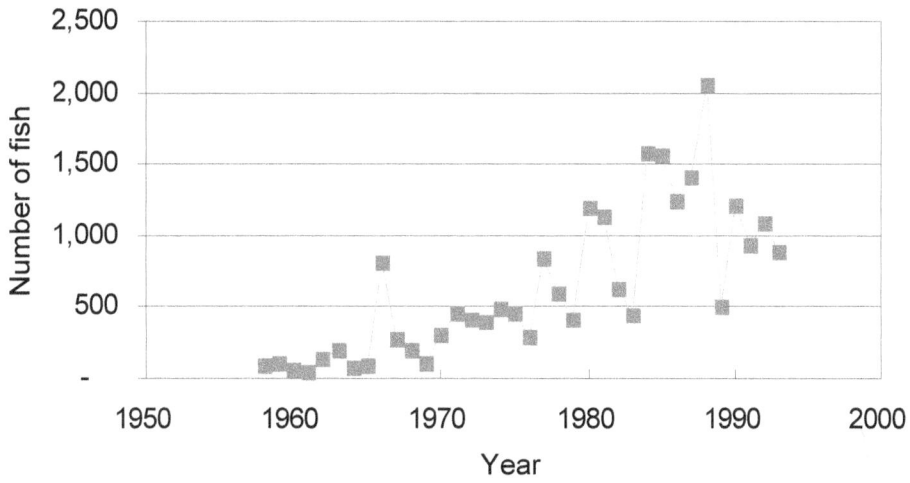

Figure 14. South Fork Skykomish River steelhead returns at the Sunset Falls trap and haul facility, 1958–1993 (based on data from T. Burns, WDFW Habitat Program, Olympia).

method produced a spawner escapement estimate at MSY of 7,742 adults. An alternate method compared adult abundance per lineal mile of stream habitat in the South Fork Skykomish River with lineal miles of accessible habitat in the Elwha River, producing an estimate of 19,143 adult coho salmon. The average of these two values (13,443) was further reduced by 10% (12,100) to account for the assumption that the information for South Fork Skykomish overestimated MSY escapement. Spawner-recruit modeling by FERC (1993) generated a recovery curve for Elwha coho salmon based on a pristine potential production of 31,758 (no harvest).

Rebuilding Curves

Using an assumed maximum sustained harvest rate of 65% and the equilibrium MSY escapement of 12,100 coho, FERC's production model predicted an MSY adult recruitment of 34,571. The harvest rate of 65% is likely an overestimate of sustainable levels for a natural stock, as was reported by the PFMC (1997) when it evaluated the affects of harvest on other Strait of Juan de Fuca naturally spawning coho salmon stocks. However, an assumed harvest rate of 60% still results in a sustained adult recruitment of more than 30,000 fish. Recovery under this production curve is estimated to occur 8 to 10 years following initialization of dam removal (Figure 15).

To verify this rebuilding rate, the South Fork Skykomish River was again used as an example. Coho salmon were introduced into that river starting in 1958. Without additional supplementation, returns increased from 1,500 fish in 1960 to more than 20,000 fish in a matter of 10 years (Figure 16). Declines observed in years following 1980 (1980–1993) are consistent with patterns seen in other Puget Sound river systems.

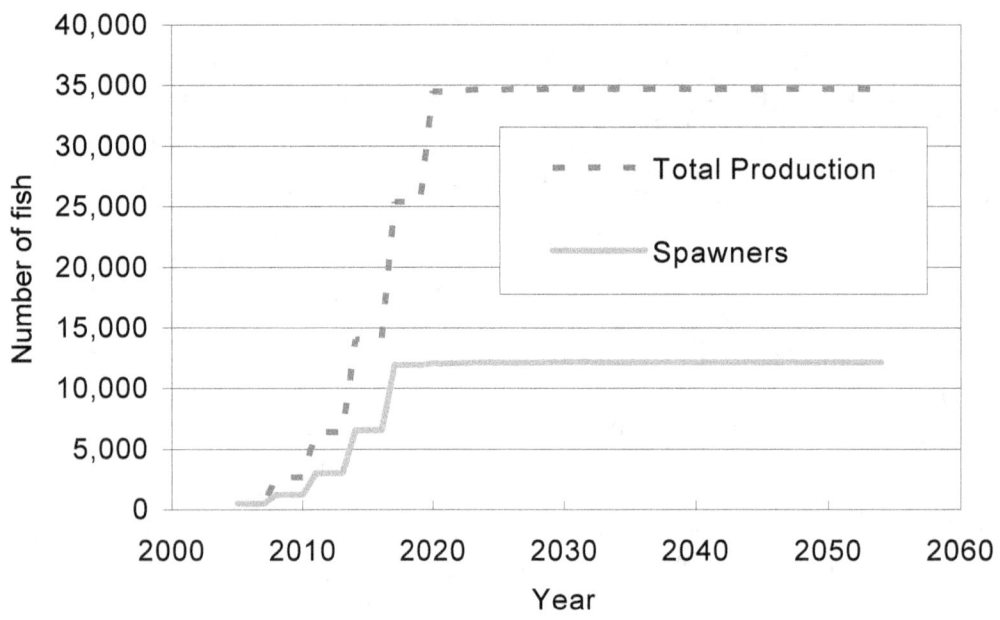

Figure 15. Predicted recovery of Elwha River coho salmon stocks using spawner-recruit model (FERC 1993).

Chum Salmon

Potential Production Estimates

Similar to the coho salmon estimates, FERC (1993) averaged two alternative methods of calculating MSY escapement levels for chum salmon in the Elwha River, resulting in an MSY escapement estimate of 18,000 fish. Assuming an exploitation rate of 50%, FERC generated a production curve back-calculating the pristine potential production of 43,219.

Rebuilding Curves

The rebuilding curves were developed from the production model, with an equilibrium MSY escapement of 18,000 chum salmon and concurrent harvest rate of 50% (total production equaling 36,000). Substantial recovery of Elwha chum salmon is estimated to occur 15 to 20 years following the initialization of dam removal (Figure 17). However, adverse habitat conditions in the lower river in the years immediately following dam removal may prolong recovery timing, as chum salmon are expected to rely almost exclusively on this habitat, which will be directly affected by dam removal.

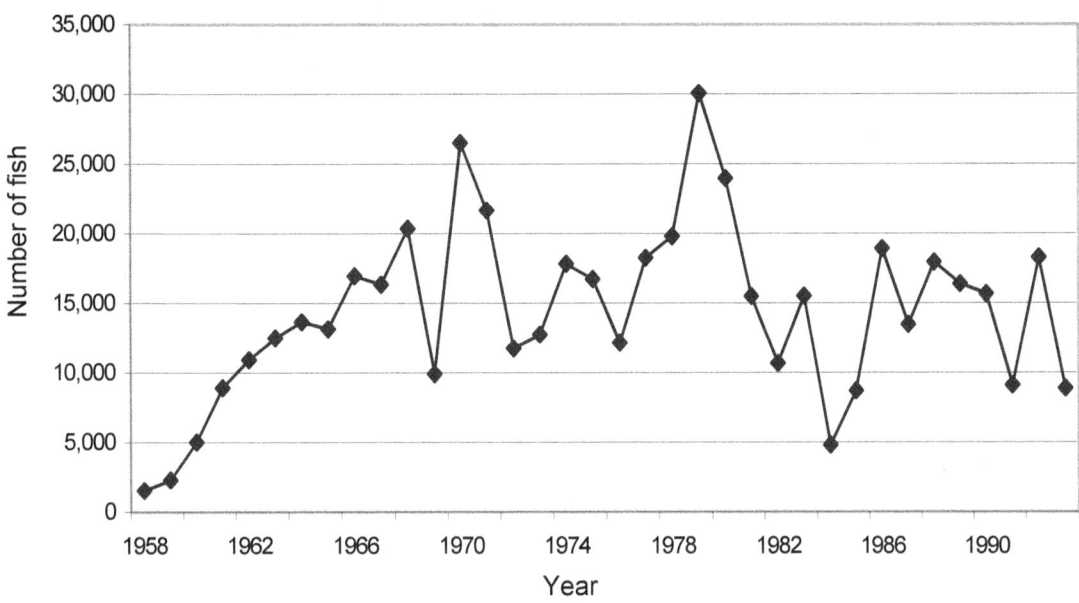

Figure 16. South Fork Skykomish River coho salmon at the Sunset Falls trap and haul facility, 1958–1993 (based on data from T. Burns, WDFW Habitat Program, Olympia).

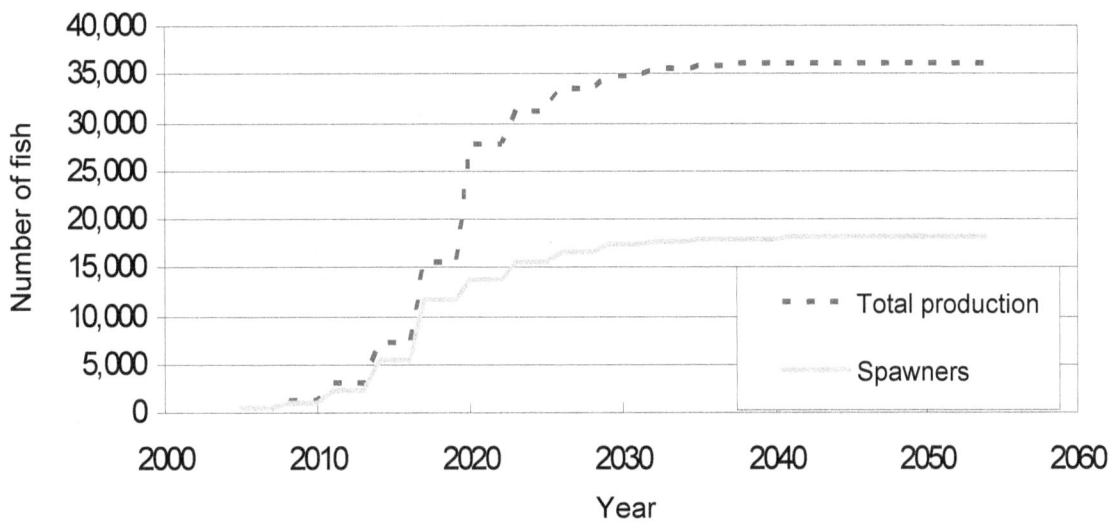

Figure 17. Predicted recovery of Elwha River chum salmon stock using spawner-recruit model (FERC 1993).

Pink Salmon

Potential Production Estimates

The estimated escapement of pink salmon to the Elwha River at MSY levels was calculated by averaging two separate estimates, (56,000 + 137,000)/2 = 96,000 (rounded to the nearest thousand). Spawner-recruit modeling by FERC (1993), assuming an MSY exploitation rate of 65%, generated a recovery curve for Elwha pink salmon with a pristine potential production of 251,968 (no harvest). Substantial recovery of this stock is estimated to occur 10 to 15 years following the start of dam removal (Figure 18). As with chum salmon, adverse habitat conditions in the lower river following dam removal may prolong recovery timing. Additionally, as with most pink salmon populations of Puget Sound, it is assumed that odd-year runs will be the predominant population.

Other Species

The other species expected to recover within the Elwha Basin include sea-run cutthroat trout, sockeye salmon, native char, lamprey, and a variety of forage fish. Though important in the restoration process, not enough information is known about these local stocks to be able to generate recovery goals. As fish monitoring activities proceed, interim goals may be established and updated as appropriate.

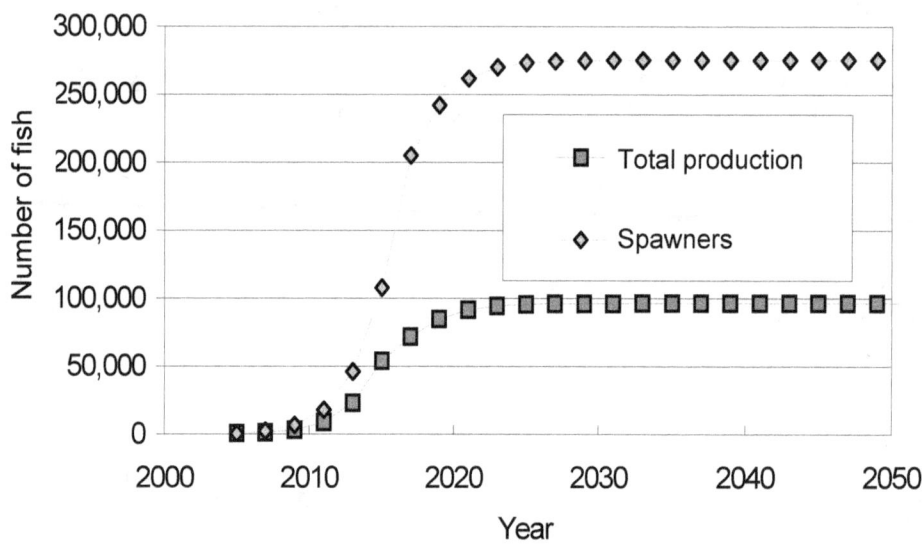

Figure 18. Predicted recovery of Elwha River pink salmon stock using spawner-recruit model (FERC 1993).

Monitoring and Adaptive Management

The Elwha Act calls for "the removal of the dams and full restoration of the Elwha River ecosystem and native anadromous fisheries." The following are goals central to implementing the act:

- Reestablish self-sustaining anadromous salmonid populations and habitats throughout the Elwha River watershed and its nearshore as quickly as possible, using the most appropriate methods.

- Maintain the integrity of the existing salmonid genetic and life history diversity before, during, and after dam removal and the subsequent periods of elevated sediment levels.

- Maintain the health of fish populations before, during, and after dam removal.

- Restore the physical and biological processes of the overall ecosystem through dam removal, including the return of viable salmonid populations (VSPs).

Additionally, a parallel goal is found in the NOAA Fisheries Service guidance documents for recovering ESA-listed salmon species: restoration efforts shall be targeted at achieving VSPs.[6]

Monitoring the fish population and ecosystem response to the removal of the Elwha River dams and implementation of appropriate adaptive management actions are critical to achievement of the above goals. Monitoring will provide information necessary to evaluate the success or failure of management actions. This information can be used to make necessary changes in management. Because of the spatial and temporal scale of the project, it will be necessary to reevaluate the restoration effort at intervals to make adjustments if assumptions of the plan are invalidated. Monitoring will also allow managers to define additional restoration actions needed outside the scope of the Elwha Act.

Adaptive Management and Monitoring Objectives

Monitoring ecosystem response in the Elwha River requires establishing clearly defined objectives. Adaptive management requires the objectives to be linked to the overall goals of the Elwha Act, as the goals form the basis for judging project effectiveness and guide adaptive management actions necessary to achieve the EFRP goals. Objectives for the EFRP include:

Objective 1: Evaluate recolonization by species (or genotype) and method of reintroduction through the examination of rebuilding rates (production), population size (abundance), spatial distribution, and habitat utilization.

---

[6] A VSP is defined as "an independent population … that has a negligible risk of extinction due to threats from demographic variation, local environmental variation, and genetic diversity changes over a 100-year time frame" (McElhany et al. 2000). The VSP concept incorporates abundance, productivity, diversity, and distribution.

Objective 2: Document the genetic structure and life history diversity of existing Elwha River fish populations. Identify how genetic structure and life history diversity are affected by dam removal and hatchery practices over time. Document how any changes affect the viability of the population.

Objective 3: Monitor fish health over time, space, and method of reintroduction.

Objective 4: Document recovery of ecosystem processes over time and space. Ecosystem recovery includes not only freshwater, but also riparian, nearshore, and terrestrial habitats.

Hypotheses Development

A suite of testable hypotheses has been developed for each of the monitoring objectives identified. In order to be linked to the adaptive management strategy, these hypotheses have been written to specify desired or expected outcomes of the recovery plan. In some cases, these desired or expected outcomes have been carefully developed through analysis of existing data (see Table 25). In other cases, the expected outcome is unknown but is intuitively inferred (e.g., ecosystem response to recolonizing salmonid populations). When a specific target has been identified, the hypotheses will reference the source. If no reference is shown, the target is inferred.

Objective 1: Recolonization

For summer steelhead, cutthroat and bull trout, sockeye salmon, brook lamprey, Pacific lamprey, and nearshore forage fish species (eulachon, Pacific sandlance [*Ammodytes hexapterus*], herring [*Clupea pallasii pallasii*], smelt spp.), the EFRP prioritizes natural colonization as the lone restoration strategy for the three restoration phases identified in the plan (before, during, and after dam removal). For winter steelhead and Chinook, coho, chum, and pink salmon, hatchery supplementation will be used to first preserve and then help restore the species during the pre-dam-removal and dam-removal phases, with a shift toward natural colonization as the priority restoration method during the post-dam-removal phase as the numbers of naturally produced fish of these species approach interim 10-year restoration targets (Table 25). Recolonization monitoring must be designed to evaluate the success of the various restoration strategies and to provide feedback on the effectiveness of these strategies over time and space.

Spatial distribution

When fish have full access to the Elwha watershed following dam removal, it is expected they will colonize the watershed at a predictable rate. It is anticipated that all species will have fully colonized the watershed within 20 to 30 years (Table 25) following dam removal. In order to test this assumption, these three hypotheses have been developed.

H_0: Rate of dispersion throughout the watershed is consistent with modeled and expected rate (Table 25).

H_0: Species are utilizing all physically appropriate and accessible habitat (Table 25).

H_0: No barriers to migration exist.

Table 25. EFRP interim restoration targets.

Species	Abundance		Productivity[a]		Spatial distribution[d]	Diversity	Harvest goals
	After 10 years[b]	After 25 years[c]	After 10 years	At MSY			
Chinook salmon	≈2,000	6,900	>1.0	4.6	Main stem to RM 42.9	Spring and summer/fall	<10 SUS[e] exploitation rate (ER)
Coho salmon	≈3,000	12,100	>1.0	2.9	Main stem (RM 42.9) and accessible tribs.	Fall	<40% (rebuilding) <20% (critical)[f]
Pink salmon	≈10,000	96,000	>1.0	2.9	Main stem (RM 16) and accessible tribs.	Early/late	<50% (rebuilding)
Chum salmon	≈3,000	18,000	>1.0	2.0	Main stem (RM 16) and accessible tribs.	Fall	<25% (rebuilding)
Sockeye salmon	TBD[g]	6,000	>1.0	TBD	Lake Sutherland	Unknown	TBD
Steelhead trout	≈1,500	5,757	>1.0	1.8	Main stem (RM 42.9) and accessible tribs.	Summer/winter	<5% (rebuilding)
Cutthroat trout	TBD	TBD	>1.0	TBD	Main stem (RM 42.9) and accessible tribs.	Unknown	TBD
Bull trout	No decline from present	1,000[h]	>1.0	TBD/increasing	Main stem (RM 44+) and accessible tribs.	Unknown	TBD

[a] Natural-origin recruits and spawners.
[b] Abundance of adults spawning naturally, regardless of origin.
[c] Abundance of adults of natural-origin spawning naturally.
[d] For accessible tributaries, see Hosey and Associates 1988b.
[e] Southern United States (Puget Sound and coasts of Washington, Oregon, and California).
[f] Established for all Strait of Juan de Fuca coho salmon populations.
[g] TBD = to be determined.
[h] From USFWS Bull Trout Recovery Plan.

Composition of spawning population

Several strategies will be used to reintroduce salmon into the watershed, including the release of hatchery produced fish at a variety of life history stages. Each strategy has an expected outcome in terms of survival to spawning adult (Table 26). It is anticipated some strategies will ultimately be more successful than others, and an important goal of the monitoring plan is to determine which strategy will be most effective. The following hypotheses are designed to test whether the restoration strategy is achieving the goals of the project.

H_o: Success of reintroduction methods is consistent with expectations (Table 26).

H_o: Composition of spawning population is consistent with expectations (Table 26).

Productivity and abundance

Juvenile production, the freshwater environment, and marine survival are keys to productivity and abundance objectives. As naturally spawning adults colonize the watershed, the production of natural-origin juveniles should increase and ultimately result in the return of spawning adults from naturally spawning parents. The underlying productivity of the freshwater environment is a key component of the rate of recovery realized and overall carrying capacity of the system. Marine survival is another component affecting the rate of recovery of natural-origin populations in the watershed. It may also be a measure of the success of various juvenile hatchery fish release strategies selected for preserving and restoring each species through the plan. Sources of marine mortality (e.g., natural vs. harvest, fishery specific) may also suggest strategies to improve marine survival over time.

The following hypotheses are designed to evaluate the success of juvenile fish production, the productivity of the freshwater environment, and postrelease survival for fish produced through various hatchery release strategies applied through the plan. Assuming the majority of postrelease mortality will occur in the marine environment because of the relatively short distance that most hatchery fish released into the Elwha River transit before reaching the estuary, the latter hypothesis will also serve to indicate marine survival affects on natural-origin components of fish populations.

H_o: Rate of recovery is consistent with modeled or expected rate (Table 26).

H_o: Juvenile NOR production is consistent with rebuilding rate expectations (Table 25).

H_o: Hatchery-origin fish postrelease survival is consistent with expectations (Table 26 and Appendix A).

Objective 2: Genetic Diversity and Population Integrity

Full restoration of the Elwha River ecosystem requires that fish species adapt to using the full range of habitat types available. Historically, this diversity of habitat conditions led to the development of different phenotypes (i.e., run timing, life history), and potential genotypes. To restore fish throughout the watershed, it will be necessary to preserve the entire spectrum of existing genetic diversity, while other traits develop or reexpress themselves.

Table 26. EFRP interim Chinook salmon hatchery targets before, during, and after dam removal.

Release period	Release strategy	Release numbers	Survival rate (total)[a]	Survival to river	Spatial distribution	Diversity
Before removal	On-station yearling	200,000	>1%	>1,000	To weir	No change[b]
	Morse Creek yearling	200,000	>1%	>500	Morse Creek	No change
	On-station fingerling	2,550,000	>0.25%	>1,000	To weir	No change
	Off-station fingerling	0	NA[c]	NA	NA	No change
Removal	On-station yearling	200,000	>1%	>1,000	To weir	No change
	Morse Creek yearling	200,000	>1%	>500	Morse Creek	No change
	On-station fingerling	2,725,000	>0.25%	>1,000	To weir	No change
	Off-station fingerling	500,000	>0.25%	>500	TBD[d]	No change
After removal	On-station yearling	200,000	>1%	>1,000	TBD	No change
	Morse Creek yearling[e]	200,000	>1%	>500	Morse Creek	No change
	On-station fingerling	2,200,000	>0.25%	>1,000	TBD	No change
	Off-station fingerling	750,000	>0.25%	>500	TBD	No change

[a] Expected survival rates for other species are found in Appendix A.
[b] No change in run timing or genetic or phenotypic composition over the duration of the hatchery program.
[c] NA = not applicable
[d] TBD = to be decided
[e] Morse Creek yearling production will be phased out following dam removal.

Run timing and spawn timing

Alterations in run timing and spawn timing are perhaps the most obvious effects of hatchery practices found in salmonid populations (Quinn 2004). Hatchery practices may alter run timing by selectively spawning fish from a limited portion of the total run through altered rearing conditions or inadvertent changes to a population's genotype (Johnson et al. 1997, Quinn 2004). Salmonid run timing and spawn timing, however, also respond to changes in habitat conditions and accessibility. The most obvious example of this in the Elwha River is the loss of the early timed component of the Chinook population in response to loss of access to the upper watershed.

A change in run timing may be detrimental, beneficial, or neutral to the success of the restoration effort. Again, using the early timed Chinook salmon population as an example, a shift to earlier run timing in fish using the upper watershed would likely benefit Chinook salmon recovery, as it would indicate fish were successfully adapting to the colder water conditions found in the upper watershed. Conversely, a shift to an earlier run timing in the lower river population of Chinook salmon could indicate that hatchery practices or changes in habitat were altering the timing, possibly leading to a less successful population. This hypothesis is designed to evaluate potential changes in timing.

H_0: Run timing and spawn timing are not changing over time (Table 25).

Genetic composition

The genetic composition of any fish population plays a critical role in its viability (McElhany et al. 2000). The genetic traits of individual salmonid populations allow that population to be uniquely adapted to a particular river. Additionally, genetic diversity improves the population's ability to adapt to changes in its environment, whether those changes are natural or anthropogenic. Conversely, the loss of diversity reduces the ability of the population to thrive over the long term. Therefore, it is imperative that restoration efforts in the Elwha River preserve the genetic diversity of populations remaining in the watershed, and that actions implemented under the plan do not lead to the further loss of diversity, but instead help enhance diversity over the long term as the various populations adapt to new habitat conditions. This is addressed in the following hypothesis.

H_0: Actions implemented under the plan do not directly alter the genetic signature of remaining populations.

Phenotypic composition

A population's phenotype is an outward expression of genetic structure and diversity, as shaped by environmental pressures. For example, Elwha River Chinook salmon were historically known for being very large bodied (up to 100 pounds) (Brannon and Hershberger 1984). Currently, Elwha Chinook salmon adults returning to the river are relatively large in average body weight (20–30 pounds round weight, LEKT test fishery data) when compared to other Puget Sound fall Chinook populations returning to natal streams (e.g., Green River Chinook salmon average 15 pounds round weight, WDFW Soos Creek Hatchery data). A small proportion of the current Elwha Chinook population entering freshwater each year remain extraordinarily large in body weight (30–60 pounds round weight) and, according to Mike McHenry, LEKT Fisheries Department, one individual in the 80 pound range was observed in 2003.

Although the population remains among the largest in average body weight within the Puget Sound region, extremely large individuals in the Elwha River appear to be rarer in occurrence than observed historically. The apparent decreased proportion of larger adult fish in the river may reflect a change in genetic diversity and a shift away from a large body phenotype that was historically advantageous, commensurate with restriction of the population to spawning in the lower five miles of the watershed. A phenotypic change resulting from artificial propagation practices is also possible, although the strategy of releasing mainly subyearling fish reared for a short duration in the hatchery makes such changes less likely (as suggested in Berejikian and Ford 2004). When fish are again exposed to the natural selective pressures found in the Elwha watershed, the large body characteristic may be allowed to reexpress itself. The following hypothesis was designed to examine change in phenotype over time.

H_0: Phenotypic composition is not changing over time.

Objective 3: Fish Health Response

One risk when artificial propagation is used as a primary means to preserve and restore fish populations is the potential catastrophic loss of hatchery and natural-origin fish due to the introduction, transfer, and amplification of fish disease pathogens. Interactions between hatchery fish and natural fish may result in the transmission of pathogens, if either the hatchery or natural fish are harboring a disease. This impact may occur in tributary areas where hatchery fish are planted and throughout migration areas where hatchery and natural-origin fish may interact. As the pathogens responsible for the most prevalent fish diseases observed in the watershed (*Dermocystidium salmonis* and bacterial kidney disease [*Renibacterium salmoninarum*]) may be present in Elwha River hatchery or natural populations, there is some uncertainty associated with determining the source of the pathogens. The hatchery-origin fish may have an increased risk of carrying fish disease pathogens because of relatively high rearing densities that increase stress and can lead to greater manifestation and spread of disease within the hatchery population.

Under natural, low density conditions, most pathogens do not lead to a disease outbreak. When fish disease outbreaks in Elwha River natural salmon populations do occur, they are often triggered by stressful high temperature and low flow conditions associated with the dams and water withdrawal practices. Under these conditions, it is possible that the release of hatchery fish may lead to the loss of natural fish, if the hatchery fish are carrying a pathogen, if that pathogen is transferred to the natural fish, and if the transfer of the pathogen leads to a disease outbreak. A disease outbreak in either the hatchery or natural populations could slow recovery and pose an increased risk to the success of the restoration effort. To address concerns of potential disease transmission from hatchery salmonids to natural-origin fish, fish health practices and monitoring are implemented so that Elwha hatchery fish are reared and released in healthy condition. The USFWS initiated a baseline assessment of the fish diseases found in wild fish within the Elwha watershed in 2004.[7] The following hypothesis is associated with the threat of disease.

H_0: Restoration strategy has not introduced, transferred, or amplified fish diseases in the watershed.

Objective 4: Ecosystem Recovery

Ecosystem recovery related to restoration efforts for salmonid populations can have a direct effect on adaptive management actions taken in the fish restoration strategy. Ecosystem recovery includes:

- habitat-forming assemblages including kelp and eelgrass systems

- linkages between habitat-forming and functional processes throughout the watershed, including the nearshore

- nonsalmonid fish species and shellfish populations

- riparian vegetation

- terrestrial wildlife

- fish habitat

As for other aspects of this project, specific hypotheses will be defined by individual research projects; however, for each of the above categories, two very general hypotheses have been described to evaluate restoration efforts for planning purposes.

H_0: The ecosystem is recovering to historic or expected conditions.

H_0: Recovery rate is consistent with expectations.

---

[7] S. Mumford, USFWS, Olympia Fish Health Center, Olympia, WA. Pers. commun., 11 July 2005.

Conceptual Design for Monitoring

A large number of research questions could be asked regarding the restoration of the Elwha River. In order to focus the plan, specific monitoring tasks must be completed in order to ensure that the goals of the Elwha Act are achieved. For example, if an anthropogenic barrier to salmonid migration remains in the river following dam removal, then fish will be unable to fully colonize the watershed. Therefore, simply documenting the migration of fish through the construction sites following dam removal will be a high priority monitoring need for the success of the project. This subsection discusses the conceptual design for the monitoring program needed to meet the objectives stated in the previous subsection, Adaptive Management and Monitoring Objectives.

Objective 1: Recolonization

As stated previously, the EFRP will use natural colonization for summer steelhead, cutthroat and bull trout, sockeye salmon, and forage fish species (eulachon, herring, smelt, etc.), while a combination of natural recolonization and hatchery outplants will be used for winter steelhead and Chinook, coho, chum, and pink salmon. Hatchery outplants will be conducted spatially in selected portions of the Elwha River watershed. Some areas of the watershed will not be outplanted and will be used as controls.

In order to evaluate spatial or temporal rates of species recolonization and to understand the effect of various recolonization strategies, it will be necessary to partition the Elwha River watershed into areas that receive no supplementation, areas that receive supplementation for one or more cycles (5 years), and areas that receive supplementation over the life of the project (20–30 years). Because of access and helicopter use limitations, the upper Elwha River (above Lake Mills) provides a control site for assessing recolonization for several species. The only species currently targeted for outplanting in this area are Chinook salmon, and these outplants may be limited by restrictions on the number of helicopter flights allowed within ONP (a maximum of 36 per year). These restrictions are a result of the biological opinion of the project designed to protect other federally protected species including marbled murrelets and spotted owls.

Natural recolonization in this reach is anticipated for summer and winter steelhead, coho salmon, and anadromous forms of cutthroat trout and char. Chum and pink salmon may not extensively colonize this reach, as stream gradient increases above Press Valley may naturally limit their distribution. Several large tributaries also represent excellent control sites in the upper river where no outplanting would occur. These tributaries include Hayes River, Lillian River, Lost River, Goldie River, and Long Creek in the upper Elwha and could be used to test specific rates of recolonization.

The reach between Elwha and Glines Canyon dams would be appropriate to test the effectiveness of hatchery supplementation over a single generation cycle (3–5 years). A single cycle was chosen as a natural time break for feedback through the adaptive management process. This area is easily accessible for truck-based outplanting, contains excellent habitat (at least 31 side channels), and should be quickly colonized by fish following removal of Elwha Dam. This reach also contains two large tributaries, Indian Creek and Little River. Little River supports a population of rainbow trout least affected by past hatchery outplanting (Phelps et al. 2001) that could also be retained for natural recolonization.

While all native species are anticipated to use this reach, only Chinook and coho salmon will be planted in significant numbers (see the Habitat Restoration section). Because of small population sizes, winter steelhead and chum and pink salmon outplants will likely be limited by availability of eggs during the first cycle following dam removal. These species could be increased in subsequent cycles based on availability of broodstock in the lower river and the success of initial efforts.

Below the Elwha Dam, supplementation efforts will be carried out according to EFRP recommendations. This is logical as the bulk of the outplanted fish will be steelhead and Chinook and coho salmon from the two hatcheries. Most of these releases are anticipated to be on station and will occur for up to 10 years. Dam removal will impact habitat conditions in the lower river for the greatest period.

In order for this portion of the monitoring plan to succeed, it is critical that all hatchery fish produced and released to the Elwha River receive marks of some type (otolith, fin clips, etc.). Older year classes of steelhead and Chinook salmon returning from smolts released 3 years prior to commencement of dam removal could potentially access upriver spawning grounds. For coho and other salmon species, returning adults from releases beginning the year of dam removal could access the upper watershed. Marking systems for Chinook salmon and steelhead currently are in place. Marking systems for all species need to be agreed to and in place no later than the year dam removal begins.

To determine the most appropriate methods for growing fish to outplant, hatchery techniques will be evaluated and focused on smolt size and timing. Emergence time and growth rate (postemergence) influence time of smolting. Age-0 smolting may occur June through October. Holding back fish that are normally released at age 0 for yearling release for Chinook salmon may result in both disease problems (due to the stress of smolting and then desmolting as underyearlings) and the production of large numbers of precocious males. Simplistically, for fish to smolt earlier, they need to grow faster and thus be larger than their nonsmolting cohorts. An experimental rearing program may be conducted to develop size, growth, and date targets for both age-0 and yearling smolts.

Monitoring Parameters and Frequency for Objective 1

Primary importance will be placed on the response of adult and juvenile fish communities to restoration. For adults it will be critical to assess the abundance, distribution, and genetics of each population over time. These assessments will be exceedingly difficult in the upper portions of the Elwha River, as the majority of the basin is accessible only on foot or horseback. Many species of salmon will return during times of the year, such as fall, when weather and flow conditions make traditional observation and sampling techniques difficult, if not impossible. For the upper Elwha River, it is reasonable to expect that the majority of spawning will occur in low gradient, unconfined valley reaches that contain side channels and in low gradient tributary reaches. These reaches can be identified, mapped, and sampled based on distance upstream.

Spatial coverage over time will indicate how long recolonization takes and at what rate stock recovery occurs. Spawning ground surveys of live or dead fish and redds can then be conducted on foot at 10- to 14-day intervals throughout the spawning period. A similar strategy can be developed for the middle reach. This area contains 31 side channels that can be stratified by function and sampled as per the upper reach. Access in the middle reach is much easier and can be assisted with drift boats and rafts as flow allows. In the lower river, LEKT and WDFW have already established adult counting indexes for Chinook and pink salmon and wild winter steelhead. These indexes will be maintained and opportunities to expand adult counts for other species examined. Flow, turbidity, and limited side-channel habitat create conditions difficult for late fall spawning foot counts.

Radio telemetry techniques could be applied to determine recolonization of remote sites in the upper basin. Individual adult fish of various species would be captured and surgically implanted with radio tags. A series of antennas would be established at remote sites along an upstream gradient in the Elwha River, so when individual fish migrated within the range of each antenna their presence would be recorded. ONP, NWFSC, and LEKT have initiated efforts to establish such a network.

Repeatable spatial and temporal monitoring of juvenile abundance using snorkeling techniques at index areas will be an important technique for monitoring response of Elwha River fish populations. Fish censuses conducted over different reaches of the river and nearshore can be used not only to monitor recolonization of habitats but changes in fish community structure over time. These changes will be particularly important in the middle and upper reaches, where rainbow trout, char, and smaller numbers of cutthroat trout dominate current fish communities. As Chinook and coho salmon and other species invade these areas, community structure is anticipated to change. Additionally, as populations rebuild and increasing numbers of salmon return to the watershed, productive capacity of the watershed will change.

Monitoring outmigrating fish, including smolt numbers using rotary screw traps, will provide information on population recovery over time. Along with data collected for adult returns and juvenile density, this information can also be used to monitor productivity of various stocks, to monitor development of different life history trajectories, and to implement new tagging programs. Multiple trap sites could also be established to monitor production from various portions of the watershed. LEKT initiated a smolt trapping program in 2003 in the lower river. It is anticipated this effort will continue and will establish baseline estimates for smolt emigration during the period leading up to dam removal. Plankton sampling will provide data on the presence or absence of forage fish larvae, suggesting successful spawning of forage fish species in the river. Water quality sampling can be conducted in conjunction with the plankton tows, providing site-specific information on suspended sediment loading at the time of forage fish spawning and emergence.

Objective 2: Genetic Diversity and Population Integrity

Because several aspects of the EFRP are based on assumptions concerning the genetic structure of the population, genetic baselines will be developed using microsatellite DNA techniques for all stocks before dam removal. This information will aid the stock selection process and will be useful for tracking the population of recolonizing stocks to the overall populations. Specifically the following will be evaluated:

- temporal segments of Chinook and chum salmon
- the composition of anadromous and resident steelhead and rainbow trout[8]
- the relation of Lake Sutherland kokanee populations to other regional stocks
- the relation of current Elwha River pink salmon population to other regional stocks
- the relation of lower, middle, and upriver char populations to each other and to Dungeness River char
- establishment of baseline genetic information for resident and anadromous cutthroat populations
- use of baseline genetic information in combination with marking programs to evaluate the effectiveness of various culture techniques

One of the most uncertain genetic relationships involves determining the structure of the steelhead and rainbow trout populations and how they will respond to dam removal over time. It is not certain whether a native summer steelhead population still exists in the lower river. Similarly, although a steelhead population consistent with the timing of wild coastal winter steelhead does still exist, it has not been assessed genetically. Existing populations of rainbow trout above Elwha and Glines Canyon dams appear to represent a gradient of native and introduced stocks (Phelps et al. 2001). These populations are known to currently produce small numbers of viable smolts (Hiss and Wunderlich 1994a); however, it is not known whether these smolts will ultimately manifest themselves as summer or winter run fish.

Monitoring Parameters and Frequency for Objective 2

Chinook salmon

Prior to construction of the Elwha River dams, there were apparently two temporal runs of Chinook salmon: one in the spring and the other during summer and fall. There is little information on the life history characteristics of these runs but, with the loss of access to the upper basin and an aggressive hatchery supplementation program, the two runs have melded over time. With construction of the dams, lower river conditions have been marginal for the early returning spring run holding in freshwater prior to spawning. Presently, a remnant of the early returning component to the summer and fall run may be expressing vestigial characteristics of the spring run or may simply be part of the normal variation in run timing expressed by the summer and fall run. The early run component of Elwha Chinook salmon was considered for selection to recolonize the upper portion of the basin; however, it is so limited in size that the preferred approach is to use Chinook salmon from across the current extant run timing. A genetic and phenetic approach will provide the opportunity to maximize variability in the

---

[8] Anadromous and resident *Oncorhynchus mykiss* stocks could include native Elwha River steelhead, nonnative steelhead, native Elwha rainbow trout, native Elwha steelhead that have residualized as rainbow trout, or any of several nonnative rainbow trout stocks that were planted in the river in the years since dam construction.

Chinook salmon stock and therefore maximize the chances of reintroduction success into the basin.

A genetic baseline for the Chinook salmon population will be established using microsatellite DNA genetic markers specifically targeting temporal components of the entire run in the lower Elwha River. Fish will be marked while taking genetic samples to assess whether early returning fish are also early spawning fish and stream spawning surveys will be tied together with genetic sampling. If an early stock of fish is recognized (either phenotypically or genotypically), juveniles from different spawning dates would be kept separate in a hatchery program and uniquely marked prior to release as yearlings. Early spawned fish would be released higher in the basin. If there is no temporal-genetic structure or temporal relationship between return time and spawning time, then the procedure proposed in the recovery plan would be best suited to the existing conditions.

Resident and anadromous *O. mykiss* stocks

Both summer and winter steelhead are indigenous to the Elwha River (WDFW and WWTIT 1994). The HSRG (2002) reported the LEKT hatchery is currently using an early running nonnative broodstock (originally from Chambers Creek and Bogachiel River). The late-running "natural" population is currently at very low population levels (<200). Various rainbow trout stocks exist upstream, some of which may represent native steelhead recently residualized above the dams. A DNA-based genetic baseline will be established for the natural, hatchery, and various rainbow trout stocks to help understand the pattern of genetic diversity among these stocks. Approximately 12 collections of 100 fish each will be necessary. Nonlethal fin clips can be taken during fieldwork. Out-of-watershed hatchery stocks will be evaluated as well. Laboratory work will proceed according to standardized procedures among regional genetics laboratories (e.g., WDFW and NWFSC).

In agreement with HSRG review, the early timed hatchery stock is deemed an inappropriate stock for recolonization of the upper watershed. LEKT is developing a broodstock from the later timed natural steelhead run.

The contribution of upriver rainbow trout stocks is poorly understood. The capacity of the various resident rainbow trout stocks to produce smolts in light of their differing levels of genetic divergence is unknown. Experiments have been designed to evaluate the life history characteristics of pertinent rainbow trout stocks versus the potential colonizing steelhead stocks (natural and hatchery) and their hybrids, particularly with regard to smolt production and juvenile migration behavior. Stocks for these experiments will be selected based on the results of the basin-wide genetic survey.

Counts of summer steelhead are considered depressed due to the loss of habitat associated with the dams on the Elwha River. Escapement of naturally produced summer steelhead is unknown but is estimated at less than 100 fish per year. Annual releases of Skamania stock in the lower basin by WDFW occurred prior to 2000. This unique life history type is included in the genetic survey.

It is important to realize that a DNA-based baseline of all potentially contributing stocks will enable monitoring of the reproductive success of the various gene pools. The agencies will be able to match genetic data from nonlethal fin clips from returning adults or outmigrating smolts against the basin-wide genetic baseline (analogous to a genetic stock identification analysis).

Sockeye salmon

Genetic studies have shown that lake populations of sockeye salmon are widely differentiated (Gustafson et al. 1997). On the Olympic Peninsula, lakes Quinault and Ozette are distinctive; moreover, kokanee in Lake Ozette are highly differentiated from the anadromous stock. Based on protein genetic data, it was shown that river-type sockeye salmon in the Skagit River had elevated values of genetic richness and resembled other river- and sea-type sockeye salmon in British Columbia (Gustafson and Winans 1999). An updated DNA-based baseline of sockeye salmon will be constructed to evaluate the relationships among Elwha basin and other peninsula stocks of sockeye salmon. This baseline will be created in cooperation with biologists at the Department of Fisheries and Oceans Canada, Nanaimo, who have constructed a thorough DNA baseline for populations in British Columbia (Beacham et al. 2006). With a DNA-based baseline of all potentially contributing stocks, reproductive success of the various gene pools can be monitored. There is a good chance that Lake Sutherland kokanee will have a unique genetic mark, which can be used to track their contribution to the recolonizing gene pool in the Elwha.

Pink salmon

A genetic survey of pink salmon stocks on the Olympic Peninsula has been undertaken, using as a comparison baseline data collected by LEKT and WDFW on the Elwha River, Dungeness River, and Morse Creek. Evidence suggests there are two discrete populations of pink salmon in the Elwha River, while Morse Creek pink salmon can be distinguished from both the Elwha and Dungeness populations (Small 2004). As it can be shown that Elwha River pink salmon are unique to the Olympic Peninsula, efforts to develop this local broodstock for restoration should be undertaken.

Char

Char species will be collected during the fieldwork of Objective 1. Fin clips will be processed using DNA microsatellite analysis to establish that all native char in the watershed are bull trout (vs. Dolly Varden), to determine the baseline signature for native char above lower Elwha Dam, and to determine whether native char located below the dam are similar to the upriver populations. Samples will also be compared to Dungeness River bull trout.

Cutthroat trout

Cutthroat trout can be nonlethally sampled during the fieldwork of Objective 1. Regional databases can be used to monitor the genetic composition of a recolonizing group of cutthroat trout. This is a critical species to consider because it hybridizes freely in some situations with *O. mykiss*, potentially compromising both species' reproductive output. Evaluation of the location and magnitude of hybridization with *O. mykiss* will be noted and tracked prior to and during recolonization.

Genetic monitoring

It is necessary to use an adaptive management approach in supplementing the upper Elwha Basin with Chinook salmon and steelhead. By maintaining a very flexible approach to supplementation, agencies will have the best chance to reestablish salmonid stocks over the long term. An essential component of adaptive management is the accurate estimation of the relative rate of recovery of stocks, especially for NORs. These estimates can only be derived from a systematic DNA-based monitoring program operated in tandem with a physical marking program that uses a number of distinctive marks. Where possible, marks should be specific down to the age at release and possibly to the geographic area of release.

Objective 3: Fish Health Response

Three discrete monitoring programs to assess changes in fish health have been proposed. They include:

1. Monitor Lake Sutherland kokanee for infectious hematopoietic necrosis virus (IHNV) and *Parvicapsula* before and after dam removal and the recolonization by sockeye salmon.

2. Monitor coho and Chinook salmon and steelhead smolts from smolt traps on the lower Elwha River.

3. Monitor fish disease events observed on the Elwha River on a case-by-case basis.

The first program, monitoring Lake Sutherland kokanee for IHNV and *Parvicapsula* before and after dam removal and the natural colonization of sockeye salmon, has two hypotheses.

H_0: The colonization of Lake Sutherland by anadromous fish after dam removal will have no impact on pathogens detected in surveys of the resident kokanee population.

H_A: The colonization of Lake Sutherland by anadromous fish after dam removal will have an impact on pathogens detected in surveys of the resident kokanee population.

There are historical accounts of kokanee in Lake Sutherland prior to the construction of the Elwha Dam in 1911, as well as records of releases of kokanee, cutthroat, and rainbow from multiple hatchery stocks. Since 1995 only Goldendale rainbow trout, reared in pathogen-free water from regulated, pathogen-free captive broodstock, have been released.

Currently the kokanee in Lake Sutherland have been isolated from anadromous fish and, therefore, from marine pathogens since 1911. With the removal of the dams in 3 to 5 years and renewed access for anadromous fish, it is anticipated that a sockeye salmon run will return to Lake Sutherland. The return of sockeye salmon has the potential to expose possibly naive resident fish populations to marine pathogens. As stated above, there is no health history available for the kokanee population or other fish populations in the lake. Sonia Mumford, USFWS, along with scientists from the various agencies involved with this plan, will sample spawning kokanee adults prior to and following dam removal as in the Hiss and Wunderlich study (1994b). Virus assays will be performed annually to determine the presence or absence of detectable levels of IHNV, to which kokanee and sockeye salmon are known to be susceptible.

Additionally, samples for PCR (polymerase chain reaction) and histology will be collected and evaluated for the presence of the parasite *Parvicapsula minibicornis*. Sixty fish will be collected annually. Other fish health monitoring activities will be performed for the USFWS's National Wild Fish Health Survey.

Gary Winans, NWFSC, is conducting a genetic evaluation of Lake Sutherland kokanee and sockeye salmon with a comparison to other regional stocks and will coordinate sampling as much as possible. Winans' effort will rely on sampling spawned out fish that are freshly dead, which may not be suitable for EFRP sampling needs. If possible the various agencies involved with EFRP will sample juvenile kokanee and sockeye salmon and monitor for the presence of IHNV, although according to Bob Wunderlich, USFWS, previous research at Lake Sutherland indicates there may be difficulty in collecting small fish.

Finally, cutthroat and rainbow trout in Lake Sutherland will be sampled if possible, and subjected to the same analysis as the kokanee and sockeye salmon (on their return). It would be important to sample these fish populations prior to dam removal so that a more complete understanding of potential parasite reservoirs is established.

The second program, monitoring coho and Chinook salmon and steelhead smolts captured in smolt traps on the lower Elwha River, has two hypotheses.

H_o: There is no detectable difference in the pathogens detected in surveys of outmigrating smolts before and after dam removal.

H_A: There is a detectable difference in the pathogens detected in surveys of outmigrating smolts before and after dam removal.

General fish health monitoring of outgoing smolts captured in a trap on the lower end of the Elwha River will take place annually in an effort to collect baseline information on pathogenic bacteria and viruses in the fish populations. The sampling will be approached in a manner consistent with the National Wild Fish Health Survey, with routine screening of 60 fish per species for viral pathogens including infectious pancreatic necrosis virus (IPNV), INHV, viral hemorrhagic septicemia (VHS), infectious salmon anaemia virus (ISAV), Oncorhynchus masou virus (OMV), and bacterial pathogens including furunculosis (*Aeromonas salmonicida*), enteric redmouth disease (*Yersinia ruckeri*), bacterial kidney disease (*Renibacterium salmoninarum*), and cold-water disease (*Flavobacterium psychrophilum*).

The trap will be in place from mid-March through mid-June. The total number of fish collected will be at least 60 fish per species. Sampling will take place in collaboration with Walt Dickhoff, NWFSC, who is studying several aspects of the reproductive physiology. Additionally, toxicology could potentially be done on the same fish. Dickhoff has proposed collecting 15 fish per species per location per date and repeating this process several times throughout the time that the smolt trap is in place.

Fish will be sampled, taking the kidney and spleen from all species for the fish health evaluation, and the cranial elements from the steelhead to monitor for whirling disease (*Myxobolus cerebralis*). Wild fish samples will be processed and analyzed by USFWS under the

National Wild Fish Health Survey. Hatchery-origin fish will be processed and analyzed by the Northwest Indian Fisheries Commission.

The third program, case-by-case monitoring of fish disease events observed on the Elwha River, has no hypotheses. It is not a hypothesis-based component, but instead a continuation of response to specific events that are brought to the attention of a fish health specialist by others taking part in the monitoring effort. These cases will be handled as diagnostic cases; it is not possible to effectively monitor in the "before and after" fashion as above. The information gathered will provide a record of the selected events over time.

Objective 4: Ecosystem Recovery

Monitoring the rate of ecosystem recovery will require the expansion of biological monitoring strategies to lower and higher trophic levels in freshwater, estuarine, and nearshore habitats. The primary producers are in the lower trophic levels, while secondary producers as well as salmon-dependent wildlife are in the higher trophic level. Additionally, linkages to changes in habitat from reestablishment of dominant physical processes including sediment, woody debris, flow, nutrient transport, and temperature regime will be necessary to understand ecosystem recovery. This work should be done in conjunction with agencies conducting sediment monitoring following dam removal in the Elwha River (Randle et al. 2003). A stratification of river habitats that includes mainstem, side-channel, and tributary sites grouped by similar physical features (gradient, confinement, and location within the watershed) represents a logical system for measuring ecosystem response.

The nearshore ecosystem of the Elwha has endured significant sediment starvation for nearly 100 years. Dam removal will provide a significant but incomplete restoration of this process. Restoration response in the nearshore depends on multiple variables, making the nearshore element of Elwha ecosystem recovery very complex (see Shaffer et al. 2005). Nearshore habitat of the Elwha ecosystem may be defined as the area within tidal influence from the riparian zone to a depth of 30 m MLLW. The primary area of the Elwha nearshore is defined as the area east of Observatory Point (west side of Freshwater Bay) to Port Angeles Harbor and includes the estuary of the river mouth.

A strategy for defining nearshore restoration response to Elwha dam removals has been developed (Shaffer et al. 2005). In general, stratification of nearshore habitats includes eroding and stable bluffs, sandy and rocky beaches, and pocket beaches that are grouped by geologic and biological parameters (McBride and Beamer 2004). Nearshore habitat rebuilding and recolonization will be largely passive, with the possible exception of some species of shellfish. An enhancement and recolonization plan for Pinto abalone (*Haliotis kamtschatkana*), urchin (*Strongylocentrotus* spp.), and sea cucumber (*Stichopus* spp.) may be initiated, if monitoring following dam removal indicates a need.

Monitoring Parameters and Frequency for Objective 4

Ecosystem recovery parameters include both measures of physical habitat and expansion of biological monitoring beyond fish populations. Ecosystem response will be assessed in both freshwater and marine (estuary and nearshore) environments. For physical habitat monitoring, a combination of in situ and remote monitoring techniques in partnership with planned sediment monitoring will be used. Remote sensing techniques including aerial photography, side scan, LIDAR (light detection and ranging using aerial laser), and hyperspectral imaging will be used to assess long-term (decadal) changes in river morphology, floodplain vegetation, and habitat features. These remote sensing techniques will be combined with field measurements that can be repeated over space and time. The field measurements may include surface flow, groundwater, sediment, water chemistry, temperature studies, and measurements of LWD.

Freshwater biological monitoring will require mostly in situ field studies primarily using sites established along an upstream gradient. These field studies will be linked with fish and wildlife studies to provide measures of ecosystem response. Here changes in ecosystem production and function can be repeatedly measured. Parameters measured will include nutrient levels, primary production, secondary production, and fish response. Monitoring response of wildlife populations will build on past and ongoing studies implemented by ONP.

Nearshore monitoring will focus on three restoration events: 1) the initial pulse of sediment that results from dam removal, 2) the post-dam-removal sediment processes anticipated to occur within 10 years of dam removal (Stolnack and Neiman 2005), and 3) additional habitat restoration actions independent of the dam removals. These habitat restoration options may include restoration of the estuary by modification of an existing fish barrier and restoration of the Elwha feeder bluffs. Monitoring will be based on geomorphic classification of habitats (McBride and Beamer 2004). Physical monitoring includes substrate type, elevation, and profile, covering control sites including Dungeness and Crescent bays, and utilizing the strategy found in "Elwha and Glines Canyon Dam Removals: Nearshore Restoration and Salmon Recovery of the Central Strait of Juan de Fuca" (Shaffer et al. 2005). Biological monitoring includes overstory and understory kelp beds, eelgrass beds, and shallow subtidal unvegetated habitats. Biological habitat structure monitoring will include standard habitat-mapping techniques including aerial surveys, side-scan sonar of shallow subtidal habitats with snorkeling and scuba for understory habitats, and on the ground mapping of beaches using scuba, snorkeling, and beach walking.

The function of these habitats for fishery resources will be defined by documenting the biological communities of each habitat type and focusing on function of habitats for forage fish spawning, juvenile salmon and forage fish migration, and shellfish presence. Methods for defining function will include mapping for forage fish spawning, snorkel and scuba surveys, and seines for fish migration. Given the extreme seasonal variability in the physical and biological habitats of the central strait, monitoring of habitat function will need to occur frequently. Mapping of biological and physical habitats should occur seasonally. In the case of fish migration, sampling should occur at a minimum of monthly and preferably at weekly intervals during early spring and summer months. Due to large variability intrinsic to the central strait nearshore and the temporal nature of the nearshore restoration that may occur, long-term monitoring should be applied.

Prioritization of Projects

Funding for the monitoring described in this section is limited. In particular, the Elwha Fish Restoration Project funding will not be capable of completing all the tasks identified as needed. Therefore, it will be necessary to prioritize projects to maximize the benefits of those funds which are available. Table 27 is the "tool kit" of monitoring activities currently envisioned for the restoration effort. It outlines the utility of each tool and identifies its relative priority for Elwha Project funding. It is important to note that the level of priority in Table 27 is defined by the tool's importance to implementing the adaptive management component of the EFRP. These same tools may have a very different priority for a different aspect of the overall project.

Adaptive Management Strategy

Adaptive management is the means by which changes are made to the restoration strategy, based on information gained from monitoring efforts, in order to achieve the goals of the project. In order for an adaptive management strategy to be effective, there must be a clearly defined decision-making process, as well as a matrix of management actions to be considered. Table 28 documents the preliminary matrix of adaptive management actions that will be implemented, if it is found that desired outcomes of the EFRP are not being achieved. It should be noted that the identified adaptive management actions are broadly described and will be refined in conjunction with the specific monitoring projects. Decision making will be facilitated through the Elwha Project manager and will include the LEKT, WDFW, NWFSC, USFWS, NPS, and BOR.

Table 27. EFRP monitoring strategy relative project priority.

Tool	Applicability	Area	Priority
Aerial surveys	Spawner abundance, distribution, timing, and composition	Entire watershed, but limited in time by ESA requirements to protect spotted owls and marbled murrelets	Medium
Wading and boat surveys	Spawner abundance, distribution, timing, and composition; also provides opportunity to recover marks and collect physical data from carcasses	Entire watershed, but limited by accessibility	Medium
Snorkel and scuba surveys	Spawner, smolt, forage fish, and other species abundance, distribution, timing, and composition; also provides an opportunity to recover marks, collect physical data, and evaluate habitat use by species	Entire watershed, including nearshore, but limited by accessibility	High
Radio telemetry	Spawner and smolt distribution, timing, and detailed freshwater migrational behavior	Entire watershed, but limited by accessibility	High
PIT tagging	Spawner and smolt distribution, timing, and detailed freshwater migrational behavior	Entire watershed, but limited by accessibility	Medium
Coded wire tags (CWT)	Survival by release strategy, contribution by strategy to natural spawning population, marine distribution, contribution to fisheries, and exploitation rates	Entire watershed, but limited by ability to collect tags at return; also, some species are not sampled for CWTs in marine fisheries (pink, chum, and sockeye salmon and steelhead)	High
Otolith marking	Survival by release strategy and contribution by strategy to natural spawning population	Entire watershed, but limited by ability to collect otoliths at return	High
Smolt trapping and net sampling	Smolt abundance, survival to emigration by release strategy, contribution of NORs to population, emigration timing; also provides an opportunity to recover marks and collect physical data	Throughout the watershed, including nearshore, depending on tool	High
Electrofishing	Juvenile abundance, survival by release strategy, contribution of NORs to population; provides an opportunity to recover marks, collect physical data; also provides information on nonsalmonid fish abundance	Entire watershed, but limited by accessibility	Medium
Habitat-mapping techniques (side-scan, remote mapping techniques)	Habitat mapping	Lower river, nearshore Elwha, comparative areas	High
Condition factor	Indication of freshwater productivity and fish health	Entire watershed, but limited by accessibility and sampling effort	Low

113

Table 27 continued. EFRP monitoring strategy relative project priority.

Tool	Applicability	Area	Priority
Scale samples	Age at emigration, age at return, and growth rates	Entire watershed, but limited by accessibility and sampling effort	High
Length and weight	Indicates changes in phenotypic characteristics of the population over time	Entire watershed, but limited by accessibility and sampling effort	Medium
Genetic sampling	Indicates changes in genetic characteristics of the population over time	Entire watershed, but limited by accessibility and sampling effort	High
Marine isotopes	Indicates ecosystem response to restoration efforts over time	Entire watershed, but limited by accessibility and sampling effort	Medium
Water chemistry	Indicates ecosystem response to restoration efforts over time; also related to ability of fish populations to use habitat below Lake Mills after dam removal	Lower and middle reaches, below Lake Mills	Medium
Habitat parameters	Indicates ecosystem response to restoration efforts over time; also related to ability of fish populations to use habitat below Lake Mills after dam removal	Lower and middle reaches, below Lake Mills; nearshore	Medium
Primary and secondary productivity assessment (e.g., macroinvertebrate, phytoplankton, and periphyton)	Indicates ecosystem response to restoration efforts over time; also related to underlying freshwater productivity	Entire watershed, but focused on lower and middle reaches below Lake Mills	Medium
Pathogen sampling	Indicates ecosystem response to restoration efforts over time; also related to salmonid production potential and productivity in the event that disease is inadvertently introduced to the watershed	Entire watershed, but limited by accessibility and sampling effort	High
Nonsalmonid aquatic population assemblages	Indicates ecosystem response to restoration efforts over time	Entire watershed, but limited by accessibility and sampling effort	Low
Terrestrial vegetation assemblages	Indicates ecosystem response to restoration efforts over time	Entire watershed, but limited by accessibility and sampling effort	Low
Terrestrial wildlife assemblages	Indicates ecosystem response to restoration efforts over time	Entire watershed, but limited by accessibility and sampling effort	Low

Table 28. Adaptive management strategy decision matrix.

Topic	Hypothesis	Desired condition	Adaptive management actions
Spatial distribution	H_0: Rate of dispersion throughout the watershed is consistent with modeled or expected rate. H_0: Species are utilizing all physically appropriate and accessible habitat. H_0: No barriers to migration exist.	Anadromous salmonids are distributed throughout their historic range in the Elwha River watershed and its associated nearshore marine environment.	1. Identify and repair anthropogenic barriers to migration. 2. Modify hatchery program to achieve recovery objectives. 3. Modify outplanting strategy to achieve program objectives. 4. Modify dam removal strategy to minimize avoidance behavior. 5. Continue to monitor.
Composition	H_0: Success of reintroduction methods is consistent with expectations. H_0: Composition of spawning population is consistent with expectations.	The historic assemblage of naturally spawning anadromous salmonid populations is restored to the Elwha River watershed.	1. Modify hatchery program to achieve recovery objectives. 2. Modify outplanting strategy to achieve program objectives. 3. Continue to monitor.
Productivity and abundance	H_0: Rate of recovery is consistent with modeled or expected rate. H_0: Juvenile production is consistent with expectations. H_0: Marine survival is consistent with expectations.	The productivity of the anadromous salmonid populations is restored to levels that support viable fisheries and the Elwha River ecosystem.	1. Modify hatchery program. 2. Modify outplanting strategy. 3. Identify and rectify anthropogenic restrictions to freshwater production. 4. Identify and rectify anthropogenic restrictions to marine production. 5. Modify harvest regimes. 6. Continue to monitor.
Diversity	H_0: Run timing and spawn timing are not changing over time. H_0: Genetic signature is not changing over time. H_0: Phenotypic composition is not changing over time.	The genotypic and phenotypic diversity of the anadromous salmonid populations in the Elwha watershed is preserved.	1. Modify hatchery program. 2. Modify outplanting strategy. 3. Identify and rectify anthropogenic alterations to habitat that may alter diversity. 4. Modify harvest regimes, within the confines of comanager capabilities. 5. Continue to monitor.
Fish health	H_0: Restoration strategy has not introduced diseases into the watershed.	Activities associated with restoration of the Elwha River do not introduce pathogens into the watershed.	1. Treat diseases in the hatcheries. 2. Alter hatchery practices to reduce potential for disease. 3. Alter outplanting strategy. 4. Continue to monitor.
Ecosystem recovery	H_0: Ecosystem is recovering to historic or expected conditions. H_0: Recovery rate is consistent with expectations.	The Elwha River ecosystem and nearshore marine environment is fully functioning and representative of historic conditions.	1. Identify and alleviate limiting factors of anthropogenic origin. 2. Alter hatchery and outplanting strategy as appropriate. 3. Reintroduce species as appropriate. 4. Consider methods to boost marine derived nutrients (e.g., carcass planting). 5. Continue to monitor.

References

Abbe, T. B., and D. M. Montgomery. 1996. Large woody debris jams, channel hydraulics, and habitat formation in large rivers. Regul. Rivers: Res. Manag. 12:201–222.

Adamire, B., and H. U. Fish. 1991. The Elwha, a river of destiny. H. U. Fish, P.O. Box 900, Carlsborg, WA 98324.

Adams, C., R. Reisenbichler, and J. Meyer. 1999. Final report to Olympic National Park, Part I: Inventory of resident fishes in the upper Elwha River. *In* Reisenbichler (ed.), Elwha River ecosystem restoration: Potential effects and restoration methods—fisheries investigations. Produced pursuant to Subagreement 27 under Cooperative Agreement CA-9000-8-007. Tech. Rep. NPS/CCSOU/NRTR-99-04, NPS D-309. USGS BRD, Western Fisheries Research Center, Seattle, WA.

Arden, W. R. 2003. Genetic analyses of steelhead in the Hood River, Oregon: Statistical analyses of natural reproductive success of hatchery and natural-origin adults passed upstream of Powerdale Dam. Draft report to Bonneville Power Administration (BPA) in partial fulfillment of BPA Contract No. 00013429. U.S. Fish and Wildlife Service, Abernathy Fish Technology Center, Longview, WA.

Beacham, T. D., R. E. Withler, and A. P. Gould. 1985. Biochemical genetic stock identification of pink salmon (*Oncorhynchus gorbuscha*) in southern British Columbia and Puget Sound. Can. J. Fish. Aquat. Sci. 42:1474–1483.

Beacham, T. D., R. E. Withler, C. B. Murray, and L. W. Barner. 1988. Variation in body size, morphology, egg size, and biochemical genetics of pink salmon in British Columbia. Trans. Am. Fish. Soc. 117:109–126.

Beacham, T. D., B. McIntosh, C. MacConnachie, K. M. Miller, and R. E. Withler. 2006. Pacific Rim population structure of sockeye salmon as determined from microsatellite analysis. Can. J. Fish. Aquat. Sci. 135:174–187.

Berejikian, B. A. 1995. The effects of hatchery and wild ancestry and experience on the relative ability of steelhead trout fry (*Oncorhynchus mykiss*) to avoid a benthic predator. Can. J. Fish. Aquat. Sci. 52:2476–2482.

Berejikian, B., and M. Ford. 2004. A review of the relative fitness of hatchery and natural salmon. U.S. Dept. Commer., NOAA Tech. Memo. NMFS-NWFSC-61.

Berejikian, B., J. Scheurer, J. Lee, D. Van Doornik, E. Volk, and T. Johnson. Unpubl. manuscr. Evaluation of conservation hatchery rearing and release strategies for steelhead recovery in the Hamma Hamma River. (Available from B. Berejikian, Northwest Fisheries Science Center, Manchester Research Station, 7305 E. Beach Dr., Port Orchard, WA 98366.)

Bjerselius, L., J. Weiming, J. H. Teeter, J. G. Seelye, P. B. Johnsen, P. J. Maniak, G. C. Grant, C. N. Polkinghorne, and P. W. Sorensen. 2000. Direct behavioral evidence that unique bile acids released by larval sea lamprey (*Petromyzon marinus*) function as a migratory pheromone. Can. J. Fish. Aquat. Sci. 57:557–569.

Blouin, M., and H. Araki. 2005. Reproductive success: Steelhead in the Hood River. End of year report for Bonneville Power Administration project number 19502 (2003-054-00), FY 2005. Oregon State University, Dept. Zoology, Corvallis.

BOR (U.S. Bureau of Reclamation). 1996. Sediment analysis and modeling of the river erosion alternative. Elwha technical series PN-95-9, August 1996. U.S. Department of the Interior, Bureau of Reclamation, Pacific Northwest Region, Boise, ID.

Brannon, E. L., and W. K. Hershberger. 1984. Elwha River fall Chinook salmon. *In* J. M. Walton and D. B. Houston (eds.), Proceedings of the Olympic wild fish conference. Peninsula College, Fisheries Technology Program, Port Angeles, WA.

Brannon, E. M. 1930. Elwha River hatchery prospect, Washington Dept. Fisheries and Game, Olympia.

Brown, B. 1982. Mountain in the clouds. Simon and Schuster, NY.

Bryant, M. D., B. J. Frenette, and K. T. Coghill. 1996. Use of the littoral zone by introduced anadromous salmonids and resident trout, Margaret Lake, Southeast Alaska. Alsk. Fish. Res. Bull. 3(2):112–122.

Bryant, M. D., B. J. Frenette, and S. J. McCurdy. 1999. Colonization of a watershed by anadromous salmonids following the installation of a fish ladder in Margaret Creek, Southeast Alaska. N. Am. J. Fish. Manag. 19(4):1129–1136.

Bugert, R., K. Petersen, G. Mendel, L. Ross, D. Milks, J. Dedloff, and M. Alexandersdottir. 1992. Lower Snake River compensation plan, Tucannon River spring Chinook salmon hatchery evaluation plan. U.S. Fish and Wildlife Service, Boise, ID.

Burger, C. V., K. T. Scribner, W. J. Spearman, C. O. Swanton, and D. E. Campton. 2000. Genetic contribution of three introduced life history forms of sockeye salmon to colonization of Frazer Lake, Alaska. Can. J. Fish. Aquat. Sci. 57(10):2096–2111.

Campton, D. E. 1995. Genetic effects of hatchery fish on wild populations of Pacific salmon and steelhead: What do we really know? Am. Fish. Soc. Symp. 15:337–353.

Chapman, D. W. 1981. Pristine production of anadromous salmonids—Elwha River. Prepared for U.S. Bureau of Indian Affairs contract no. P00C14206447, July 28, 1981. Bureau of Indian Affairs, Portland, OR.

Chilcote, M. 2002. The adverse reproductive consequences of supplementing natural steelhead populations in Oregon with hatchery fish. Draft. (Available from Oregon Dept. Fish and Wildlife, Portland, OR.)

Chilcote, M. 2003. Relationship between natural productivity and the frequency of wild fish in mixed spawning population of wild and hatchery steelhead (*Oncorhynchus mykiss*). Can. J. Fish. Aquat. Sci. 60:1057–1067.

Chilcote, M. W., S. A. Leider, and J. J. Loch. 1986. Differential reproductive success of hatchery and wild summer-run steelhead under natural conditions. Trans. Am. Fish. Soc. 115:726–735.

Clallam County MRC (Marine Resource Committee). 2004. Proceedings of the technical workshop on nearshore restoration in the central Strait of Juan de Fuca. Clallam County MRC, Port Angeles, WA. Online at http://www.clallammrc.org/CCMRC/allframes.html [accessed 5 October 2007].

Close, D. 2002. Pacific lamprey research and restoration project. Project no. 1994-02600. Bonneville Power Administration Report DOE/BP-00005455-3. Online at http://www.efw.bpa.gov/publications/I00005455-3.pdf [accessed 5 October 2007].

Cook-Tabor, C. 1995. A literature review of the effects of suspended sediments on salmonids. U.S. Fish and Wildlife Service, Western Washington Resource Office, Olympia, WA.

Dilley, S. J., and R. C. Wunderlich. 1990. Juvenile Chinook passage at Glines Canyon Dam, Elwha River, 1989–1990. U.S. Fish and Wildlife Service, Fisheries Assistance Office, Olympia, WA.

DOI (U.S. Department of the Interior) and BOR (U.S. Bureau of Reclamation). 1996. Sediment analysis and modeling of the river erosion alternative. Elwha technical series PN-95-9. U.S. Department of the Interior, Bureau of Reclamation, Pacific Northwest Region, Boise, ID.

DOI (U.S. Department of the Interior), NMFS (National Marine Fisheries Service), and Lower Elwha Klallam Tribe. 1994. The Elwha report: Restoration of the Elwha River ecosystem and native anadromous fisheries: A report submitted pursuant to Public Law 102-495. Olympic National Park, Port Angeles, WA.

DOI (U.S. Department of the Interior), NMFS (National Marine Fisheries Service), and Lower Elwha Klallam Tribe. 1995. Elwha River ecosystem restoration. Final Environmental Impact Statement, June 1995. Olympic National Park, Port Angeles, WA. Online at http://www.nps.gov/olym/elwha/docs/eis0695/eis0695toc.htm [accessed 5 October 2007].

DOI (U.S. Department of the Interior), NMFS (National Marine Fisheries Service), and Lower Elwha Klallam Tribe. 1996. Elwha River restoration implementation. Draft environmental impact statement, April 1996. Olympic National Park, Port Angeles, WA. Online at http://www.nps.gov/olym/elwha/docs/eis0496/eis0496toc.htm [accessed 5 October 2007].

DOI (U.S. Department of the Interior) and ONP (Olympic National Park). 2006. Glines Canyon Dam–Lake Mills reservoir revegetation plan. Final draft. (Available from Olympic National Park, Port Angeles, WA.)

DOI (U.S. Department of the Interior) and USFWS (U.S. Fish and Wildlife Service). 2004. 50 CFR Part 17 USFWS. Proposed rules: Petition to list three species of lampreys as threatened or endangered. Federal Register [Docket No. 04-28167, 27 December 2004] 69(247):77158–77167.

DOI (U.S. Department of the Interior). 2005. Elwha River ecosystem restoration implementation, final supplement to the final Environmental Impact Statement. NPS D-377A. Department of the Interior, National Park Service, Olympic National Park, Port Angeles, WA.

Elwha-Dungeness Planning Unit. May 2005. Elwha-Dungeness watershed plan, water resource inventory area 18 (WRIA 18) and Sequim Bay in west WRIA 17. Published by Clallam County. Online at http://www.clallam.net/environment/html/wria_18_draft_watershed_plan.htm [accessed 5 October 2007].

FERC (Federal Energy Regulatory Commission). 1993. Proposed Elwha (FERC No. 2683) and Glines Canyon (FERC No. 588) hydroelectric projects, Washington. Office of Hydropower Licensing (now the Division of Hydropower Licensing within the FERC Office of Energy Projects). Federal Energy Regulatory Commission, Washington, DC.

Ford, M. J., H. Fuss, B. Boelts, E. LaHood, J. J. Hard, and J. M. Miller. 2006. Changes in run timing and natural smolt production in a naturally spawning coho salmon (*Oncorhynchus kisutch*) stream after 60 years of intensive hatchery supplementation. Can. J. Fish. Aquat. Sci. 63:2343–2355.

Gharrett, A. J., C. Smoot, A. J. McGregor, and P. B. Holmes. 1988. Genetic relationships of even-year northwestern Alaskan pink salmon. Trans. Am. Fish. Soc. 117(6):536-545.

Gibbons, R. G., P. K. Hahn, and T. H. Johnson. 1985. Methodology for determining MSH steelhead spawning escapement requirements. Washington Dept. Game, Olympia, WA.

Ging, G., and F. Seavey. 1995. Marine resources of the Elwha River estuary, Clallam County, Washington. Prepared for Olympic National Park by U.S. Fish and Wildlife Service, North Pacific Coast Eco-region, Olympia, WA.

Groot, C., and L. Margolis. 1991. Pacific salmon life histories. UBC Press, Vancouver, BC.

Gustafson, R. G., T. C. Wainwright, G. A. Winans, F. W. Waknitz, L. T. Parker, and R. S. Waples. 1997. Status review of sockeye salmon from Washington and Oregon. U.S. Dept. Commer., NOAA Tech. Memo. NMFS-NWFSC-33.

Gustafson, R. G., and G. A. Winans. 1999. Distribution and population genetic structure of river/sea-type sockeye salmon in western North America. Ecol. Freshw. Fish 8:181–193.

Hard, J. J., R. G. Kope, W. S. Grant, F. W. Waknitz, L. T. Parker, and R. S. Waples. 1996. Status review of pink salmon from Washington, Idaho, Oregon, and California. U.S. Dept. Commer., NOAA Tech. Memo. NMFS-NWFSC-25.

Hayes, M. C., and R. W. Carmichael. 2002. Salmon restoration in the Umatilla River: A study of straying and risk containment. Fisheries 27(10):10–19.

Helle, J. H. 1966. Behavior of displaced adult pink salmon. Trans. Am. Fish. Soc. 95:188–195.

Hiss, J. 1995. Elwha River chum salmon (*Oncorhynchus keta)*: Spawner survey and escapement estimate, 1994–1995. Prepared for the National Park Service, Olympic National Park, Port Angeles, WA, by the U.S. Fish and Wildlife Service, Olympia, WA.

Hiss, J. M., and R. C. Wunderlich. 1994a. Salmonid availability and migration in the middle Elwha River system. Prepared for the National Park Service, Olympic National Park, Port Angeles, WA, by the U.S. Fish and Wildlife Service, Western Washington Fishery Resource Office, Olympia, WA.

Hiss, J., and R. Wunderlich. 1994b. Status of kokanee salmon (*Oncorhynchus nerka*) in the Lake Sutherland basin and prospects for sockeye salmon restoration. U.S. Fish and Wildlife Service, Western Washington Fishery Resource Office, Olympia, WA.

Hosey and Associates. 1987. Applicant's 3-month report. Filed with FERC (Federal Energy Regulatory Commission) 28 August 1987. Elwha Project and Glines Project, James River II Inc. Hosey and Associates Engineering Company, Bellevue, WA.

Hosey and Associates. 1988a. Response to request for additional information of 28 May 1977. Elwha Project (FERC No. 2683) and Glines Project (FERC No. 588) James River II Inc. Vol. 2 of 4. Prepared by Hosey and Associates for Perkins Coie, May 27, 1988. Hosey and Associates Engineering Company, Bellevue, WA.

Hosey and Associates. 1988b. Response to request for additional information of 28 May 1977. Elwha Project (FERC No. 2683) and Glines Project (FERC No. 588) James River II Inc. Vol. 3 of 4. Prepared by Hosey and Associates for Perkins Coie, May 27, 1988. Hosey and Associates Engineering Company, Bellevue, WA.

HSRG (Hatchery Scientific Review Group). 2002. Scientific framework and hatchery reform program. (Available from Long Live the Kings, 1305 Fourth Ave., Suite 810, Seattle, WA 98101.) Online at: www.hatcheryreform.org [accessed 5 October 2007].

HSRG (Hatchery Scientific Review Group). 2004. Letter dated 9 November 2004 to the Elwha Recovery Team. (Available from L. Ward, Lower Elwha Klallam Tribe, 51 Hatchery Rd., Port Angeles, WA 98363.)

Johnson, O. W., W. S. Grant, R. G. Kope, K. Neely, F. W. Waknitz, and R. S. Waples. 1997. Status review of chum salmon from Washington, Oregon, and California. U.S. Dept. Commer., NOAA Tech. Memo. NMFS-NWFSC-32.

Johnson, P. R. 1997. Elwha River historical narrative. Olympic National Park, Port Angeles, WA.

JFWA (Joint Fish and Wildlife Agencies). 1988. Comments in response to FERC (Federal Energy Regulatory Commission) request for additional information of 28 May 1987.

Kapuscinski, A., and L. Miller. 1993. Genetic hatchery guidelines for the Yakima/Klickitat fisheries project. Co-Aqua, St. Paul, MN.

Katz, M., D. E. Weitkamp, and R. F. Campbell. 1975. Compensation for Elwha River game fish losses. Document #75-0228-013FR. Submitted to Crown Zellerbach Corp. by Parametrix Inc., Seattle, WA.

Kostow, K. 2002. Oregon lampreys: Natural history status and problem analysis. Oregon Dept. Fish and Wildlife, Corvallis.

Lane and Lane Associates. 1990. The conflict between Indian terminal fisheries and hydropower on the Elwha River. Prepared for the Lower Elwha Klallam Tribe, Lower Elwha Indian Reservation, Port Angeles, WA. Lane and Lane Associates.

Leary, R. F., and F. W. Allendorf. 1997. Genetic confirmation of sympatric bull trout and Dolly Varden in western Washington. Trans. Am. Fish. Soc. 126:715–720.

LEKT (Lower Elwha Klallam Tribe). 2003a. Hatchery and genetic management plan: Lower Elwha fish hatchery. Coho salmon. Lower Elwha Klallam Tribe, Port Angeles, WA.

LEKT (Lower Elwha Klallam Tribe). 2003b. Hatchery and genetic management plan: Lower Elwha fish hatchery. Chum salmon. Lower Elwha Klallam Tribe, Port Angeles, WA.

LEKT (Lower Elwha Klallam Tribe). 2003c. Hatchery and genetic management plan: Lower Elwha fish hatchery. Steelhead salmon. Lower Elwha Klallam Tribe, Port Angeles, WA.

LEKT (Lower Elwha Klallam Tribe). 2006. Spawner escapement database. Lower Elwha Klallam Tribe, Port Angeles, WA.

Leopold, L. B., M. G. Wolman, and J. P. Miller. 1964. Fluvial processes in geomorphology. W. H. Freeman, San Francisco.

McBride, A., and E. Beamer. 2004. Geomorphic classification for estuaries and shorelines within Whidbey Basin. Skagit River System Cooperative, La Conner, WA.

McElhany, P., M. H. Ruckelshaus, M. J. Ford, T. C. Wainwright, and E. P. Bjornstedt. 2000. Viable salmonid populations and the recovery of evolutionarily significant units. U.S. Dept. Commer., NOAA Tech. Memo. NMFS-NWFSC-42.

McHenry, M. L., J. Lichatowich, and R. Kowalski-Hagaman. 1996. Status of Pacific salmon and their habitats on the Olympic Peninsula, Washington. Lower Elwha Klallam Tribe, Department of Fisheries, Port Angeles, WA.

McHenry, M. L., J. Petersen, and R. McCoy. Unpubl. manuscr. Elwha River project: A summary of restoration activities during 1999–2000. (Available from M. McHenry, Lower Elwha Klallam Tribe, Fisheries Department, 51 Hatchery Rd., Port Angeles, WA 98363.)

Milner, A. M., and York, G. S. 2001. Salmonid colonization of a new stream in Kenai Fjords National Park, Southeast Alaska. Arch. Hydrobiol. 151:627–647.

Montgomery, D. R., and J. M. Buffington. 1993. Channel classification, prediction of channel response, and assessment of channel condition. Report TFW-SH10-93-002. Washington Dept. Natural Resources, Olympia.

Morrill, D. M., and M. McHenry. Unpubl. manuscr. Elwha River fish community study. (Available from M. McHenry, Lower Elwha Klallam Tribe, Fisheries Department, 51 Hatchery Rd., Port Angeles, WA 98363.)

Myers, J. M., R. G. Kope, G. J. Bryant, D. Teel, L. J. Lierheimer, T. C. Wainwright, W. S. Grant, F. W. Waknitz, K. Neely, S. T. Lindley, and R. S. Waples. 1998. Status review of Chinook salmon from Washington, Idaho, Oregon, and California. U.S. Dept. Commer., NOAA Tech. Memo. NMFS-NWFSC-35.

NMFS (National Marine Fisheries Service). 1999. Endangered and threatened species: Threatened status for three Chinook salmon evolutionarily significant units (ESUs) in Washington and Oregon, and endangered status of one Chinook salmon ESU in Washington. Final rule, notice of determination. Federal Register [Docket No. 990303060-9071-02, 24 March 1999] 64(56):14308–14328.

NMFS (National Marine Fisheries Service). 2003. Decision memorandum on a joint tribal and state resource management plan submitted under Limit 6 of the 4(d) Rule by the Puget Sound Treaty Tribes and Washington Dept. Fish and Wildlife for salmon fisheries and steelhead net fisheries affecting Puget Sound Chinook salmon.

NMFS (National Marine Fisheries Service). 2005a. Endangered and threatened species; final listing determinations; final rules and proposed rules. Federal Register [Docket No. 040525161-5155-02, 28 June 2005] 70(123):37160–37204.

NMFS (National Marine Fisheries Service). 2005b. Endangered and threatened species; recovery plans. Federal Register [Docket No. E5-7852, 27 December 2005] 70(247):76445–76447.

NMFS (National Marine Fisheries Service). 2006. Listing endangered and threatened species and designating critical habitat: 12-month finding on petition to list Puget Sound steelhead as an endangered or threatened species under the Endangered Species Act. Federal Register [Docket No. 060313064-6064-01, 29 March 2006] 71(60):15666–15680.

NMFS (National Marine Fisheries Service). 2007. Endangered and threatened species: Final listing determination for Puget Sound steelhead. [Docket No. 070123015-7086-02, 11 May 2007] 72(91):26722–26735.

NOPLE (North Olympic Peninsula Lead Entity). 2005a. North Olympic Peninsula Lead Entity strategy and process, version 4. Prepared by Peninsula Lead Entity Group, Port Angeles, WA. Online at http://noplegroup.org/NOPLE/ [accessed 1 October 2007].

NOPLE (North Olympic Peninsula Lead Entity). 2005b. Draft. North Olympic Peninsula Lead Entity nearshore strategy, version 4. Prepared by Peninsula Lead Entity Group, Port Angeles, WA. Online at http://noplegroup.org/NOPLE/ [accessed 1 October 2007].

Pess, G. R., M. McHenry, T. Beechie, and J. Daives. In press. Biological impacts of the Elwha River dams and potential salmonid responses to dam removal. Northwest Sci.

PFMC (Pacific Fishery Management Council). 1997. Puget Sound Salmon Stock Review Group report, 1997: An assessment of the status of Puget Sound Chinook and Strait of Juan de Fuca coho stocks as required under the salmon fishery management plan. PFMC, Portland, OR.

Phelps, R. P., J. M. Hiss, and R. J. Peters. 2001. Genetic relationships of Elwha River *Oncorhynchus mykiss* to hatchery-origin rainbow trout and Washington steelhead. Prepared for the National Park Service, Olympic National Park, Port Angeles, WA.

PNPTC (Point No Point Treaty Council), WDFW (Washington Dept. Fish and Wildlife), and Makah Tribe. 2003. 2003 management framework plan and salmon runs' status for the Strait of Juan de Fuca region. WDFW, Olympia.

PNPTC (Point No Point Treaty Council), WDFW (Washington Dept. Fish and Wildlife), Lower Elwha Klallam Tribe, and Makah Tribe. 2005. 2005 management framework plan and salmon runs' status for the Strait of Juan de Fuca region. WDFW, Olympia.

Pohl, M. M. 1999. The dams of the Elwha River, Washington: Downstream impacts and policy implications. Doctoral dissertation. Arizona State Univ., Tempe.

Powell, Madison. 1997. Summary report from tissue samples of kokanee and sockeye salmon. Submitted by letter to Roger Peters, USFWS, 17 February 1997. USFWS Fisheries Resource Office, Olympia, WA.

PSC (Pacific Salmon Commission). 2000. Pacific Salmon Treaty: 1999 revised annexes, memorandum of understanding (1985), and exchange of notes. (Available from PSC, 1155 Robson St., Suite 600, Vancouver, BC V6E 189.)

PSMFC (Pacific States Marine Fisheries Commission). 2006. Regional mark information system (RMIS). Portland, OR. Online at http://www.rmpc.org/ [accessed 13 July 2006].

PSIT (Puget Sound Indian Tribes) and WDFW (Washington Dept. Fish and Wildlife). 2004. Comprehensive management plan for Puget Sound Chinook: Harvest management component, 1 March 2004. Washington Dept. Fish and Wildlife, Olympia, WA. Online at http://wdfw.wa .gov/fish/papers/ps_chinook_management/harvest/ps_chinook_harvest.pdf [accessed 16 November 2007].

PSTT (Puget Sound Treaty Tribes) and WDFW (Washington Dept. Fish and Wildlife). 2004. Resource management plan: Puget Sound hatchery strategies for steelhead, coho salmon, chum salmon, sockeye salmon, and pink salmon, 31 March 2004. Northwest Indian Fisheries Commission, Lacey, WA.

Quinn, T. P. 1993. A review of homing and straying of wild and hatchery-produced salmon. Fish. Res. 18:29–44.

Quinn, T. P. 2004. The behavior and ecology of Pacific salmon and trout. University of Washington Press, Seattle.

Quinn, T. P., J. L. Nielson, C. Gan, M. J. Unwin, R. J. Wilmot, C. M. Guthrie, and F. M. Utter. 1996. Origin and genetic structure of Chinook salmon (*Oncorhynchus tshawytscha*) transplanted to New Zealand. Fish. Bull. 94:506–521.

Randle, T. J., C. A. Young, J. T. Melena, and E. M. Ouellette. October 1996. Sediment analysis and modeling of the river erosion alternative. Elwha Technical Series PN-95-9. U.S. Department of the Interior, Bureau of Reclamation, Boise, ID.

Randle, T. J., J. Bountry, B. Jackson, and G. Smillie. 2003. Elwha River restoration draft sediment monitoring and management plan: Recommendations of the Elwha River physical processes monitoring workshop, 13–17 August 2001. U.S. Bureau of Reclamation, Port Angeles, WA.

Reisenbichler, R. R., and J. D. McIntyre. 1977. Genetic differences in growth and survival of juvenile hatchery and wild steelhead trout, *Salmon gairdneri*. J. Fish. Res. Board Can. 34:123–128.

Reisenbichler, R. R., and S. R. Phelps. 1989. Genetic variation in steelhead trout (*Salmon gairdneri*) from the north coast of Washington State. Can. J. Fish. Aquat. Sci. 46:66–73.

Reisenbichler, R. R., and S. P. Rubin. 1999. Genetic changes from artificial propagation of Pacific salmon affect the productivity and viability of supplemented populations. ICES J. Mar. Sci. 56:459–466.

Rieman, B. E., and F. W. Allendorf. 2001. Effective population size and genetic conservation criteria for bull trout. N. Am. J. Fish. Manag. 21:756–764.

Rieman, B. E., and J. D. McIntyre. 1993. Demographic and habitat requirements for conservation of bull trout. General Tech. Rep. INT-302. U.S. Forest Service, Intermountain Research Station, Ogden, UT.

Ruckelshaus, M. H., K. P. Currens, W. H. Graeber, R. R. Fuersterberg, K. Rawson, N. J. Sands, and J. B. Scott. 2006. Independent populations of Chinook salmon in Puget Sound. U.S. Dept. Commer., NOAA Tech. Memo. NMFS-NWFSC-78.

Salmon Recovery Science Review Panel. 2001. Report for meeting held 27–29 August 2001. Northwest Fisheries Science Center, Seattle, WA.

Schwartz, M. L. 1994. Beach geomorphology of the Elwha river delta in connection with removal of the Elwha and Glines canyon dams. Coastal Consultants Inc., Bellingham, WA.

Scott, W. B., and E. J. Crossman. 1973. Freshwater fishes of Canada. Fisheries Research Board of Canada, Ottawa.

Seiler, D. 1991. Coho production potential above Snoqualmie Falls. Washington Dept. Fisheries memorandum from D. Seiler to B. Gerke dated 15 January 1991. (Available from D. Morrill, Lower Elwha Klallam Tribe, 51 Hatchery Road, Port Angeles, WA 98363.)

Seiler, D. 2000. Natural production of anadromous salmonids in three western Washington watersheds formerly inaccessible to migratory fish. Presentation to the 2000 Annual Western Division American Fisheries Society Meeting, 16–20 July 2000. Telluride, CO.

Shaklee, J. B., D. C. Klaybor, S. Young, and B. A. White. 1991. Genetic stock structure of odd-year pink salmon, *Oncorhynchus gorbuscha*, from Washington and British Columbia and potential mixed-stock fisheries applications. J. Fish Biol. 39:21–34.

Shaffer, J. A. 2000. Seasonal variation in understory kelp bed habitats of the Strait of Juan de Fuca. J. Coast. Res. 16(3):768–775.

Shaffer, J. A., P. Crain, B. Winter, and M. McHenry. 2004. Nearshore restoration of the central Strait of Juan de Fuca and the Elwha and Glines Canyon dams removal. *In* Proceedings, Restore America's Estuaries Conference, September 2004, Seattle. Restore America's Estuaries (RAE), Arlington, VA.

Shaffer, J. A., L. Ward, P. Crain, B. Winter, K. Fresh, and C. Lear. 2005. Elwha and Glines Canyon dam removals: Nearshore restoration and salmon recovery of the central Strait of Juan de Fuca. *In* Proceedings of the 2005 Puget Sound Georgia Basin Research Committee, 29-31 March 2005. Puget Sound Action Team, Olympia, WA.

Shared Salmon Strategy for Puget Sound. 2005. Draft salmon recovery plan for Puget Sound, 30 June 2005—Revised December 2005, vols. 1 and 2. Submitted to NOAA Fisheries Service by Shared Strategy Development Committee, Seattle, WA.

Small, M. 2004. Elwha, Dungeness, and Morse pink salmon report, January 2003. Draft report, 6 January 2004. Washington Dept. Fish and Wildlife, Olympia.

Stolnack, S., and R. Neiman. 2005. Summary of research and education activities in the Elwha River watershed and adjacent coastal zone. Univ. Washington, School of Aquatic and Fishery Sciences, Seattle.

Thom, R. M., and L. K. Hallum (Wetland Ecosystem Team). 1991. Long-term changes in the extent of tidal marshes, eelgrass meadows, and kelp forests of Puget Sound. Final report to EPA. FRI-UW-9008 and EPA 910/91-005. Univ. Washington. School of Aquatic and Fishery Sciences, Fisheries Research Institute, Seattle.

Thrower, F. P., and J. E. Joyce. 2004. Effects of 70 years of freshwater residency on survival, growth, early maturation, and smolting in a stock of anadromous rainbow trout from Southeast Alaska. Am. Fish. Soc. Symp. 44:485–496.

Tipping, J. 2003. Using acclimation ponds in the rearing of salmon. *In* Hatchery Scientific Review Group (HSRG), April 2004, Hatchery reform: Principles and recommendations of the HSRG, p. B68–B74. (Available from Long Live the Kings, 1305 Fourth Ave., Suite 810, Seattle, WA 98101.) Online at: www.hatcheryreform.org [accessed 5 October 2007].

USDOS (U.S. Department of State), and NMFS (National Marine Fisheries Service). 1999. Biological opinion: Approval of the Pacific Salmon Treaty by the U.S. Department of State and management of the southeast Alaska salmon fisheries subject to the Pacific Salmon Treaty. Endangered Species Act—Reinstated section 7 consultations.

USFWS (U.S. Fish and Wildlife Service). 2000. Appendix B: Final biological opinion for the Elwha River restoration project (FWS Ref: 1-3-00-F-0606). Memorandum to Superintendent, Olympic National Park, Port Angeles, WA.

USFWS (U.S. Fish and Wildlife Service). 2004. Draft recovery plan for Coastal-Puget Sound distinct population segment of bull trout (*Salvelinus confluentus*), vol. II (of II). Olympic Peninsula Management Unit. Portland, OR. Online at http://www.fws.gov/pacific/bulltrout/jcs/documents/OlyPenPt1.pdf [accessed 5 October 2007].

USFWS (U.S. Fish and Wildlife Service). 2005. Natural reproductive success and demographic effects of hatchery-origin steelhead in Abernathy Creek, Washington. Annual Rep., January 2005–December 2005. U.S. Fish and Wildlife Service, Abernathy Fish Technology Center, Longview, WA.

USGS (U.S. Geological Survey). Unpubl. data. McDonald Bridge gauge. Online at http://wa.water.usgs.gov/cgi/adr.cgi?12045500 [accessed 5 October 2007].

VanBlaricom, G. R., and M. D. Chambers. 2003. Testing a charismatic paradigm: Consequences of a growing sea otter population for nearshore benthic communities along the south shore of the Strait of Juan de Fuca. U.S. Geological Survey, Washington Cooperative Fish and Wildlife Research Unit, Biological Resources Division, and Univ. Washington, School of Aquatic and Fishery Sciences, Seattle.

Vernon, E. H. 1966. Enumeration of migrant pink salmon fry in the Fraser River estuary. Int. Pac. Salmon Fish. Comm. Bull. 19.

Waples, R. S. 1991. Genetic interactions between hatchery and wild salmonids: Lessons from the Pacific Northwest. Can. J. Fish. Aquat. Sci. 48(Suppl. 1):124–133.

Waples, R. S. 1999. Dispelling some myths about hatcheries. Fisheries 24(2):12–29.

Wampler, P. L. 1984. Radio telemetry assessment of adult summer run steelhead behavior following release in the upper Elwha River. U.S. Fish and Wildlife Service, Fisheries Assistance Office, Olympia, WA.

WDF (Washington Dept. Fisheries). 1971. Elwha River fisheries studies. Financed by Crown Zellerbach Corp., contract no. 0313. Washington Dept. Fisheries, Management Research Division, Olympia.

WDF (Washington Dept. Fisheries). 1981. Methods for estimating escapement objectives for north coastal Washington salmon stocks. Washington Dept. Fisheries, Olympia.

WDF (Washington Dept. Fisheries), and Crown Zellerbach Corp. 1975. 25 April 1975 settlement agreement regarding licensing of Elwha Dam (FERC No. 2663) and Glines Canyon Dam (FERC No. 588). Washington Dept. Fisheries, Olympia.

WDFW (Washington Dept. Fish and Wildlife). 1996. Memorandum 10 September 1996 from L. LeClair and S. Phelps (WDFW) to D. Morrill (Lower Elwha Klallam Tribe). Subject: Elwha River chum salmon analysis. Washington Dept. Fish and Wildlife, Olympia.

WDFW (Washington Dept. Fish and Wildlife). 2002. Hatchery and genetic management plan—Elwha River summer/fall Chinook. Washington Dept. Fish and Wildlife, Olympia.

WDFW (Washington Dept. Fish and Wildlife). 2005. Hatchery and genetic management plan: Elwha summer/fall Chinook. August 2005 draft. Washington Dept. Fish and Wildlife, Fish Program, Science Division, Olympia.

WDFW (Washington Dept. Fish and Wildlife) and PNPTC (Point No Point Treaty Council). 2005. 2004 Progress report on Hood Canal summer chum salmon. Memorandum dated 10 February 2005. Washington Dept. Fish and Wildlife, Olympia.

WDFW (Washington Dept. Fish and Wildlife) and PNPTC (Point No Point Treaty Council). 2006. 2005 Progress report on Hood Canal summer chum salmon. Memorandum dated 1 March 2006. Washington Dept. Fish and Wildlife, Olympia.

WDFW (Washington Dept. Fish and Wildlife) and PNPTT (Point No Point Treaty Tribes). 2003. Report on summer chum salmon stock assessment and management activities for 2001 and 2002. Supplemental Rep. No. 4, Summer chum salmon conservation initiative: An implementation plan to recover summer chum in the Hood Canal and Strait of Juan de Fuca. October 2003. Washington Dept. Fish and Wildlife, Olympia.

WDFW (Washington Dept. Fish and Wildlife) and PSTT (Puget Sound Treaty Tribes). 2004. Puget Sound Chinook salmon hatcheries, a component of the comprehensive Chinook salmon management plan. 31 March 2004. Northwest Indian Fisheries Commission, Lacey, WA.

WDFW (Washington Dept. Fish and Wildlife) and WWTIT (Western Washington Treaty Indian Tribes). 1994. 1992 Washington state salmon and steelhead stock inventory: Appendix one Puget Sound stocks, Hood Canal and Strait of Juan de Fuca, Vol. 1. Washington Dept. Fish and Wildlife, Olympia.

WDG (Washington Dept. Game). 1973. Preliminary analysis of game fish and wildlife resources of Elwha River drainage affected by Elwha and Glines Dams and preliminary proposals for compensation of project related losses. Washington Dept. Game, Olympia.

Winans, G. A., M. L. McHenry, J. Baker, A. Elz, A. Goodbla, E. Iwamoto, D. Kuligowski, K. M. Miller, M. P. Small, P. Spruell, and D. Van Doornik. In press. Genetic inventory of anadromous Pacific salmonids of the Elwha River prior to dam removal. Northwest Sci. 82.

WSCC (Washington State Conservation Commission). 2000. Salmon and steelhead habitat limiting factors—Water Resource Inventory Area 18, Dungeness/Elwha Watershed. Washington State Conservation Commission, Olympia.

Wunderlich, R. C., and S. Dilley. 1990. Chinook and coho emigration in the Elwha River. U.S. Fish and Wildlife Service, Fisheries Assistance Office, Olympia, WA.

Wunderlich, R. C., S. J. Dilley, and E. E. Knudsen. 1989. Timing, exit selection, and survival of steelhead and coho smolts at Glines Canyon Dam. U.S. Fish and Wildlife Service, Fisheries Assistance Office, Olympia, WA.

Wunderlich, R. C., S. Hager, and Lower Elwha Klallam Tribe. 1993. Elwha River spring Chinook stock status evaluation. U.S. Fish and Wildlife Service, Fisheries Assistance Office, Olympia, WA.

Wunderlich, R. C., C. Pantaleo, and R. Wiswell. 1994. Elwha River chum salmon surveys, 1993–1994. September 1994. Prepared for Olympic National Park. U.S. Fish and Wildlife Service, Olympia, WA.

Wunderlich, R., and C. Pantaleo. 1995. A review of methods to re-introduce anadromous fish in the Elwha River. U.S. Fish and Wildlife Service, Western Washington Fishery Resource Office, Olympia, WA.

Zillges, G. 1977. Methodology for determining Puget Sound coho escapement goals, escapement estimates, 1977 pre-season run size prediction, and in-season run assessment. Tech. Rep. No. 28. Washington Dept. Fisheries, Olympia.

Appendix A: Hatchery Production Matrices

This appendix provides matrices of hatchery production data related to the Elwha River Fish Restoration Plan. For each species, the accompanying 35 tables provide data for estimated production and restoration strategies broken down in stages (before, during, and after removal of the Elwha and Glines Canyon dams on the Elwha River, Olympic National Park).

Table A-1. Estimated Chinook salmon (*Oncorhynchus tshawytscha*) production before, during, and after dam removal.*

Adults returning		Production projections			
Total	Female	Green eggs	Eyed eggs	Age-0 smolts	Yearling smolts
100	50	250,000	225,000	200,000	180,000
200	100	500,000	450,000	400,000	360,000
500	250	1,250,000	1,125,000	1,000,000	900,000
750	375	1,875,000	1,687,500	1,500,000	1,350,000
1,000	500	2,500,000	2,250,000	2,000,000	1,800,000
2,000	1,000	5,000,000	4,500,000	4,000,000	3,600,000
4,000	2,000	10,000,000	9,000,000	8,000,000	7,200,000
>4,000	4,000	20,000,000	18,000,000	16,000,000	14,400,000

*Assumptions: Adult capture weir is in place for adult collection; sex ratio is 0.5; Eggs per female = 5,000. Rates of survival: green, 1; eyed, 0.9; age 0, 0.8; and yearling, 0.72. Egg equivalence rate (egg equivalents are the number of green eggs necessary to produce this amount of eggs or fish): green, 1; eyed, 0.9; age 0, 0.8; and yearling, 0.72.

Table A-2. Chinook salmon restoration strategies before dam removal.[a]

Release strategy employed	Adults returning[b]							
	100	200	500	750	1,000	2,000	4,000	>4,000
Captive brood								
Elwha Channel yearling smolts	X	X	X	X	X	X	X	X
Morse Creek yearlings	X	X	X	X	X	X	X	X
Elwha Channel age-0 smolts			X	X	X	X	X	X
Natural spawners[c]				X	X	X	X	X
Adults upstream								
Eggs upstream								
Fry upstream								
Age-0 smolts upstream								
Yearling smolts upstream								

[a] Assumptions: Adult capture weir is in place for adult collection. Upstream access and passage: No upstream access by adults.

[b] If egg takes exceed targeted levels, outplants of eyed eggs and fry will be considered.

[c] At returns of 750 to 1,000 minimum, 250 adult brood are needed for natural spawning; at returns of 1,000 to 2,000 maximum, 500 adult brood are needed for natural spawning.

Table A-3. Chinook salmon restoration production numbers before dam removal.[a]

Programming production options	Adults returning							
	100	200	500	750	1,000	2,000	4,000	>4,000
Potential egg production available[b]	250,000	500,000	1,250,000	1,875,000	2,500,000	5,000,000	10,000,000	20,000,000
Release strategy								
Elwha Channel yearling smolts	175,000	180,000	200,000	200,000	200,000	200,000	200,000	200,000
Morse Creek yearlings		180,000	200,000	200,000	200,000	200,000	200,000	200,000
Morse Creek age-0 smolts								
Elwha Channel age-0 smolts			555,000	1,050,000	1,050,000	2,550,000	3,526,000	3,665,000
Age-0 smolts LEKT								
Natural spawners[c]				65	315	565	2,077	5,945
Adults upstream								
Eggs upstream								
Fry upstream								
Age-0 smolts upstream								
Yearling smolts upstream								
Total egg programmed production[d]	0	0	0	162,500	787,500	1,412,500	5,192,500	14,862,500
Total age-0 programmed production[d]	0	0	555,000	1,050,000	1,050,000	2,550,000	3,526,000	3,665,000
Total yearling smolt programmed production[d]	175,000	360,000	400,000	400,000	400,000	400,000	400,000	400,000
Total programmed production	175,000	360,000	955,000	1,612,500	2,237,500	4,362,500	9,118,500	18,927,500
Unprogrammed egg production	6,944	0	694	0	0	0	0	694

[a] Assumptions: Adult capture weir is in place for adult collection. Upstream access and passage: No upstream access by adults. Programming assumptions: re age-0 Washington Department of Fish and Wildlife (WDFW), production goal is 125 to 250 adults back per year or 500 to 1,000 adults per generation; re yearling WDFW, survival = 0.3%; 40,000 to 80,000 release for targeted return of 125 to 500 adults.
[b] If egg takes exceed targeted levels, outplants of eyed eggs and fry will be considered.
[c] 250 = minimum adult brood needed for natural spawning; 500 = maximum adult brood needed for natural spawning.
[d] Programmed production includes deduction of eggs from adults into the system.

Table A-4. Chinook salmon restoration strategies during dam removal.[a]

Release strategy employed	Adults returning							
	100	200	500	750	1,000	2,000	4,000	>4,000
Captive brood								
Elwha Channel yearling smolts	X	X	X	X	X	X	X	X
Morse Creek yearlings	X	X	X	X	X	X	X	X
Morse Creek age-0 smolts								
Elwha Channel age-0 smolts			X	X	X	X	X	X
Age-0 smolts LEKT[b]								
Natural spawners						X	X	X
Adults upstream						X	X	X
Eggs upstream								
Fry upstream								
Age-0 smolts upstream								
Yearling smolts upstream								

[a] Assumptions: Adult capture weir is in place for adult collection; water production limited to 22 cfs. Water quality: Maximum sediment impacts occurring. Upstream access and passage: No upstream access for adults; outplanted fry upstream will have access to the upstream areas. Assumes no natural spawners, but there may be some anyway. If egg takes exceed targeted levels, outplants of eyed eggs and fry will be considered.
[b] Lower Elwha Klallam Tribe hatchery.

Table A-5. Chinook salmon restoration production numbers during dam removal.[a]

Programming production options	Adults returning							
	100	200	500	750	1,000	2,000	4,000	>4,000
Potential egg production available[b]	250,000	500,000	1,250,000	1,875,000	2,500,000	5,000,000	10,000,000	20,000,000
Release strategy								
Elwha Channel yearling smolts	175,000	180,000	200,000	200,000	200,000	200,000	200,000	200,000
Morse Creek yearlings		180,000	200,000	200,000	200,000	200,000	200,000	200,000
Morse Creek age-0 smolts								
Elwha Channel age-0 smolts			555,000	805,000	855,000	1,250,000	1,250,000	1,250,000
Age-0 smolts LEKT								
Natural spawners								
Adults upstream						903	2,778	6,778
Eggs upstream								
Fry upstream								
Age-0 smolts upstream[c]				250,000	250,000	500,000	750,000	750,000
Yearling smolts upstream								
Total egg programmed production[d]	0	0	0	0	0	2,257,500	6,945,000	16,945,000
Total age-0 programmed production[d]	0	0	555,000	1,055,000	1,105,000	1,750,000	2,000,000	2,000,000
Total yearling smolt programmed production[d]	175,000	360,000	400,000	400,000	400,000	400,000	400,000	400,000
Total programmed production	175,000	360,000	955,000	1,455,000	1,505,000	4,407,500	9,345,000	19,345,000
Unprogrammed egg production	6,944	0	694	694	563,194	−556	−556	−556

[a] Assumptions: Adult capture weir is in place for adult collection; water production limited to 22 cfs. Water quality: Maximum sediment impact period. Upstream access and passage: Adults will have upstream access 2 years before dam removal. Programming assumptions: Age-0 WDFW: production goal is 125 to 250 adults back per year or 500 to 1,000 adults per generation. Yearling WDFW: survival = 0.3%; 40,000 to 80,000 release for targeted return of 125 to 500 adults.
[b] If egg takes exceed targeted levels, outplants of eyed eggs and fry will be considered.
[c] Fingerlings released on station as subyearling smolts 2 years before dam removal.
[d] Programmed production includes deduction of eggs from adults into the system.

133

Table A-6. Chinook salmon restoration strategies after dam removal.[a]

Release strategy employed	Adults returning							
	100	200	500	750	1,000	2,000	4,000	>4,000
Captive brood								
Elwha Channel yearling smolts	X	X	X	X	X	X	X	X
Morse Creek yearlings								
Morse Creek age-0 smolts[b]								
Elwha Channel age-0 smolts			X	X	X	X	X	X
Age-0 smolts LEKT								
Natural spawners[c, d]			X	X	X	X	X	X
Adults upstream								
Directed fishery								
Eggs upstream[e]								
Fry upstream								
Age-0 smolts upstream				X	X	X	X	X
Yearling smolts upstream				X	X	X	X	X

[a] Assumptions: Adult capture weir is in place and will be phased out. Water quality: Sediment impacts peaking and reducing; potential for major sediment impacts remains. Hatchery water systems: Water treatment system off-line; hatchery water is raw surface water supplemented by groundwater. Upstream access and passage: Full upstream and downstream access is available.

[b] Out-of-basin release and recovery program will be phased out as a tool for Elwha ecosystem restoration.

[c] At returns of 750 to 2,000 adults at minimum, 250 adult brood needed for natural spawning. At higher return rates, all additional fish will be permitted to spawn naturally.

[d] Natural spawners include adults in both upstream and downstream populations.

[e] If egg takes exceed targeted levels, outplants of eyed eggs and fry will be considered.

Table A-7. Chinook salmon restoration production numbers after dam removal.[a]

Programming production options	Adults returning							
	100	200	500	750	1,000	2,000	4,000	>4,000
Potential egg production available[b]	250,000	500,000	1,250,000	1,875,000	2,500,000	5,000,000	10,000,000	20,000,000
Release strategy employed								
Captive brood								200,000
Elwha Channel yearling smolts	180,000	180,000	200,000	200,000	200,000	200,000	200,000	200,000
Morse Creek yearlings[c]		180,000	200,000	200,000	200,000	200,000	200,000	200,000
Morse Creek age-0 smolts								
Elwha Channel age-0 smolts			500,000	546,000	805,000	2,200,000	2,200,000	2,200,000
Age-0 smolts LEKT								
Natural spawners[d, e]			250	250	250	490	2,365	6,303
Adults upstream[b]								
Eggs upstream[b]								
Fry upstream								
Age-0 smolts upstream				120,000	250,000	500,000	750,000	750,000
Yearling smolts upstream				100,000	200,000	200,000	200,000	200,000
Total egg programmed production[f]	0	0	625,000	625,000	625,000	1,225,000	5,912,500	15,757,500
Total age-0 programmed production[f]	0	0	500,000	666,000	1,055,000	2,700,000	2,950,000	2,950,000
Total yearling smolt programmed production[f]	180,000	360,000	400,000	300,000	400,000	400,000	400,000	400,000
Total programmed production	180,000	360,000	1,525,000	1,591,000	2,080,000	4,325,000	9,262,500	19,107,500
Unprogrammed egg production	0	0	0	833	694	0	0	−556

[a] Assumptions: Adult capture weir is in place and will be phased out; off-station outplants will be phased out as stocks rebuild; on-station releases and objectives will be reevaluated. Water quality: Surface water treatment system is off-line; hatchery water will be raw surface water supplemented with groundwater. Upstream access and passage: Adults will have upstream access.

[b] If egg takes exceed targeted levels, outplants of eyed eggs and fry will be considered.

[c] Out-of-basin release and recovery program will be phased out as a tool for Elwha ecosystem restoration.

[d] Goal: minimum 250 fish. At higher return rates, all additional fish will be permitted to spawn naturally.

[e] Natural spawners include adults in both upstream and downstream populations.

[f] Programmed production includes deduction of eggs from adults into the system.

135

Table A-8. Estimated winter steelhead (*Oncorhynchus mykiss*) production before, during, and after dam removal.*

Adults returning		Production projections				
Total	Female	Green eggs	Eyed eggs	Age-0 smolts	Yearling smolts	Two-year-old smolts
100	50	150,000	127,500	117,000	102,000	78,000
500	250	750,000	637,500	585,000	510,000	390,000
1,000	500	1,500,000	1,275,000	1,170,000	1,020,000	780,000
1,500	750	2,250,000	1,912,500	1,755,000	1,530,000	1,170,000
2,000	1,000	3,000,000	2,550,000	2,340,000	2,040,000	1,560,000
5,000	2,500	7,500,000	6,375,000	5,850,000	5,100,000	3,900,000
7,500	3,750	11,250,000	9,562,500	8,775,000	7,650,000	5,850,000
10,000	5,000	15,000,000	12,750,000	11,700,000	10,200,000	7,800,000
15,000	7,500	22,500,000	19,125,000	17,550,000	15,300,000	11,700,000

*Assumptions: Fish are at upper limit of return numbers; survival of fish is reduced due to use of wild stock. Sex ratio is 0.5. Eggs per female = 3,000. Rates of survival: green, 1; eyed, 0.85; age 0, 0.78; yearling, 0.68; and 2-year-old smolt, 0.52. Egg equivalence rate (egg equivalents are the number of green eggs necessary to produce this amount of eggs or fish): green, 1; eyed, 0.85; age 0, 0.78; yearling, 0.68; and 2-year-old smolt, 0.52.

Table A-9. Winter steelhead restoration strategies before dam removal.[a]

Release strategy employed	Adults returning[b]					
	100	500	1,000	1,500	2,000	5,000
Yearling on-station (late component)	X	X	X	X	X	X
Natural spawners[c]		X	X	X	X	X
Fishery[d]		X	X	X	X	X
Adults upstream					X	X
Eggs upstream[e]		X	X	X	X	X
Fry upstream[e]		X	X	X	X	X
Presmolts upstream[e, f]		X	X	X	X	X
Smolts upstream[e, f]					X	X
2-year-old smolts upstream						

[a] Assumptions: Adult capture weir is not in place during adult return period; alternate brood capture methods will be employed. Water availability: Hatchery water use is limited by current reduced production capabilities. Upstream access and passage: Upstream access by adults is not possible.

[b] Late-timed native-origin return (NOR) winter run stock is primary enhancement stock for restoration.

[c] Incidental natural spawning will occur, but is unprogrammed.

[d] Fishery is targeted on early timed component of run and will not harvest late component.

[e] First outplant of presmolts, smolts is three years before dam removal.

[f] Restoration program allotted total 36 helicopter flights per season.

Table A-10. Winter steelhead restoration production numbers before dam removal.[a]

Programming production options	Adults returning					
	100	500	1,000	1,500	2,000	5,000
Potential egg production available	150,000	750,000	1,500,000	2,250,000	3,000,000	7,500,000
Release strategy						
Yearling on-station (late component)[b]	102,000	125,000	125,000	125,000	125,000	125,000
Natural spawners[c]		100	577	1,077	1,577	4,577
Fishery[d]						
Adults upstream						
Eggs upstream		100,000	100,000	100,000	100,000	100,000
Fry upstream		220,000	250,000	250,000	250,000	250,000
Presmolts upstream (late component)[e]		20,000	20,000	20,000	20,000	20,000
Smolts upstream (late component)						
2-year-old smolts upstream						
Total egg programmed production[f]	0	250,000	965,500	1,715,500	2,465,500	6,965,500
Total age-0 programmed production[f]	0	220,000	250,000	250,000	250,000	250,000
Total yearling smolt programmed production[f]	102,000	145,000	145,000	145,000	145,000	145,000
Total programmed production	102,000	615,000	1,360,500	2,110,500	2,860,500	7,360,500
Unprogrammed egg production	0	4,713	752	752	752	752

[a] Assumptions: Adult capture weir is not in place during adult return period; alternate brood capture methods will be employed. Water quality: Hatchery water is raw surface water supplemented with groundwater. Water availability: Hatchery water use is limited by current reduced production capabilities. Upstream access and passage: Upstream access by adults is not possible. Production assumptions: Hatchery enhancement of early timed portion of run will continue during this period; late component of run is severely depressed; and capture of adults sufficient to achieve program goals may not occur during this period.
[b] Late-timed NOR winter run stock is primary enhancement stock for restoration.
[c] Incidental natural spawning will occur, but is unprogrammed.
[d] Fishery is targeted on early timed component of run and will not harvest late component.
[e] First outplanting of presmolts 3 years before dam removal.
[f] Programmed production includes deduction of eggs from adults into the system.

Table A-11. Winter steelhead restoration strategies during dam removal.[a]

Release strategy employed	Adults returning					
	100	500	1,000	1,500	2,000	5,000
Yearling on-station (late component)[b]	X	X	X	X	X	X
Natural spawners[c]						
Fishery[d]		X	X	X	X	X
Adults upstream[e]					X	X
Eggs upstream[f]					X	X
Fry upstream[g]					X	X
Presmolts upstream[h]	X	X	X	X	X	X
Smolts upstream[h]					X	X
2-year-old smolts upstream[i]		X	X	X	X	X

[a] Assumptions: Adult capture weir is not in place during return period; other adult capture methods will be used when necessary. Water quality: Maximum sediment impacts occurring. Upstream access and passage: Adults will have assisted access to the upstream areas.

[b] Late-timed NOR winter run stock is primary enhancement stock for restoration.

[c] Incidental natural spawning will occur, but is unprogrammed.

[d] Fishery is targeted primarily on early timed component of run. Harvest on late component implemented following stock status assessment.

[e] 100 adults needed for radio telemetry project.

[f] Start 4 years before dam removal.

[g] Start 3 years before dam removal via helicopter (outplant 2 years before dam removal, emigrate 1 year before dam removal).

[h] Outplants of presmolts and smolts to begin the year of dam removal.

[i] Production need for 2-year-old smolts to be based on fish response to hatchery environment.

Table A-12. Winter steelhead restoration production numbers during dam removal.[a]

Programming production options	Adults returning					
	100	500	1,000	1,500	2,000	5,000
Potential egg production available	150,000	750,000	1,500,000	2,250,000	3,000,000	7,500,000
Release strategy						
Yearling on-station (late component)[b]	80,000	100,000	100,000	100,000	100,000	100,000
Natural spawners[c]						
Fishery[d]						
Adults upstream[e]		39	537	1,037	1,537	4,537
Eggs upstream[f]		100,000	100,000	100,000	100,000	100,000
Fry upstream[g]		272,000	275,000	275,000	275,000	275,000
Presmolts upstream[h]	22,000	20,000	20,000	20,000	20,000	20,000
Smolts upstream[h]		25,000	25,000	25,000	25,000	25,000
2-year-old smolts upstream[i]		15,000	15,000	15,000	15,000	15,000
Total egg programmed production[j]	0	158,500	905,500	1,655,500	2,405,500	6,905,500
Total age-0 programmed production[j]	0	272,000	275,000	275,000	275,000	275,000
Total yearling smolt programmed production[j]	102,000	145,000	145,000	145,000	145,000	145,000
Total 2-year-old smolt programmed production[j]	0	15,000	15,000	15,000	15,000	15,000
Total programmed production	102,000	575,500	1,340,500	2,075,500	2,825,500	7,325,500
Unprogrammed egg production	0	701	-146	-146	-146	-146

[a] Assumptions: Lower river is not suitable for natural spawning. Water quality: Hatchery water is treated surface water, and groundwater is seasonally available. Water availability: Hatchery water use is limited by reduced treatment facility production capabilities. Upstream access and passage: Access to upper watershed by adults and downstream migration by juveniles possible.
[b] Late-timed NOR winter run stock is primary enhancement stock for restoration.
[c] Incidental natural spawning will occur, but is unprogrammed.
[d] Fishery is targeted primarily on early timed component of run harvest on late component implemented following stock status assessment.
[e] 100 adults needed for radio telemetry project.
[f] Start 2 years before dam removal.
[g] Start 2 years before dam removal via helicopter (outplant 2 years before dam removal, emigrate 1 year before dam removal).
[h] Outplants of presmolts and smolts to begin the year of dam removal.
[i] Production need for 2-year-old smolts to be based on fish response to hatchery environment.
[j] Programmed production includes deduction of eggs from adults into the system.

140

Table A-13. Winter steelhead restoration strategies after dam removal.[a]

Release strategy employed	Adults returning					
	100	500	1,000	1,500	2,000	5,000
Yearling on-station (late component)[b]	X	X	X	X	X	X
Natural spawners[c]		X	X	X	X	X
Fishery[d]		X	X	X	X	X
Eggs upstream[b]					X	X
Fry upstream[b]			X	X	X	X
Presmolts upstream[b]	X	X	X	X	X	X
Smolts upstream[b]		X	X	X	X	X
2-year-old smolts upstream[e]		X	X	X	X	X

[a] Assumptions: Water treatment system is off-line. Water quality: Maximum sediment impacts occurring. Hatchery water systems: Water treatment system is off-line; hatchery water is raw surface water supplemented by groundwater. Upstream access and passage: full upstream and downstream access.
[b] Hatchery production of late component will phase out as natural production increases to sustainable numbers.
[c] Natural spawners includes both upstream and downstream populations.
[d] Fishery is targeted primarily on early timed component of run. Harvest on late component implemented following stock status assessment.
[e] Production need for 2-year-old smolts to be based on fish response to hatchery environment.

Table A-14. Winter steelhead restoration production numbers after dam removal.[a]

Programming production options	Adults returning					
	100	500	1,000	1,500	2,000	5,000
Potential egg production available	150,000	750,000	1,500,000	2,250,000	3,000,000	7,500,000
Release strategy						
Yearling on-station[b]	80,000	100,000	100,000	100,000	100,000	100,000
Natural spawners[c, d]		37	537	1,037	1,537	4,537
Fishery[e]						
Eggs upstream[b]		100,000	100,000	100,000	100,000	100,000
Fry upstream[b]		275,000	275,000	275,000	275,000	275,000
Presmolts upstream[b]	22,000	20,000	20,000	20,000	20,000	20,000
Smolts upstream[b]		25,000	25,000	25,000	25,000	25,000
2-year-old smolts upstream[f]		15,000	15,000	15,000	15,000	15,000
Total egg programmed production[g]	0	155,500	905,500	1,655,500	2,405,500	6,905,500
Total age-0 programmed production[g]	0	275,000	275,000	275,000	275,000	275,000
Total yearling smolt programmed production[g]	102,000	145,000	145,000	145,000	145,000	145,000
Total 2-year-old smolt programmed production[g]	0	15,000	15,000	15,000	15,000	15,000
Total programmed production	102,000	575,500	1,325,500	2,075,500	2,825,500	7,325,500
Unprogrammed egg production	0	−146	−146	−146	−146	−146

[a] Assumptions: Water treatment system is off-line. Water quality: Hatchery water is raw surface water supplemented by groundwater. Water availability: Full complement of water is available. Upstream access and passage: Full watershed access is possible.

[b] Hatchery production of late component will phase out as natural production increases to sustainable numbers.

[c] Dungeness brood used if female numbers are less than 125.

[d] Natural spawners include both upstream and downstream populations.

[e] Fishery is targeted primarily on early timed component of run. Harvest on late component implemented following stock status assessment.

[f] Production need for 2-year-old smolts to be based on fish response to hatchery environment.

[g] Programmed production includes deduction of eggs from adults into the system.

Table A-15. Estimated coho salmon (*Oncorhynchus kisutch*) production before, during, and after dam removal.*

Adults returning		Production projections			
Total	Female	Green eggs	Eyed eggs	Age-0 smolts	Yearling smolts
100	50	125,000	112,500	100,000	90,000
500	250	625,000	562,500	500,000	450,000
1,000	500	1,250,000	1,125,000	1,000,000	900,000
1,500	750	1,875,000	1,687,500	1,500,000	1,350,000
2,000	1,000	2,500,000	2,250,000	2,000,000	1,800,000
5,000	2,500	6,250,000	5,625,000	5,000,000	4,500,000
7,500	3,750	9,375,000	8,437,500	7,500,000	6,750,000
10,000	5,000	12,500,000	11,250,000	10,000,000	9,000,000
15,000	7,500	18,750,000	16,875,000	15,000,000	13,500,000

*Assumptions: Fish are at upper limit of return numbers. Sex ratio is 0.5. Eggs per female = 2,500. Rates of survival: green, 1; eyed, 0.9; age 0, 0.8; yearling, 0.72. Egg equivalence rate (egg equivalents are the number of green eggs necessary to produce this amount of eggs or fish): green, 1; eyed, 0.9; age 0, 0.8; and yearling, 0.72.

Table A-16. Coho salmon restoration strategies before dam removal.[a]

Release strategy employed	Adults returning								
	100	500	1,000	1,500	2,000	5,000	7,500	10,000	15,000
Yearling on-station	X	X	X	X	X	X	X	X	X
Dungeness egg importations[b]	X	X							
Natural spawners[c]	X	X	X	X	X	X	X	X	X
Fishery[d]	X	X	X	X	X	X	X	X	X
Adults upstream									
Eggs upstream					X	X	X	X	X
Fry upstream					X	X	X	X	X
Presmolts upstream									
Smolts upstream									

[a] Assumptions: adult capture weir is not in place during return period; other adult capture methods will be used when necessary. Upstream access and passage: Upstream access by adults is not possible.
[b] Dungeness brood used if female numbers are less than 125 (hatchery returns and adult brood capture efforts).
[c] Incidental natural spawning will occur, but is unprogrammed.
[d] Fishery implemented if hatchery escapement goal is reached.

144

Table A-17. Coho salmon restoration production numbers before dam removal.[a]

Programming production options	Adults returning								
	100	500	1,000	1,500	2,000	5,000	7,500	10,000	15,000
Dungeness importations[b]	187,500								
Potential egg production available	312,500	625,000	1,250,000	1,875,000	2,500,000	6,250,000	9,375,000	12,500,000	18,750,000
Release strategy									
Yearling on-station	225,000	450,000	750,000	750,000	750,000	750,000	750,000	750,000	750,000
Natural spawners[c]									
Fishery[d]			166	666	1,166	4,166	6,666	9,166	14,166
Adults upstream[e]									
Eggs upstream									
Fry upstream									
Presmolts upstream									
Smolts upstream									
Total egg programmed production[f]	0	0	207,500	832,500	1,457,500	5,207,500	8,332,500	11,457,500	17,707,500
Total age-0 programmed production[f]	0	0	0	0	0	0	0	0	0
Total yearling smolt programmed production[f]	225,000	450,000	750,000	750,000	750,000	750,000	750,000	750,000	750,000
Total programmed production	225,000	450,000	957,500	1,582,500	2,207,500	5,957,500	9,082,500	12,207,500	18,457,500
Imported off station production	187,500	0	0	0	0	0	0	0	0
Unprogrammed egg production	0	0	833	833	833	833	833	833	833

[a] Assumptions: Adult capture weir is not in place during return period; other adult capture methods will be used when necessary. Water quality: Hatchery water is raw surface water supplemented with groundwater. Water availability: Hatchery water use is limited by current reduced production capabilities. Upstream access and passage: Upstream access by adults is not possible. Production assumptions: Rate of return of 0.5%; 125 to 250 adults return from release of 50,000 smolts.

[b] Dungeness brood used if female numbers are less than 125.

[c] Incidental natural spawning will occur, but is unprogrammed.

[d] Fishery implemented if hatchery escapement goal is reached.

[e] 100 = adult brood needed for radio telemetry project.

[f] Programmed production includes deduction of eggs from adults into the system.

Table A-18. Coho salmon restoration strategies during dam removal.[a]

Release strategy employed	Adults returning								
	100	500	1,000	1,500	2,000	5,000	7,500	10,000	15,000
Yearling on-station	X	X	X	X	X	X	X	X	X
Dungeness egg importations[b]	X	X							
Natural spawners[c]									
Fishery									
Adults upstream					X	X	X	X	X
Eggs upstream[d]					X	X	X	X	X
Fry upstream[e]					X	X	X	X	X
Presmolts upstream[f]					X	X	X	X	X
Smolts upstream[f]					X	X	X	X	X

[a] Assumptions: Adult capture weir is not in place during return period; other adult capture methods will be used when necessary. Water quality: Maximum sediment impacts occurring. Upstream access and passage: Adults will have assisted access to the upstream areas.
[b] Dungeness brood used if female numbers are less than 125 (to maintain minimum effective spawning population).
[c] Incidental natural spawning will occur, but is unprogrammed.
[d] Start by the year of dam removal.
[e] Start 1 year before dam removal via helicopter (outplant 1 year before dam removal; emigrate the year of dam removal).
[f] Outplants of presmolts and smolts to begin the year of dam removal.

146

Table A-19. Coho salmon restoration production numbers during dam removal.[a]

Programming production options	Adults returning								
	100	500	1,000	1,500	2,000	5,000	7,500	10,000	15,000
Dungeness egg importations[b]	187,500								
Potential egg production available	312,500	625,000	1,250,000	1,875,000	2,500,000	6,250,000	9,375,000	12,500,000	18,750,000
Release strategy									
Yearling on-station	225,000	425,000	425,000	425,000	425,000	425,000	425,000	425,000	425,000
Natural spawners[c]									
Fishery									
Adults upstream[d]			110	531	1,031	4,031	6,531	9,031	14,031
Eggs upstream[e,f]				100,000	100,000	100,000	100,000	100,000	100,000
Fry upstream[g]			300,000	300,000	300,000	300,000	300,000	300,000	300,000
Presmolts upstream[h]		15,000	75,000	75,000	75,000	75,000	75,000	75,000	75,000
Smolts upstream[h]		10,000	30,000	30,000	30,000	30,000	30,000	30,000	30,000
Total egg programmed production[i]	0	0	137,500	763,750	1,388,750	5,138,750	8,263,750	11,388,750	17,638,750
Total age-0 programmed production[i]	0	0	300,000	300,000	300,000	300,000	300,000	300,000	300,000
Total yearling smolt programmed production[i]	225,000	450,000	530,000	530,000	530,000	530,000	530,000	530,000	530,000
Total programmed production	225,000	450,000	967,500	1,593,750	2,218,750	5,968,750	9,093,750	12,218,750	18,468,750
Imported off station production	187,500	0	0	0	0	0	0	0	0
Unprogrammed egg production	0	0	1,389	139	139	139	139	139	139

[a] Assumptions: Lower river is not suitable for natural spawning. Water quality: Hatchery water is treated surface water; groundwater is seasonally available. Water availability: Hatchery water use is limited by reduced treatment facility production capabilities. Upstream access and passage: Access to upper watershed by adults and downstream migration by juveniles is possible.

[b] Dungeness brood used if female numbers are less than 125 (to maintain minimum effective spawning population).

[c] Incidental natural spawning will or may occur, but is unprogrammed.

[d] The ability to hold adults for transfer upstream above the Elwha Dam may be limited by water available at the hatchery.

[e] Start 2 years before dam removal.

[f] The ability to release fry upstream may be limited by water available for rearing at the hatchery.

[g] Helicopter outplants, start 2 years before dam removal (outplant 1 year before dam removal, emigrate the year of dam removal).

[h] Outplants of presmolts and smolts to begin 1 year before dam removal.

[i] Programmed production includes deduction of eggs from adults into the system.

Table A-20. Coho salmon restoration strategies after dam removal.[a]

Release strategy employed	Adults returning								
	100	500	1,000	1,500	2,000	5,000	7,500	10,000	15,000
Yearling on-station[b]	X	X	X	X	X	X	X	X	X
Dungeness egg importations[c]	X	X							
Natural spawners[d]	X	X	X	X	X	X	X	X	X
Fishery[e]		X	X	X	X	X	X	X	X
Eggs upstream[b]					X	X	X	X	X
Fry upstream[b]			X	X	X	X	X	X	X
Presmolts upstream[b]		X	X	X	X	X	X	X	X
Smolts upstream[b]		X	X	X	X	X	X	X	X

[a] Assumptions: Water treatment system is off-line. Water quality: Maximum sediment impacts occurring. Hatchery water systems: Water treatment system is off-line; hatchery water is raw surface water supplemented by groundwater. Upstream access and passage: Full upstream and downstream access.

[b] Hatchery production will phase out as natural production increases.

[c] Dungeness brood used if female numbers are less than 125.

[d] Natural spawners include both upstream and downstream populations.

[e] Fishery implemented if hatchery escapement goal is reached.

148

Table A-21. Coho salmon restoration production numbers after dam removal.[a]

Programming production options	Adults returning								
	100	500	1,000	1,500	2,000	5,000	7,500	10,000	15,000
Dungeness importations[b]	187,500								
Potential egg production available	312,500	625,000	1,250,000	1,875,000	2,500,000	6,250,000	9,375,000	12,500,000	18,750,000
Release strategy									
Yearling on-station[c]	225,000	425,000	425,000	750,000	750,000	750,000	750,000	750,000	750,000
Natural spawners[d]			286	425	845	2,345	3,845	4,845	9,845
Fishery[e]						1,500	2,500	4,000	4,000
Eggs upstream[c]					100,000	100,000	100,000	100,000	100,000
Fry upstream[c]			125,000	125,000	125,000	125,000	125,000	125,000	125,000
Presmolts upstream[c]		15,000	75,000	75,000	75,000	75,000	75,000	75,000	75,000
Smolts upstream[c]		10,000	30,000	30,000	30,000	30,000	30,000	30,000	30,000
Total egg programmed production[f]	0	0	357,500	531,250	1,156,250	4,906,250	8,031,250	11,156,250	17,406,250
Total age-0 programmed production[f]	0	0	125,000	125,000	125,000	125,000	125,000	125,000	125,000
Total yearling smolt programmed production[f]	225,000	450,000	530,000	855,000	855,000	855,000	855,000	855,000	855,000
Total programmed production	225,000	450,000	1,012,500	1,511,250	2,136,250	5,886,250	9,011,250	12,136,250	18,386,250
Imported off station production	187,500	0	0	0	0	0	0	0	0
Unprogrammed egg production	0	0	139	0	0	0	0	0	0

[a] Assumptions: Water treatment system is off-line. Water quality: Hatchery water is raw surface water supplemented by groundwater. Water availability: Full complement of water is available. Upstream access and passage: Full watershed access is possible.
[b] Dungeness brood used if female numbers are less than 125.
[c] Hatchery production will phase out as natural production increases.
[d] Natural spawners include both upstream and downstream populations.
[e] Fishery implemented if hatchery escapement goal is reached and natural escapement goal is met.
[f] Programmed production includes deduction of eggs from adults into the system.

Table A-22. Estimated chum salmon (*Oncorhynchus keta*) production (fall early and late runs) before, during, and after dam removal.*

| Adults returning | | Production projections | | |
Total	Female	Green eggs	Eyed eggs	Age-0 smolts
50	12.5	37,500	33,750	30,000
100	50.0	150,000	135,000	120,000
200	100.0	300,000	270,000	240,000
500	250.0	750,000	675,000	600,000
750	375.0	1,125,000	1,012,500	900,000
1,000	500.0	1,500,000	1,350,000	1,200,000
2,000	1,000.0	3,000,000	2,700,000	2,400,000

*Assumptions: Fish are at upper limit of return numbers. Sex ratio is 0.5. Eggs per female = 3,000. Rates of survival: green, 1; eyed, 0.9; and age 0, 0.8. Egg equivalence rate (egg equivalents are the number of green eggs necessary to produce this amount of eggs or fish): green, 1; eyed, 0.9; and age 0, 0.8.

Table A-23. Chum salmon restoration strategies (fall early and late runs) before dam removal.*

| Release strategy employed | Adults returning | | | | | | |
	50	100	200	500	750	1,000	2,000
Age-0 LEKT hatchery releases	X	X	X	X	X	X	X
Age-0 Elwha Channel releases				X	X	X	X
Eyed egg outplants			X	X	X	X	X
Natural spawners							
Adults upstream							
Eggs upstream							
Fry upstream							
Age-0 upstream							

*Assumptions: Adult capture weir will not be used for adult acquisition. Upstream access and passage: No upstream access by adults.

Table A-24. Chum salmon restoration production numbers (fall early and late runs) before dam removal.[a]

Programming production options	Adults returning						
	50	100	200	500	750	1,000	2,000
Potential egg production available	37,500	150,000	300,000	750,000	1,125,000	1,500,000	3,000,000
Release strategy							
Age-0 LEKT hatchery releases	31,000	75,000	75,000	75,000	75,000	75,000	75,000
Age-0 Elwha Channel releases		40,000	100,000	450,000	450,000	450,000	450,000
Eyed egg outplants			75,000	100,000	100,000	100,000	100,000
Natural spawners					250	500	1,500
Adults upstream							
Eggs upstream							
Fry upstream							
Total egg programmed production[b]	0	0	75,000	100,000	475,000	850,000	2,350,000
Total age-0 fingerling programmed production[b]	31,000	115,000	175,000	525,000	525,000	525,000	525,000
Total programmed production	31,000	115,000	250,000	625,000	1,000,000	1,375,000	2,875,000
Unprogrammed egg production	-1,250	6,250	6,250	-6,250	-6,250	-6,250	-6,250

[a] Assumptions: Adult capture weir will not be used for adult acquisition. Upstream access and passage: No upstream access by adults. Programming assumptions: re age-0 LEKT hatchery releases, assumed that LEKT hatchery capacity would be limited to 75,000 during hatchery construction period; re age-0 Elwha Channel releases, WDFW will be able to take on any additional chum production temporarily; re eyed egg outplants, assumed that 100 Jordan-Scotty incubators would be maximum possible outplanting effort; re natural spawners, received remaining potential production to reduce unprogrammed eggs to zero.
[b] Programmed production includes deduction of eggs from adults into the system.

Table A-25. Chum salmon restoration strategies (fall early and late runs) during dam removal.[a]

Release strategy employed	Adults returning					
	100	200	500	750	1,000	2,000
Age-0 LEKT hatchery releases	X	X	X	X	X	X
Age-0 Elwha Channel releases						
Eyed egg outplants	X	X	X	X	X	X
Natural spawners[b]	X	X	X	X	X	X
Adults upstream[b]				X	X	X
Eggs upstream[b]			X	X	X	X
Fry upstream[b]				X	X	X

[a] Assumptions: Adult capture weir will not be used for adult acquisition. Water quality: Maximum sediment impacts occurring. Upstream access and passage: No upstream access for adults; outplanted fry upstream will have access to the upstream areas.
[b] Enhancement to begin in the year of dam removal.

Table A-26. Chum salmon production numbers (fall early and late runs) during dam removal.[a]

Programming production options	Adults returning						
	50	100	200	500	750	1,000	2,000
Potential egg production available	37,500	150,000	300,000	750,000	1,125,000	1,500,000	3,000,000
Release strategy							
Age-0 LEKT hatchery releases	31,000	75,000	165,000	500,000	650,000	650,000	650,000
Age-0 Elwha Channel releases		40,000					
Eyed egg outplants			100,000	100,000	100,000		
Natural spawners[b]				20	140	460	1,460
Adults upstream							
Eggs upstream							
Fry upstream							
Total egg programmed production[c]	0	0	100,000	130,000	310,000	690,000	2,190,000
Total age-0 fingerling programmed production[c]	31,000	115,000	165,000	500,000	650,000	650,000	650,000
Total programmed production	31,000	115,000	265,000	630,000	960,000	1,340,000	2,840,000
Unprogrammed egg production	–1,250	6,250	–6,250	–5,000	2,500	–2,500	–2,500

[a] Assumptions: Adult capture weir will not be used for adult acquisition. Water quality: Maximum sediment impact period. Upstream access and passage: Adults will have upstream access in the year of dam removal. Programming assumptions: re age-0 LEKT hatchery releases, maximum engineered production potential of 650,000 assumed; re age-0 Elwha Channel releases, rearing potential of 40,000 assumed for Elwha Channel facility; re eyed egg outplants, assumed that 100 Jordan-Scotty incubators would be maximum possible outplanting effort; re natural spawners, received remaining potential production to reduce unprogrammed eggs to zero.

[b] Enhancement to begin with the year of dam removal.

[c] Programmed production includes deduction of eggs from adults into the system.

Table A-27. Chum salmon restoration strategies (fall early and late runs) after dam removal.*

Release strategy employed	Adults returning						
	50	100	200	500	750	1,000	2,000
Age-0 LEKT hatchery releases	X	X	X	X	X	X	X
Age-0 Elwha Channel releases							
Eyed egg outplants				X	X	X	X
Natural spawners				X	X	X	X
Adults upstream							
Eggs upstream				X	X	X	X
Fry upstream						X	X

*Assumptions: Adult capture weir will not be used for adult acquisition. Water quality: Sediment impacts peaking and reducing; potential for major sediment impacts remain. Hatchery water systems: Water treatment system off-line; hatchery water is raw surface water supplemented by groundwater. Upstream access and passage: Full upstream and downstream access is available.

Table A-28. Chum salmon production numbers (fall early and late runs) after dam removal.[a]

Programming production options	Adults returning						
	50	100	200	500	750	1,000	2,000
Potential egg production available	37,500	150,000	300,000	750,000	1,125,000	1,500,000	3,000,000
Release strategy							
Age-0 LEKT hatchery releases	31,000	120,000	240,000	300,000	300,000	300,000	300,000
Age-0 Elwha Channel releases							
Eyed egg outplants				250,000	250,000	250,000	250,000
Natural spawners				83	333	292	1,292
Adults upstream							
Eggs upstream							
Fry upstream					350,000	350,000	350,000
Total egg programmed production[b]	0	0	0	374,500	749,500	688,000	2,188,000
Total age-0 programmed production[b]	31,000	120,000	240,000	300,000	300,000	650,000	650,000
Total programmed production	31,000	120,000	240,000	674,500	1,049,500	1,338,000	2,838,000
Unprogrammed egg production	-1,250	0	0	500	500	-500	-500

[a] Assumptions: Adult capture weir will not be used for adult acquisition, off-station outplants will be phased out as stocks rebuild, and on-station releases and objectives will be reevaluated. Water quality: Surface water treatment system is off-line. Hatchery water systems: Hatchery water will be raw surface water supplemented with groundwater. Upstream access and passage: Adults will have upstream access. Programming assumptions: re age-0 LEKT hatchery releases, maximum production level of 300,000 assumed; re eyed egg outplants, 250 Jordan-Scotty incubators will be maximum outplanting effort; re natural spawners, received remaining potential production to reduce unprogrammed eggs to zero; re fry upstream, 350,000 will be maximum incubation and rearing potential.
[b] Programmed production includes deduction of eggs from adults into the system.

155

Table A-29. Estimated pink salmon (*Oncorhynchus gorbuscha*) production before, during, and after dam removal.*

Adults returning		Production projections		
Total	Female	Green eggs	Eyed eggs	Age-0 smolts
50	25	37,500	33,750	30,000
100	50	75,000	67,500	60,000
200	100	150,000	135,000	120,000
500	250	375,000	337,500	300,000
750	375	562,500	506,250	450,000
1,000	500	750,000	675,000	600,000
2,000	1,000	1,500,000	1,350,000	1,200,000

*Assumptions: Fish are at upper limit of return numbers. Sex ratio is 0.5. Eggs per female = 1,500. Rates of survival: green, 1; eyed, 0.9; and age 0, 0.8. Egg equivalence rate (egg equivalents are the number of green eggs necessary to produce this amount of eggs or fish): green, 1; eyed, 0.9; and age 0, 0.8.

Table A-30. Pink salmon restoration strategies before dam removal.*

Release strategy employed	Adults returning						
	50	100	200	500	750	1,000	2,000
Age-0 LEKT hatchery releases	X	X	X	X	X	X	X
Age-0 Elwha Channel releases				X	X	X	X
Eyed egg outplants			X	X	X	X	X
Natural spawners							X
Adults upstream							
Eggs upstream							
Fry upstream							
Age-0 upstream							

*Assumptions: Adult capture weir is in place. Upstream access and passage: No upstream access by adults.

Table A-31. Pink salmon restoration production numbers before dam removal.[a]

Programming production options	Adults returning						
	50	100	250	500	750	1,000	2,000
Potential egg production available[b]	37,500	75,000	150,000	375,000	562,500	750,000	1,500,000
Release strategy							
Age-0 LEKT hatchery releases	30,000	60,000	75,000	75,000	75,000	75,000	75,000
Age-0 Elwha Channel releases			45,000	225,000	375,000	450,000	450,000
Eyed egg outplants						93,750	100,000
Natural spawners							495
Adults upstream							
Eggs upstream							
Fry upstream							
Total egg programmed production[c]	0	0	0	0	0	0	0
Total age-0 fingerling programmed production[c]	30,000	60,000	120,000	300,000	450,000	525,000	525,000
Total programmed production	30,000	60,000	120,000	300,000	450,000	618,750	1,367,500
Unprogrammed egg production	0	0	0	0	0	0	1,250

[a] Assumptions: Adult capture weir is in place. Upstream access and passage: No upstream access by adults.
[b] Captive brood may be developed through egg collections from redds or capture of outmigrating smolts.
[c] Programmed production includes deduction of eggs from adults into the system.

157

Table A-32. Pink salmon restoration strategies during dam removal.*

Release strategy employed	Adults returning						
	50	100	200	500	750	1,000	2,000
Age-0 LEKT hatchery releases	X	X	X	X	X	X	X
Age-0 Elwha Channel releases							
Eyed egg outplants	X	X	X	X	X	X	
Natural spawners	X	X	X	X	X	X	
Adults upstream				X	X	X	X
Eggs upstream			X	X	X	X	
Fry upstream				X	X	X	

*Assumptions: Adult capture weir is in place; other capture strategies to be employed where necessary. Water quality: Maximum sediment impacts are occurring. Upstream access and passage: No upstream access for adults; outplanted fry upstream will have access to the upstream areas.

Table A-33. Pink salmon restoration production numbers during dam removal.[a]

Programming production options	Adults returning						
	50	100	200	500	750	1,000	2,000
Potential egg production available[b]	37,500	75,000	150,000	375,000	562,500	750,000	1,500,000
Release strategy							
Age-0 LEKT hatchery releases	30,000	60,000	120,000	300,000	450,000	600,000	650,000
Age-0 Elwha Channel releases							
Eyed egg outplants							100,000
Natural spawners							391
Adults upstream							
Eggs upstream							
Fry upstream							
Total egg programmed production[c]	0	0	0	0	0	0	686,500
Total age-0 fingerling programmed production[c]	30,000	60,000	120,000	300,000	450,000	600,000	650,000
Total programmed production	30,000	60,000	120,000	300,000	450,000	600,000	1,336,500
Unprogrammed egg production	0	0	0	0	0	0	1,000

[a] Assumptions: Adult capture weir is in place during adult return period. Water quality: Maximum sediment impact period. Upstream access and passage: Adults will have upstream access in the year of dam removal.
[b] Captive brood may be developed through egg collections from redds or capture of outmigrating smolts.
[c] Programmed production includes deduction of eggs from adults into the system.

Table A-34. Pink salmon restoration strategies after dam removal.*

Release strategy employed	Adults returning						
	50	100	200	500	750	1,000	2,000
Age-0 LEKT hatchery releases	X	X	X	X	X	X	X
Age-0 Elwha Channel releases							
Eyed egg outplants				X	X	X	X
Natural spawners				X	X	X	X
Adults upstream							
Eggs upstream				X	X	X	X
Fry upstream						X	X

*Assumptions: Adult capture weir is in place and will be phased out. Water quality: Sediment impacts peaking and reducing; potential for major sediment impacts remain. Hatchery water systems: Water treatment system is off-line; hatchery water is raw surface water supplemented by groundwater. Upstream access and passage: Full upstream and downstream access is available.

Table A-35. Pink salmon restoration production numbers after dam removal.[a]

Programming production options	Adults returning						
	50	100	200	500	750	1,000	2,000
Potential egg production available[b]	37,500	75,000	150,000	375,000	562,500	750,000	1,500,000
Release strategy							
Age-0 LEKT hatchery releases	30,000	60,000	120,000	300,000	450,000	600,000	650,000
Age-0 Elwha Channel releases							
Eyed egg outplants							100,000
Natural spawners							391
Adults upstream							
Eggs upstream							
Fry upstream							
Total egg programmed production[c]	0	0	0	0	0	0	686,500
Total age-0 programmed production[c]	30,000	60,000	120,000	300,000	450,000	600,000	650,000
Total programmed production	30,000	60,000	120,000	300,000	450,000	600,000	1,336,500
Unprogrammed egg production	0	0	0	0	0	0	1,000

[a] Assumptions: Adult capture weir is in place and will be phased out, off-station outplants will be phased out as stocks rebuild, and on-station releases and objectives will be reevaluated. Water quality: Surface water treatment system is off-line. Hatchery water systems: Hatchery water will be raw surface water supplemented with groundwater. Upstream access and passage: Adults will have upstream access.
[b] Captive brood may be developed through egg collections from redds or capture of outmigrating smolts.
[c] Programmed production includes deduction of eggs from adults into the system.

Appendix B: Chinook Salmon Harvest Management

[Editor's note: Chris Weller, Point No Point Treaty Council, wrote the Chinook Salmon Harvest Management for the Elwha chapter of the Puget Sound Salmon Recovery Plan and allowed it to be incorporated into this plan as Appendix B.]

Elwha Chinook salmon (*Oncorhynchus tshawytscha*) levels are in a depressed state and have been listed as a threatened component population of the Puget Sound Chinook salmon evolutionarily significant unit (ESU) (NMFS 1999). Because of this status, they are not specifically targeted for fisheries harvest. However, some Elwha Chinook salmon are harvested in mixed stock Chinook salmon fisheries where they are a relatively small portion of the catch (e.g., U.S. saltwater recreational, U.S. troll, and Canadian and Alaskan fisheries) or are incidentally caught in fisheries for other species (e.g., coho [*O. kisutch*], sockeye [*O. nerka*] , and pink [*O. gorbuscha*] salmon). Currently the harvest management objective is to limit the incidental impacts of these fisheries on Elwha Chinook salmon to low levels. In the future, as Elwha Chinook salmon recover, existing restrictions on these fisheries may be relaxed. Furthermore, when recovery occurs, fisheries specifically directed at Elwha Chinook salmon may be implemented. Such fisheries would be closely managed to maintain a healthy, sustainable population (Note: No plan currently exists for any fisheries specifically targeting Elwha Chinook salmon).

Current fish harvest management potentially affecting Elwha Chinook salmon may be viewed in three categories: 1) within the Elwha River and Freshwater Bay, 2) within Washington State, and 3) in Canadian and Alaskan waters. Each category is addressed below, followed by a description of available information on harvest and escapement of Elwha Chinook salmon.

Harvest Management within the Elwha River and Freshwater Bay

Currently for coho salmon, steelhead (*O. mykiss*), and trout (*Salvelinus* spp.) in the Elwha River, there are treaty Indian commercial and subsistence fisheries as well as nontreaty recreational fisheries. There are also nontreaty recreational fisheries and treaty subsistence fisheries for coho salmon in Freshwater Bay. There is no fishery for Chinook salmon in these terminal areas. The timing of the coho salmon fisheries is managed to minimize incidental capture of Chinook salmon adults during the fall. Coho salmon recreational, subsistence, and commercial fisheries may not be opened in the river until after 15 September (although recreational fisheries are generally not opened until 1 October) (PNPTC et al. 2003). The start of the treaty net fishery in the river may be adjusted (area or time closures) to avoid Chinook salmon bycatch.

During the period of dam removal and for 2 years following (approximately 5 years), no in-river fisheries (treaty and nontreaty) are planned. In-river fisheries for any species will not be reopened until it is clear that the additional stress caused by fishing will not adversely affect recovery.

Harvest Management within the State of Washington

Chinook salmon harvest management planning in Washington State and adjacent areas of the Pacific Ocean is complex, involving a multiplicity of federal and state management agencies, treaty tribes, and other entities interacting through formalized processes in the early part of each year. The outcome of the annual planning effort is a fisheries plan containing specific regulations that will be implemented to manage salmon harvests. Following is a brief description of the major processes involved in Chinook salmon planning, followed by a discussion of how Elwha Chinook salmon are affected.

Each year planning for fisheries of Chinook (and coho) salmon in Washington is implemented through a process known as the Pacific Fishery Management Council (PFMC) North of Falcon preseason planning. PFMC is a federally mandated council that, among other things, proposes to the Secretary of Commerce management provisions for the ocean salmon fisheries within the U.S. exclusive economic zone that extends 200 miles off the coast. North of Falcon identifies the region from Cape Falcon (just south of the Columbia River, on the Oregon coast) to the U.S.-Canada border, within the PFMC's jurisdiction in which the relevant preseason planning occurs.

Because ocean fisheries planning cannot effectively take place without consideration of the inside fisheries (i.e., for the Columbia River, Washington coast, Strait of Juan de Fuca, and Puget Sound), preseason planning for inside fisheries is incorporated into the process. Preseason planning takes place in March, but includes preparation beginning the previous December or earlier and involves follow up in April, often extending into the summer and fall fishing season. The process occurs in a series of scheduled meetings and depends on results of simulation modeling of alternative fisheries scenarios, using the Fisheries Resource Assessment Model (FRAM).

Another process that affects annual Chinook fisheries planning in Washington is that of the Pacific Salmon Commission (PSC) and its southern panel, which oversee the implementation of the Pacific Salmon Treaty between the United States and Canada. A treaty annex specifies how salmon resources are to be managed, protected, and any harvests shared between the countries. (See also the following subsection, Harvest Management within Alaska and Canada under the Pacific Salmon Treaty [PST].) Each year, details of abundance forecasts, fisheries assessments, monitoring, and fishing proposals are reviewed and decisions made on fisheries implementation and management. Of primary importance to Washington Chinook salmon fisheries planning is the annual forecast of Canadian interceptions of U.S. Chinook salmon that are authorized by the PST and predicted to occur. This forecast is an essential input for the FRAM modeling. The PSC process begins in January and intersects with the PFMC/North of Falcon process in March.

The fact that Chinook salmon of the Puget Sound Chinook salmon ESU, of which Elwha is a component, are listed as a threatened species under the Endangered Species Act (ESA), has brought another process into Chinook salmon fisheries planning. To meet requirements for permitting of fisheries under section 4(d) of the ESA, the Puget Sound Treaty Tribes and Washington Department of Fish and Wildlife (WDFW) have prepared a Puget Sound Chinook salmon harvest management plan such that fisheries managed in accordance with the plan are found to meet the requirements of the 4(d) Rule for Puget Sound Chinook and are exempt from take prohibitions. The latest version of the harvest management plan (PSIT and WDFW 2004) is applicable for fishing years 2004 through 2009 (30 April 2010). The plan includes specific provisions for protecting individual Chinook salmon populations (including Elwha) based on their status relative to critical and rebuilding thresholds. The provisions of this Chinook salmon harvest management plan are used to shape fishing seasons during the PMFC/North of Falcon fisheries planning process.

An understanding of how harvest management is applied to Elwha Chinook salmon each year may be best described by walking through the annual fisheries planning process:

1. A preliminary forecast of the expected return to the Elwha River, under average prior fisheries interceptions, is made in January. This forecast, along with similar forecasts for other Chinook salmon populations, is entered into the FRAM simulation to generate initial projections of fishery harvests and escapements. From this a preliminary assessment is made to determine population status relative to critical and rebuilding thresholds and the appropriate objective to guide management. This information on the status of populations helps inform the continuing FRAM simulation process, the results of which provide the basis for management decisions.

   The criteria for determining a population's status vary depending on the specific population. With respect to Elwha Chinook salmon, if the forecasted escapement is less than 1,000 fish (500 natural spawners and 500 hatchery fish), the population is deemed to be at critical status; if it is between 1,000 and 2,200 fish, it is deemed to be at recovering status. If the Elwha Chinook salmon escapement is projected to be above 2,200 fish, southern U.S. exploitation rates are kept at or below 10% and the population is managed to meet or exceed its management threshold.

2. If a population is at critical or rebuilding status, defined limits to harvest exploitation rates (again varying depending on the population) are implemented in evaluating fisheries alternatives. In recent years Elwha Chinook salmon have not been at critical status. The protective limits for Elwha Chinook salmon are: a) if the forecast escapement places the population at rebuilding status, subsequent planning for southern U.S. fisheries (using FRAM) is limited to an Elwha Chinook salmon harvest exploitation rate not to exceed 10%; and b) if the forecast escapement places the population at critical status, subsequent southern U.S. fisheries planning is limited by an Elwha Chinook salmon exploitation rate ceiling of 6%, and may be further limited, based on additional fisheries modeling criteria (PSTT and WDFW 2004).

3. As the PFMC North of Falcon fisheries planning proceeds, information is updated and FRAM simulations are generated, looking for the appropriate fishing levels and balances to protect Chinook salmon populations based on their status. This process involves considering management controls such as the timing and locations of the various fisheries from the ocean to the terminal areas. Using FRAM accumulates exploitation rates for each population to check against the exploitation rate ceiling defined by the population's status.

4. Once FRAM runs have been completed and alternative fisheries regimes have been reviewed, PFMC makes a decision on ocean fisheries and the WDFW and the tribes agree on an annual plan for the inside fisheries (e.g., Strait of Juan de Fuca and Puget Sound). This fisheries plan includes the specific times, locations, and other provisions (e.g., Chinook salmon release requirement, size limits) of all the inside fisheries to occur that year. Fisheries may be adjusted in season as additional information becomes available. The PFMC and inside fisheries are managed so that the aggregate impacts of the two groups of fisheries—also taking into account harvest-related impacts in Alaska and Canada—are consistent with the harvest objectives defined in the harvest management plan.

As described previously, the Elwha River and Freshwater Bay fisheries are designed to avoid capture of Chinook salmon and thus have little to no impact on Elwha Chinook salmon (but even the occasional nonlanded mortalities are accounted as part of the southern U.S. fisheries). The level of limited impacts from southern U.S. fisheries on Elwha Chinook salmon depends on the population status and the results of fisheries planning for the year. Currently the southern U.S. (i.e., south of the Canadian border) incidental harvest of Elwha Chinook salmon that does occur is due primarily to marine recreational fisheries and to a lesser degree, U.S. troll, net, and subsistence fisheries. Harvests and escapements of Elwha Chinook salmon are described in a subsection below.

Harvest Management within Alaska and Canada under the Pacific Salmon Treaty

As mentioned previously, the PST adds another layer to the management of Chinook salmon harvest. Harvest management under jurisdiction of the PST is considered here because Canadian fisheries, and to a lesser extent Alaska fisheries, currently have the greatest fishery-related impact on Elwha Chinook salmon.

The salmon life history includes migration through waters outside the salmon origin country, where they are susceptible to harvest by the other country. The PST addresses the concerns of both the United States and Canada about the other country's harvest effect on its home-origin fish and about each country's right to harvest fish in its waters irrespective of fish origin. The treaty includes specific harvest management provisions to address these concerns. Coincidentally, the treaty provisions affecting Alaska fisheries bear not only on Alaskan interceptions of Canadian-origin fish but also on Alaskan interceptions of fish originating from the southern United States.

The PST was signed in 1985. Annexes to the treaty contain the specific salmon management provisions. The most recent update to the annexes was agreed to in 1999 and is applicable through 2008. Annex IV, Chapter 3, applies to southern Chinook salmon, originating from central and southern British Columbia and the southern United States (PSC 2000). Under the PST, Chinook-intercepting fisheries are divided into two types: aggregate abundance-based management (AABM) fisheries and individual stock-based management (ISBM) fisheries. Specific rules apply to each category separately.

The AABM fisheries are managed by planning and accounting for the aggregated catch of stocks within each fishery's area and time frame. Management focus is on the aggregate abundance of the specific fishery, not for individual stocks. For each fishery, the annual target catch level is selected using a harvest rate index (also called abundance index and expressed as a portion of the catch for the 1979–1982 base period) that is determined by the annual Chinook salmon preseason abundance forecast or in-season abundance estimate, whichever is applicable. Annual fishery regulations (including fishing area, time openings, and fish size limits) are prepared and implemented to achieve the target catch level of each AABM fishery. A computer model is used to calculate catch levels and help determine the annual fishery regulations. The three AABM fisheries are southeast Alaska (sport, net, and troll), northern British Columbia (troll) and Queen Charlotte Islands (sport), and west coast of Vancouver Island (troll and outside sport).

The ISBM fisheries are based on the abundance of individual stocks or groups of stocks, the intent being to achieve maximum sustained yield or another agreed upon biologically based objective. The pool of ISBM fisheries includes the various British Columbia "inside fisheries" and southern U.S. fisheries (north of Cape Falcon, as well as Oregon marine net, sport, and troll fisheries, and Idaho freshwater sport and net fisheries). Indicator Chinook salmon stocks, representative of each ISBM fishery, are monitored through a coast-wide coded wire–tagging program. The Strait of Juan de Fuca marine net, troll, and sport and freshwater sport and net are in combination; a designated ISBM fishery with Hoko River Chinook salmon as its indicator stock. A defined index, computed preseason based on forecasted abundance and fishing plans (and evaluated postseason), was to be used to manage the individual ISBM fisheries, the planning and evaluation being based in part on the indicator stocks; however, use of this approach requires first that the escapement-dependent objectives be reviewed and agreed on by the two countries.

Because no agreement on ISBM stock escapement objectives currently exists, the default management approach is to reduce the total mortality rate, relative to a 1979–1982 base period, by 36.5 and 40% respectively for Canadian and U.S. fisheries. Again computer simulation modeling is used to help determine the annual fisheries controls necessary to meet the mortality rate criteria. The ISBM fishery management controls currently are not the primary limit constraining management of southern U.S. Chinook salmon fisheries. Interceptions by Canada and Alaska of southern U.S.-origin Chinook salmon are estimated, as part of the AABM and ISBM fisheries planning effort, and are made available to the PFMC/North of Falcon planning process to assist with preparation of the annual fisheries plan for Washington State (as noted above).

Because Puget Sound Chinook salmon were listed as threatened under ESA, the U.S. federal government was required under section 7 of the act to conduct consultations that considered the impacts of Chinook salmon harvest management under the PST. The consultations were completed and the U.S. Department of State (USDOS) and National Marine Fisheries Service (NMFS) issued a biological opinion in November 1999 (USDOS and NMFS 1999). The analysis within the biological opinion included estimates of recovery exploitation rates (RERs) for some northern Puget Sound Chinook salmon populations that had sufficient coded wire tag information to allow such estimates. These RERs were target exploitation rates considered low enough to allow rebuilding of the populations to viable population levels.

An assessment was made that suggested limitations on exploitation rates under the PST were insufficient to meet the RERs for several Puget Sound Chinook salmon populations (and by implication other Chinook salmon populations for which inadequate information existed to develop RERs). However, it was decided that rejection of the treaty provisions (i.e., the 1999 treaty updates) by the United States was unlikely to result in a better or more restrictive management regime in the near future. Also, the U.S. government noted that mechanisms existed within the treaty provisions to address deficiencies that become apparent with respect to individual populations (though conditions must be met for these mechanisms to be implemented) and expressed concern about the loss of other benefits associated with the treaty. In conclusion, the U.S. government decided that management actions under the PST were not likely to jeopardize continued existence of Puget Sound Chinook salmon.

The WDFW and the tribes remain concerned about the increased risk of underescapement for some depressed Puget Sound Chinook salmon under current levels of Canadian and Alaskan impacts and the additional constraints on Washington fisheries required to protect Chinook salmon. The topic is to be discussed during the development of a new Chinook salmon regime to replace the current annex which expires in 2008. In the interim, tribal, state, and federal managers have indicated their intent to continue to work with Canadian managers both to employ the mechanisms of the agreement and to find opportunities for reductions beyond those provided in the agreement that may be needed to address critical conservation concerns and provide additional benefits for Puget Sound Chinook salmon populations.

Harvest and Escapement of Elwha Chinook Salmon

Tagging information on Elwha Chinook salmon provides an estimate of the average distribution of fishery-related mortality for management years 1996 to 2000 (NMFS 2003) as follows:

Area	Percent
Alaska	10.0
British Columbia	69.2
Washington troll	4.7
Puget Sound net	3.8
Washington recreational	12.3

It is apparent that the vast majority of fishery interceptions occur in Canada. Alaska also harvests a relatively large proportion compared to Washington fisheries. Most of the Washington fishery mortality is from the recreational fisheries, the majority of which occurs in marine waters.

Table B-1 describes Elwha Chinook salmon spawning escapement estimates from 1986 through 2002 (PNPTC et al. 2003). Escapement has been above the critical threshold of natural and hatchery spawners in most years. However, the population failed to achieve the 500 natural spawner objective from 1994 to 1996. This was a period of extremely low total returns to the river, resulting from the complete loss of a brood year due to a suspected outbreak of viral hemorrhagic septicemia at the Sol Duc Hatchery. Based on the final FRAM run of Washington fisheries at the conclusion of the 2003 PFMC North of Falcon fisheries planning effort, the

Table B-1. Natural escapement and hatchery broodstock for Elwha River Chinook salmon.

Return year	Terminal run	Hatchery rack	Gaff-seine removals	Prespawning mortality	Natural spawning
1988	8,666	2,089	506	478	5,593
1989	5,703	1,135	905	560	3,103
1990	3,605	586	886	224	1,909
1991	3,761	970	857	108	1,826
1992	4,002	97	672	2,611	622
1993	1,669	165	771	7	726
1994	1,580	365	749	330	136
1995	1,814	145	518	662	489
1996	1,877	214	1,177	267	219
1997	2,527	318	624	10	1,575
1998	2,409	138	1,551	51	669
1999	1,625	113	609	23	880
2000	1,913	177	1,021	62	653
2001	2,246	195	1,396	38	617
2002	2,416	473	1,080	40	823
Average	3,054	479	888	365	1,323

anticipated exploitation rates and escapement for Elwha Chinook salmon for 2003 (NMFS 2003) were as follows:

Area	Percent
River and bay exploitation rate	0.1
Southern U.S. preterminal exploitation rate	0.5
Southern U.S. exploitation rate	4.6
Total exploitation rate (includes Canada and Alaska)	22.1
Projected natural spawning escapement = 2,126	

The exploitation rates are calculated as the expected number of fishery-related mortalities divided by the expected total run size including the escapement. Table B-1 shows that the previously noted relatively high levels of Canadian and Alaskan fisheries impacts were expected to continue in 2003. The projected distribution of impacts for 2004 is likely to be similar to these 2003 preseason estimates.

Estimated exploitation rates for recent years are substantially lower than the rates of the 1980s. The following table shows the estimated average total exploitation rates of Strait of Juan de Fuca Chinook salmon for the periods 1983–1987, 1998–2000, and 2001–2003 (PSTT and WDFW 2004). Percentage differences (declines) in exploitation rates between 1983 and 1987 and the latter two periods are also shown. The numbers have been generated using FRAM.

Period	Percentage	Percentage decline
1983–1987 average	76	
1998–2000 average	38	50.0
2001–2003 average	18	76.3

Exploitation rate declines have also occurred in other regions of Puget Sound (59% decline for Puget Sound spring Chinook salmon and 47% for Puget Sound fall Chinook salmon since the early 1980s).[9] These declines indicate the substantial curtailment of fisheries catches now being affected by harvest management conservation efforts.

In summary, the WDFW and tribes have worked through complicated management processes, addressing all Washington fisheries as well as those of Canada and Alaska, to substantially limit harvest effects on depressed Chinook salmon populations including those of the Elwha River. Currently no fisheries are specifically directed at Elwha Chinook salmon and incidental impacts from southern U.S. fisheries are kept at a low level. The WDFW and tribes will attempt to incorporate management provisions that better protect at-risk Washington Chinook salmon populations from the impacts of Canadian and Alaskan fisheries in the future.

---

[9] S. Bishop, NOAA Fisheries Service, Seattle, WA. Pers. commun., 4 October 2006.